FREEDOM AND THE SUBJECT OF THEORY
ESSAYS IN HONOUR OF CHRISTINA HOWELLS

LEGENDA

LEGENDA is the Modern Humanities Research Association's book imprint for new research in the Humanities. Founded in 1995 by Malcolm Bowie and others within the University of Oxford, Legenda has always been a collaborative publishing enterprise, directly governed by scholars. The Modern Humanities Research Association (MHRA) joined this collaboration in 1998, became half-owner in 2004, in partnership with Maney Publishing and then Routledge, and has since 2016 been sole owner. Titles range from medieval texts to contemporary cinema and form a widely comparative view of the modern humanities, including works on Arabic, Catalan, English, French, German, Greek, Italian, Portuguese, Russian, Spanish, and Yiddish literature. Editorial boards and committees of more than 60 leading academic specialists work in collaboration with bodies such as the Society for French Studies, the British Comparative Literature Association and the Association of Hispanists of Great Britain & Ireland.

The MHRA encourages and promotes advanced study and research in the field of the modern humanities, especially modern European languages and literature, including English, and also cinema. It aims to break down the barriers between scholars working in different disciplines and to maintain the unity of humanistic scholarship. The Association fulfils this purpose through the publication of journals, bibliographies, monographs, critical editions, and the MHRA Style Guide, and by making grants in support of research. Membership is open to all who work in the Humanities, whether independent or in a University post, and the participation of younger colleagues entering the field is especially welcomed.

ALSO PUBLISHED BY THE ASSOCIATION

Critical Texts
Tudor and Stuart Translations • *New Translations* • *European Translations*
MHRA Library of Medieval Welsh Literature

MHRA Bibliographies
Publications of the Modern Humanities Research Association

The Annual Bibliography of English Language & Literature
Austrian Studies
Modern Language Review
Portuguese Studies
The Slavonic and East European Review
Working Papers in the Humanities
The Yearbook of English Studies

www.mhra.org.uk
www.legendabooks.com

Portrait of Christina Howells by Sophia Spring, courtesy of the photographer
and the Warden and Fellows of Wadham College.

Freedom and the Subject of Theory

Essays in Honour of Christina Howells

EDITED BY
OLIVER DAVIS AND COLIN DAVIS

LEGENDA
Modern Humanities Research Association
2019

Published by Legenda
an imprint of the Modern Humanities Research Association
Salisbury House, Station Road, Cambridge CB1 2LA

ISBN 978-1-78188-733-2

First published 2019

Copy-Editor: Charlotte Brown

CONTENTS

ACKNOWLEDGEMENTS

The Editors would like to thank Charlotte Brown and Graham Nelson for their meticulous work on the typescript and proofs, Clare Woods for kind permission to use an image of her painting on the cover and Sophia Spring and the Warden and Fellows of Wadham College for permission to reproduce the photographic portrait of Christina. Earlier versions of most of these essays were presented at a conference held in March 2017. That event was generously supported by the School of Modern Languages and Cultures and the Humanities Research Centre at the University of Warwick, the Faculty of Medieval and Modern Languages and Literatures at the University of Oxford, Wadham College, Oxford, and the Society for French Studies.

O.D, C.D., April 2019

NOTES ON THE CONTRIBUTORS

Jeremy Ahearne is Professor of French Studies at Warwick University. His publications include: 'International Recognition Regimes and the Projection of France', *International Journal of Cultural Policy*, 24.6 (December 2018), 696–709; 'Cultural Insecurity and its Discursive Crystallisation in Contemporary France', *Modern and Contemporary France*, 25, 3 (2017), 265–80; 'Cultural Policy through the Prism of Fiction (Michel Houellebecq)', *International Journal of Cultural Policy*, 23, 1 (January 2017), 1–16; *Government through Culture and the Contemporary French Right* (Palgrave Macmillan, 2014); *Intellectuals, Culture and Public Policy in France: Approaches from the Left*, (Liverpool University Press, 2010); *Between Cultural Theory and Policy: The Cultural Policy Thinking of Pierre Bourdieu, Michel de Certeau and Régis Debray*, Centre for Cultural Policy Studies, University of Warwick, Research Papers, 7 (2004); *Michel de Certeau: Interpretation and its Other* (Polity Press, 1995).

Gary E. Aylesworth is Professor of Philosophy and former chair of the philosophy department at Eastern Illinois University. He also serves as co-director of the International Philosophical Seminar. His publications include *The Textual Sublime: Deconstruction and Its Differences* (co-edited with Hugh J. Silverman; SUNY Press, 1990), and translations of Martin Heidegger's *Basic Concepts* and *The Heidegger-Jaspers Correspondence*. He has also published articles on postmodernism, Heidegger, Nietzsche, hermeneutics, deconstruction, and other topics in contemporary Continental philosophy.

Patrick Chambers is reading for a DPhil in Modern Languages at Keble College, Oxford, working under the supervision of Professor Christina Howells. His research focuses on questions of subjectivity in Sartre's later thought, looking in particular at the role and status of the *project* in *Critique de la raison dialectique* and *L'Idiot de la famille*, with the final aim of exploring the relationship between a spectral Sartrean subject and the ghosts of Derridean deconstruction.

Martin Crowley is Reader in Modern French Thought and Culture at the University of Cambridge. He is the author of: *L'Homme sans: politiques de la finitude* (with an afterword by Jean-Luc Nancy; Lignes, 2009); *The New Pornographies: Explicit Sex in Recent French Fiction and Film* (co-authored with Victoria Best; Manchester University Press, 2007); *Robert Antelme: l'humanité irréductible* (Lignes/Léo Scheer, 2004); *Robert Antelme: Humanity, Community, Testimony* (Legenda, 2003); and *Duras, Writing, and the Ethical: Making the Broken Whole* (Oxford University Press, 2000). His current research explores the politics of distributed agency, particularly in the work of Bruno Latour, Bernard Stiegler, and Catherine Malabou.

Colin Davis is Professor of French and Comparative Literature at Royal Holloway, University of London. His work is principally concerned with the relations between philosophy, literature, and film. His publications include *Critical Excess: Over-reading in Derrida, Deleuze, Levinas, Žižek and Cavell* (Stanford University Press, 2010); *Postwar Renoir: Film and the Memory of Violence* (Routledge, 2012); *Traces of War: Interpreting Ethics and Trauma in Twentieth-Century French Writing* (Liverpool University Press, 2018); and *Storytelling and Ethics: Literature, Visual Arts and Power of Narrative* (co-edited with Hanna Meretoja; Routledge, 2018).

Oliver Davis is Reader in French Studies at Warwick University. His current research addresses modern administering power and its techniques of (in)security. Recent publications include: 'Mettray Revisited in Jean Genet's *Le Langage de la muraille*', *French History*, 30, 4 (December 2016), 546–66; 'Managing (in)Security in Paris in Mai 68', special issue of *Modern & Contemporary France*, guest-edited by Oliver Davis, *The Anti-Police of Mai '68 Fifty Years On*, 26, 2 (May 2018), 129–43; 'Foucault and the Queer Pharmatopia', in *After Foucault: Culture, Theory, and Criticism in the 21st Century*, ed. by Lisa Downing (Cambridge University Press, 2018), pp. 170–84. Earlier publications include *Jacques Rancière* (Polity Press, 2010), *Rancière Now* (Polity Press, 2013), and 'Desublimation in Education for Democracy', in *Stiegler and Technics*, ed. by Christina Howells and Gerald Moore (Edinburgh University Press, 2013), pp. 165–78.

Henry Dicks is adjunct teacher in environmental ethics at the Faculty of Philosophy, Université Jean Moulin Lyon 3. His current research focuses on the philosophy of biomimicry. Recent publications include: 'Thinking the Clearing in the Age of the Earth System: Heidegger and the City as Forest', in *Heidegger and the Global Age*, ed. A. Cerella and L. Odysseos (Rowman and Littlefield, 2018); 'From Anthropomimetic to Biomimetic Cities: The Place of Humans in Cities like Forests', *Architecture Philosophy*, 3, 1 (2018), 91–106; 'A New Way of Valuing Nature: Articulating Biomimicry and Ecosystem Services', *Environmental Ethics*, 39, 3 (2017), 281–99; 'The Poetics of Biomimicry: The Contribution of Poetic Concepts to Philosophical Inquiry into the Biomimetic Principle of Nature as Model', *Environmental Philosophy*, 14, 2 (2017), 191–219; 'Environmental Ethics and Biomimetic Ethics: Nature as Object of Ethics and Nature as Source of Ethics', *Journal of Agricultural and Environmental Ethics*, 30, 2 (2017), 255–74; 'The Philosophy of Biomimicry', *Philosophy & Technology*, 29, 3 (2016), 223–43.

Paul Earlie is Lecturer in French at the University of Bristol. His research interests are in French thought, with a focus on how it is communicated through a variety of media. A monograph on Derrida and Freud is forthcoming, and he is currently co-authoring a book on rhetorical theory with Michel Meyer. He has recently edited a special issue of the *Revue internationale de philosophie* on the topic of new approaches to psychoanalysis and literature.

Seán Hand is Professor of French and Deputy Pro-Vice-Chancellor (Europe) at the University of Warwick. He was previously founding Dean of the Graduate School of the University of Warwick in California project (2016–17) and founding head of the University of Warwick's School of Modern Languages and Cultures (2014–16). He is the author of *Emmanuel Levinas* (Routledge, 2008), *Alter Ego: The Critical Writings of Michel Leiris* (Legenda, 2004), and *Michel Leiris: Writing the Self* (Cambridge University Press, 2002). He has edited *Post-Holocaust France and the Jews 1945–1955* (NYU Press, 2015), *Facing the Other: The Ethics of Emmanuel Levinas* (Routledge, 1996), and *The Levinas Reader* (Blackwell, 1989); and has translated several philosophers, including Levinas, Kristeva, and Deleuze. He is a *Chevalier des Palmes Académiques*, a Senior Fellow of the UK Higher Education Academy, and a member of the Academia Europæa.

Jane Hiddleston is Professor of Literatures in French at the University of Oxford, and Official Fellow in French at Exeter College, Oxford. She has published widely in the areas of francophone literature and postcolonial theory, including most recently *Decolonising the Intellectual: Politics, Culture, and Humanism at the End of the French Empire* (Liverpool University Press, 2014) and *Writing After Postcolonialism: Francophone North African Literature in Transition* (Bloomsbury, 2017). She is currently a Co-Investigator on the Oxford-led AHRC-funded 'Creative Multilingualism', while also working on a focused study of Fanon and literature.

Ian James completed his doctoral research on the fictional and theoretical writings of Pierre Klossowski at the University of Warwick in 1996. He is a Fellow of Downing College and a Reader in Modern French Literature and Thought in the Department of French at the University of Cambridge. He is the author of *Pierre Klossowski: The Persistence of a Name* (Legenda, 2000), *The Fragmentary Demand: An Introduction to the Philosophy of Jean-Luc Nancy* (Stanford University Press, 2006), *Paul Virilio* (Routledge, 2007), *The New French Philosophy* (Polity Press, 2012), and *The Technique of Thought: Nancy, Laruelle, Malabou, and Stiegler After Naturalism* (Minnesota University Press, 2019).

Marc Lafrance is an Associate Professor of Sociology at Concordia University. Focusing on contemporary cultural theory, Marc is interested in present-day debates pertaining to subjectivity and embodiment and how they account — or fail to account — for lived experience. Through critical readings of twentieth-century poststructural and psychoanalytic texts, he aims to provide cultural theorists with new tools for making sense of embodied subjectivity. To this end, Marc has published on philosopher Michel Foucault and has been internationally recognized for his work on psychoanalyst Didier Anzieu and the 'psychoanalysis of skin'. He guest-edited a recent double issue of the peer-reviewed journal *Body and Society* entitled *Skin Matters: Thinking Through the Body's Surfaces*.

Ian Maclachlan is Professor of French Literature at the University of Oxford, where he is a Fellow of Merton College. He is the author of *Marking Time: Derrida, Blanchot, Beckett, des Forêts, Klossowski, Laporte* (Rodopi, 2012) and *Roger Laporte: The Orphic Text* (Legenda, 2000). He has edited various collections, including: *Reading Derrida's 'Of Grammatology'* (with Sean Gaston; Continuum, 2011); a special issue of *Forum for Modern Language Studies* entitled *The Writer and Responsibility* (2006); *Jacques Derrida: Critical Thought* (Ashgate, 2004); and *Sensual Reading* (with Michael

Syrotinski; Bucknell University Press, 2001). He is also an editor of *Paragraph: A Journal of Modern Critical Theory*.

Gerald Moore is Associate Professor in French at Durham University, and previously spent three years as Stipendiary Lecturer in French, under Christina Howells, at Wadham College, Oxford. He is author of *Politics of the Gift: Exchanges in Poststructuralism* (Edinburgh University Press, 2011) and co-editor, with Christina, of *Stiegler and Technics* (Edinburgh University Press, 2013). The essay in this volume is a reworked version of material due to appear in a future monograph, *Anthropocene Animals: Towards a Critique of Adaptationist Reason*.

Marieke Mueller completed her DPhil on Sartre's *L'Idiot de la famille* under the supervision of Christina Howells in 2016. She has co-edited a special edition of *Sartre Studies International* on new approaches to Sartre and has written articles on Sartre, Pierre Bourdieu, Didier Eribon, Edouard Louis, on theories of violence, and on approaches to reading. Her research interests include twentieth-century French thought, modern and contemporary French literature, and she is currently working on a new research project on the theme of 'destiny' in modern French literature and thought. She teaches at Aberystwyth University.

Sinan Richards is a DPhil researcher at Wadham College, Oxford, working at the intersection of twentieth-century French philosophy and German Idealism. He has recently published 'The Violence of Politeness: Implicit *Bienséance* in the Sadian Universe', in *Early Modern French Studies*, 39.1 (2017), 75–88. He currently teaches at the École normale supérieure, Paris.

Serge Trottein is *chargé de recherche* at the Centre national de la recherche scientifique, UMR 8230, École normale supérieure, PSL Research University, Paris, and Co-Director of the International Philosophical Seminar. His field of research is philosophical aesthetics from the Renaissance to the Enlightenment, and to Postmodernity. His publications and presentations range from the theories of Agostino Nifo and Federico Zuccaro to the philosophies of Diderot, Kant, Hegel, Nietzsche, and Heidegger, and include readings of Derrida, Lyotard, Stiegler, and Nancy. Editor of *L'Esthétique naît-elle au XVIIIe siècle?* (PUF, 2000), he is currently working on the function of aesthetics in postmodern philosophy.

Robert J. C. Young is Silver Professor of English and Comparative Literature, New York University. He is the author of *White Mythologies: Writing History and the West* (Routledge, 1990), *Colonial Desire* (Routledge, 1995), *Postcolonialism: An Historical Introduction* (Blackwell, 2001), *The Idea of English Ethnicity* (Blackwell, 2008), and *Empire, Colony, Post-Colony* (2015), among other works.

INTRODUCTION

Pathways to Freedom in the Work of Christina Howells

Colin Davis and Oliver Davis

I

Freedom has been an abiding concern of Continental thought. Are our actions, values, and self-identifications freely chosen, or imposed on us by a complex interplay of unconscious motivations, culture, history, institutions, and the pressure of others? Is the human subject a self-defining, self-creating autonomous agent, or merely the product or plaything of forces beyond its control? Is the Other an ally in the project to realize freedom, or an unmovable obstacle which forever stands in our way? If we knew how to embrace freedom, would it be a blessing or a curse, a joyous epiphany or a dreadful burden? And does the brutal fact of mortality make a nonsense of our human striving to be free?

The question of freedom is inextricable from that of the subject. Freedom has to be *mine* if it is to be meaningful, but what does it mean to be *me*? The first person singular must be more than a grammatical position if it is to have any real significance. Unless I am in some sense — however complex and mitigated that sense might be — an autonomous, free, spontaneous, really-existing subject, then it is hard to see how I can be held accountable for anything I might think or do: my acts do not belong to me; I am not responsible for my ethical and political choices. And where do values — *my* values, the ones which regulate what I do, how I understand the world, and how I treat other people, other creatures, or the environment — come from? Do they exist outside me, or have I created and chosen them, rationally or irrationally, carefully or carelessly?

The freedom of the subject is also bound up with the question of *theory*, both as a discipline based in academic institutions (sometimes reviled, sometimes celebrated), and as a defining activity of the human subject as theorizing being, straining to understand its place in the world. The subject here is both *subject to* and the *subject of* theory: it theorizes, and in large measure it theorizes about itself; and in so doing it creates itself as both the subject and object of theory. I theorize, therefore I am (the subject who theorizes). Subjectivity and theory are therefore inseparable, and deeply implicated in the problem of freedom: does the subject freely make theory, or is there a reciprocal relationship, a mutually determining sense in which theory also helps constitute the subject?

These are the questions which this volume addresses; moreover, it addresses them through a lens fashioned by Christina Howells, whose work has pioneered their investigation in the English-speaking world.

II

It is of course simplistic and trivial to find a lifetime's intellectual project encapsulated in a single sentence. Nevertheless, there is something premonitory in the last sentence of the first paragraph on the first page of Christina Howells's first book, *Sartre's Theory of Literature*. For Sartre, according to Howells, imagination is constitutive of the world as we know it. She continues: 'It [imagination] appears moreover as the correlative of the freedom of human consciousness; and it is this which permits Sartre to bring his interest in art within his overriding preoccupation with human liberty and social commitment'.[1] What Howells says of Sartre might also be said of Howells. Key terms of what will go on to be her abiding interests are already in place here: imagination, freedom, commitment.

Within an instant, however, matters become bewilderingly difficult. The next sentence, introducing the second paragraph of the book, indicates that this will be no easy journey:

> But Sartre's attitude to the imaginary is nonetheless ambiguous: imagination permits man to overcome his *embourbement* in reality, it allows his *pour-soi* to escape the toils of the *en-soi*, it is vital to any project of change; yet it can also alienate that very liberty it makes possible, leading man to deny the real and to value fantasy above reality.[2]

Imagination may both express and alienate freedom; it both gives me a world and risks making it inaccessible to me. From this starting-point *Sartre's Theory of Literature* develops into an exemplary philosophical exposition of Sartre's ambiguous, paradoxical, unrelenting contribution to literary theory, and to the complex conceptual and imaginative negotiations between committed literature and pure art.

It is important to remember that when this book was published in 1979 Sartre was still alive but some of his most important work, particularly *L'Idiot de la famille* [The Family Idiot], was largely unread; and the very topic of theory was deeply controversial within anglophone universities. Howells's first contribution to this debate was uncompromising without being confrontational: art and the imagination *matter* as part of a committed emancipatory politics; Sartre had more to contribute than his detractors believed (and in some cases would continue to believe); theory must be part of any mature intellectual debate; and it is possible to talk sanely and with clarity about even the most demanding theoretical material. To read the work of Christina Howells is to enter a no-nonsense zone. Theory may be difficult, but it does not have to be needlessly obscure; and it matters because, at its best, it always deals with questions which are pressingly important to us as desiring, divided, flawed human subjects.

Sartre has remained a decisive influence on Howells's thinking throughout her career. Her second book, *Sartre: The Necessity of Freedom*, continues her reflection on the issues outlined above whilst offering a much more comprehensive account of Sartre's work, from his early philosophy, through his novels and plays, his great philosophical works *L'Être et le néant* [Being and Nothingness] and *Critique de la raison dialectique* [Critique of Dialectical Reason], his biographies and autobiography, and his never-completed projects for an ethics.[3] The book is still the indispensable study of Sartre. But being a committed Sartrean — or at least a consistent admirer of Sartre's work — did not block interest in later intellectual developments in France. Howells championed the work of female French thinkers through her edited volume *French Women Philosophers: A Contemporary Reader*, which showcased texts by nearly thirty authors, many of whom were virtually unknown in the English-speaking world at that point.[4] She was also increasingly drawn to the work of Jacques Derrida, the subject of her third monograph, *Derrida: Deconstruction from Phenomenology to Ethics.*[5]

Derrida belonged to a generation which often seemed scornful of its existentialist forebears, of whom Sartre was the most prominent representative. From a post-structuralist perspective, Sartre was an outdated throwback to a discredited vocabulary of freedom and being, which could now be consigned to history. Derrida's early references to Sartre tend to be critical, dismissive, or just plain wrong. The 1968 essay 'Les Fins de l'homme' [The Ends of Man] caricatures Sartre as a philosopher of presence.[6] In his reading of the writer Jean Genet in *Glas* of 1974, Derrida seems reluctant even to name Sartre. He mocks Sartre as the 'onto-phenomenologist of freedom'; and his allusions to Sartre's monumental *Saint Genet, comédien et martyr* [Saint Genet, Actor and Martyr] attack the book on spurious grounds without acknowledging its extraordinary impact on the interpretation of Genet's work, not to mention on Genet's own self-understanding. In an interview in *Le Nouvel Observateur* in 1983, while professing affection for Sartre, Derrida describes his influence as 'néfaste et catastrophique' [nefarious and catastrophic].[7] He concedes that it was through Sartre that he discovered authors such as Bataille, Blanchot, and Ponge, but he insists that Sartre's renown speaks badly of French society:

> Que doit être une société comme la nôtre pour qu'un homme qui, à sa façon, a rejeté ou méconnu tant d'événements théoriques ou littéraires de son temps — disons pour faire vite la psychanalyse, le marxisme, le structuralisme, Joyce, Artaud, Bataille, Blanchot — , qui a multiplié et diffusé d'incroyables contresens sur Heidegger, parfois sur Husserl, en vienne à dominer la scène culturelle, jusqu'à devenir une grande figure populaire?[8]

> [What must a society like ours be if a man who, in his way, rejected or got wrong so many of the theoretical or literary events of his time — let us mention for the sake of speed psychoanalysis, Marxism, structuralism, Joyce, Artaud, Bataille, Blanchot — , who multiplied and broadcast unbelievable nonsense on Heidegger, sometimes on Husserl, if a such a man could come to dominate the cultural scene to the point of becoming a great popular figure?]

In short, Derrida concludes, Sartre's works do not belong to those which have any importance for him. Only belatedly, in an essay in the fiftieth-anniversary edition of *Les Temps modernes* published in 1996, does Derrida express anything like respect for the work of Sartre, who had died in 1980.[9]

What did Derrida owe to Sartre? Not very much, if his own early comments on the matter are to be believed; more than he was sometimes prepared to admit, if Howells has got the matter right. Both Sartre and Derrida served a philosophical apprenticeship studying and writing about Husserl; they both opposed Hegel's totalizing syntheses; they shared an interest in writers such as Genet and Mallarmé; both had a fraught but important relation to Marx and Marxism; and their views on issues such as subjectivity, ethics, and politics sometimes appear to be remarkably close. Howells thinks there is more going on here than routine misreading, neglect, or indifference. Derrida was, of course, as capable of making a mistake as any of us, with the sole difference that his mistakes are generally more interesting than ours. But Howells, respectfully viewing Derrida through the suspicious lenses he was accustomed to using himself, sees in his misreading of Sartre something more like a philosophical psychodrama. According to Howells, Derrida's *La Voix et le phénomène* [Voice and Phenomenon] 'repeated in part, and probably unwittingly, Sartre's own deconstruction of the Husserlian subject'; moreover, she continues, 'Twenty years later, Derrida still seems unwilling to acknowledge that Sartre is not merely a forerunner but a real originator of much of what Deconstruction has to say on the subject'.[10] Sartre is an unacknowledged precursor; and Derrida's failure to recognize his importance is associated with a Bloomian anxiety of influence following the operation of which — again, according to Howells — 'Derrida attributes to [Sartre] positions diametrically opposed to those he in fact holds'.[11] Having thus falsified Sartre's views, Derrida himself 'appears to be repeating the broad lines of an analysis he is unwilling to recognize as constituting a precursor text'.[12] Howells calls this a form of parricide: the latecomer seeks to assert his autonomy by denying the father his due, killing him and claiming as his own what in fact was his father's. It is only when Sartre is *actually* dead that Derrida can overcome his parricidal anxiety. By 1996 Derrida has apparently had what Howells calls 'a partial change of heart', and his reappraisal of Sartre is 'generous-spirited, dignified, and an appropriate tribute from one of the two most influential French philosophers of the twentieth century to the other'.[13]

Howells's crucial point is that — despite these simplifying, parricidal generational conflicts — Derrida can be understood as continuing Sartre's work rather than decisively breaking with it. And this is particularly significant when it comes to the decentering, dividing, splitting, death, or survival of the subject. The concluding essay to her edited *Cambridge Companion to Sartre*, entitled 'Sartre and the Deconstruction of the Subject', is Howells's most important statement on this issue. She begins by describing the polarized terms in which the subject has been described:

> Autonomous, independent, spontaneous foundation of knowledge, under-standing, feeling, imagination? Alienating, idealist, bourgeois humanist, phallogocentric delusion? Does the subject lie between these two polar opposite descriptions of it, does it span them and, like a Pascalian paradox, fill all the space between, or does it lie elsewhere entirely, perhaps in a utopia?[14]

What follows has two aims: to describe the philosophical route by which Sartre came to conceive of the subject as riven, longing for but incapable of self-presence and self-knowledge; and to show how Sartre's philosophical successors, Derrida in particular, often reproduced aspects of Sartre's thinking even whilst misrepresenting and repudiating it. Sartre turns out to be both a forerunner and an originator of the deconstruction of the subject. Most importantly, however tattered, embattled, and undermined it may be, the subject survives, for Sartre as for Derrida: 'The subject may be deferred, dissolved, and deconstructed, but it is not relinquished'.[15]

This is not so much a rehabilitation of the subject as an endeavour to understand and to accept it in all its tensions, paradoxes, inconsistencies, and failings. There is as yet, though, one element that remains to be added if the pathos and dignity of the subject are to be fully grasped: mortality. This would be the topic of Howells's most recent and perhaps most deeply-felt monograph, *Mortal Subjects: Passions of the Soul in Late Twentieth-Century French Thought*. This book begins with a simple and searching question: how do we reconcile philosophical reflection with lived experience? Mortality is central here because, as Howells puts is, 'All experience is predicated on its ultimate transience, in other words on its death'.[16] Everything that matters to us is permeated by the foreboding of death. There is no love, friendship, or passion for an other without the certainty of loss: one of us will die and leave the other bereft and grieving. So death is at the very core of subjectivity.

In its scholarly range, *Mortal Subjects* is an exemplary study of love and death in late twentieth-century French thought, taking in Sartre, Beauvoir, Ricœur, Levinas, Lacan, Kristeva, Derrida, Nancy, and many others. It is also, most powerfully, a reflection on love and loss, death and grief, as constituent parts of subjectivity and being human. Mortality, Howells tells us, 'is the condition of possibility and the condition of impossibility of subjectivity'.[17] Death: can't live with it, can't live without it. It underlies my ability to love and my fore-knowledge of loss, because the two are inextricably bound up with one another. Across Howells's writing we have seen the subject emerge as split and deluded, but nevertheless yearning for freedom. *Mortal Subjects* concludes that it is also 'mortal, finite, passionate, and always incomplete'.[18] Therein lies both its heroism and its tragedy.

III

This volume continues the work of Christina Howells. The contributors are students and/or colleagues who have learned important lessons from her about what it means to be a subject, to be a subject of theory, and to be subject to theory. Gary Aylesworth's substantial opening essay explicates the double reference to the 'subject of theory' in this volume's title (the subject who theorizes / the subject as object of its own and others' theorizing) by tracing it back to, and forward from, Kant's account of subjectivity, according to which reason (as power of synthesis) makes a free (unconditioned) demand for unconditioned knowledge reflecting the free, unconditioned, unity of its own act. Aylesworth tracks the vicissitudes of this Kantian subject through German Idealism (Fichte, Schelling, Hegel) before contrasting Hegel's vision of philosophy, or theory, and the subject with those of

Kierkegaard and Nietzsche. Along the way, this opening essay registers the gradual process by which theory worked free of metaphysics and religion.

The subsequent essays have been grouped into four parts, in the first of which three of Christina's current or recent doctoral students address freedom and the subject in Sartre's late work. Patrick Chambers considers the subject's freedom to theorize in the constraining shared material environment characterized by Sartre as the 'practico-inert'. Chambers explores Sartre's theorization of this shared material field — figuratively, the 'football pitch' — on which intersubjective conflicts and cooperation are played out and which is constituted by an accumulation, or sedimentation, of past praxes. He argues that the practico-inert mediates human action in a manner reminiscent of Derridean iteration and his essay offers a wide-ranging and lucid exploration of this key concept in Sartre's *Critique of Dialectical Reason*. Marieke Mueller's essay discusses the freedom afforded the reader in Sartre's late literary theory (in particular as this is implicit in *L'Idiot de la famille*), by contrast with his earlier and better-known views in *Qu'est-ce que la littérature?* [*What is Literature?*]. Whereas in that earlier work Sartre suggested that the author guides the reader through the text, in his late literary theory Mueller argues that the author is an intention imagined by the reading subject and that this new theorization in turn frees the reader from the author. Mueller's essay also offers a substantial discussion of Sartre's analysis, in *L'Idiot de la famille*, of the different types of reading in which Flaubert engaged. Sinan Richards starts out, in his essay, from Christina's discussion of *qui perd gagne* [loser wins] as shorthand for Sartre's account of subjectivity in *L'Être et le néant* [Being and Nothingness] and argues that it can also serve as a succinct summary of the overarching theme of Lacan's twenty-first seminar, *les non-dupes errent* [the undeceived are mistaken]. Richards thus shows that Lacan was indebted to Sartre's existential philosophy in ways which Lacan himself very forcefully denied — before suggesting rather mischievously that this structure of subjectivity was already present in Shakespeare.

In the second part contributors address freedom and necessity in the work of Jacques Derrida, the second major focus of Christina's work. Paul Earlie confronts Anthony Kenny's dismissive verdict on Derrida's work — that it is unduly rhetorical — by resituating it within a wide-ranging discussion of style and rhetoric in philosophy and looking closely at Derrida's own comments on the question of style, including in his critical engagements with Foucault, Nietzsche, and Cixous. Earlie returns to Derrida's reading of Plato's *Phaedrus* in 'La Pharmacie de Platon' [Plato's Pharmacy] to suggest that Plato (and Derrida) were in fact more concerned with the dangers of rhetoric than those of writing. Seán Hand's essay focuses on Derrida's influential late text, *Voyous* [Rogues], written in the aftermath of the 11 September terrorist attacks. Hand offers a thorough exposition and analysis of its principal themes and focuses in particular on Derrida's critique of Jean-Luc Nancy's 'fraternal' conception of democracy and community. Hand suggests that Derrida echoed critical analyses by Chomsky and Blum which presented the US as the most rogue of 'rogue states' and makes the case for a 'Derridean dynamic of governance' which retains incalculable singularity within the promise of democracy to come.

In the third part contributors explore freedom and the subject in contemporary philosophy and theory. Taking his cue from Christina's discussion in *Mortal Subjects*, Ian Maclachlan discusses Nancy's *L'Expérience de la liberté* [The Experience of Freedom], reflects on Derrida's aforementioned engagement with this work in *Voyous* and focuses in particular on the nature of the 'interval' in Nancy. Ian James also focuses on Nancy's *L'Expérience* and has more to say about the 'interval' and its spatial and temporal structure. James emphasizes the formative role of this philosopher's early readings of Kant and likens them in this respect to Derrida's of Husserl. James argues that Nancy's reading of Kant overcomes a narrowly ontological and anthropological conception of freedom, yet nevertheless articulates an ontology that is realist without being foundationalist. He then examines Nancy's ontology in relation to two other realist ontologies, from contemporary science, advanced by Lee Smolin and Roger Penrose. James argues that Smolin's conception of the universe as a singular relational structure evolving dynamically over time 'resonates' with Nancy's ontology of freedom.

Martin Crowley contextualizes Bernard Stiegler's philosophy of technology in relation to other French theorists, including Sartre, who have been preoccupied with the tension between freedom and determinism. Crowley offers a sympathetic exploration of Stiegler's account of the co-constitution of the human and the technical and asks to what extent that account really allows room for the transformative agency which Stiegler repeatedly exhorts his readers to exercise. Henry Dicks takes his cue from a parenthetical question about Heidegger in Christina's abovementioned essay, 'Sartre and the Deconstruction of the Subject': Dicks responds by discussing Peter Sloterdijk's Heideggerian 'paleo-ontology' — the study of the ancient disclosure of Being — and its illumination of the motif of the clearing. Dicks argues that it was the ecological shift of early humans from forested to open environments that made necessary the domesticating adaptations discussed by Sloterdijk and makes a case for an ecological rather than anthropological understanding of the concept of the clearing.

Jeremy Ahearne considers how Axel Honneth works through his doubts about whether recognition theory can be used in International Relations to understand state-to-state relations and reflects on the manner in which Honneth treads ground which is less familiar to him. Ahearne contemplates Honneth's position as a subject of Theory (the Theory of International Relations) and the interruption which this being subjected effects to the very self-confidence which Honneth had elsewhere suggested is necessary for an 'unbroken' relation of the subject to himself. Serge Trottein closes these reflections on freedom and the subject in contemporary theory by envisaging a gesture of 'franking', or *affranchissement*, by which the subject could free itself from theory and free freedom from its historical entanglements with subjectivity. Trottein's franking also works to question critically the 'Frenchness' of so called 'French theory'.

In the fourth part, contributors consider pathologies and therapeutics of freedom. Marc Lafrance presents a comparative discussion of Christina's *Mortal Subjects* alongside the work of philosopher Drew Leder: both thinkers, Lafrance argues, build on the work of Merleau-Ponty in particular to show that greater epistemic and ethical prominence should be given in our thinking of embodiment to the vulnerable, fragile, ill, and mortal body. Drawing on the work of Bernard Stiegler and contemporary neuroscience, Gerald Moore then considers addicted bodies and minds in terms of automatism.

Jane Hiddleston asks how Frantz Fanon's interest in literature relates to his psychiatric, political, and philosophical work. She argues that across these different areas Fanon developed a coherent theory of embodiment, according to which the body is potentially a form of self-expression that is shaped and channelled by language. Colonialism and racism suppress these expressive possibilities with their destructive 'schéma corporel'. Hiddleston argues that literature allowed Fanon to express a visceral sense of bodily agency through the immediacy of a call to revolt. In the volume's closing essay, Robert Young draws on his recent co-edited collection (with Jean Khalfa) of Fanon's writings on psychiatry and politics. Young recontextualizes Fanon's political writing in relation to his professional field of expertise, neurology, and French psychiatry of the 1950s and 60s more broadly. Young develops Henri Ey's suggestion, as taken up by Fanon, that psychiatry's therapeutic field was delineated by the pathologies of freedom.

This volume honours the work of Christina Howells. It originated in a conference held in Venice in March 2017, organized by Oliver Davis. All contributors are past or present students of Christina or friends and colleagues, or several of these. Its aim is not to settle prematurely the legacy of her work, but to demonstrate its ongoing and immediate importance for thought in the humanities today.

Notes to the Introduction

1. Christina Howells, *Sartre's Theory of Literature* (London: Modern Humanities Research Association, 1979), p. 1.
2. Ibid., p. 2.
3. See Christina Howells, *Sartre: The Necessity of Freedom* (Cambridge: Cambridge University Press, 1988).
4. See *French Women Philosophers: A Contemporary Reader*, ed. by Christina Howells (London & New York: Routledge, 2004).
5. See Christina Howells, *Derrida: Deconstruction from Phenomenology to Ethics* (Cambridge: Polity Press, 1999).
6. See Jacques Derrida, 'Les Fins de l'homme', in *Marges de la philosophie* (Paris: Minuit, 1972), pp. 129–64.
7. Jacques Derrida, 'Desceller ("la vieille neuve langue")', interview with Catherine David, in Derrida, *Points de suspension* (Paris: Galilée, 1992), pp. 123–40 (p. 130); first published as 'Derrida l'insoumis', in *Le Nouvel Observateur*, 9–15 September 1983.
8. Derrida, *Points de suspension*, p. 131. All translations are the authors' own unless otherwise stated.
9. See Jacques Derrida, '"Il courait mort": Salut, salut. Notes pour un courrier aux *Temps Modernes*', *Les Temps Modernes*, 587 (1996), 7–54.
10. Christina Howells, 'Sartre and the Deconstruction of the Subject', in *The Cambridge Companion to Sartre*, ed. by Christina Howells (Cambridge: Cambridge University Press, 1992), pp. 318–52 (p. 349). See also Howells, *Derrida*, p. 143.
11. Ibid., p. 28.
12. Ibid.

13. Ibid., p. 143.
14. Howells, 'Conclusion', p. 318.
15. Ibid., p. 342.
16. Christina Howells, *Mortal Subjects: Passions of the Soul in Late Twentieth-Century French Thought* (Cambridge: Polity Press, 2011), p. 2.
17. Ibid., p. 219.
18. Ibid., p. 227.

CHAPTER 1

Subjects,
Autonomous and Otherwise

Gary E. Aylesworth

In *Mortal Subjects*, Christina Howells writes: 'we desire the impossible combination of liberty and identity — to know (and be) who we are while still remaining fully free'.[1] This impossible combination structures much of what is casually referred to as 'French Theory', including figures such as Bataille, Foucault, Derrida, Blanchot, Deleuze, and Nancy. In this context, the mortality of the subject includes not only death as an unthinkable and un-appropriable limit to subjectivity, but also the passions of love and mourning as breaches in subjective identity, both for the individual and the community. As Howells points out, the radical finitude or mortality of this subject is, paradoxically, the condition of its freedom. This condition has the structure of an aporia, whose shorthand is *qui perd gange* [loser wins], and it has played out over more than two centuries of theorizing.

The notion of 'the subject of theory', as it has developed in the West since the Enlightenment, is structured by an internal tension that is evident in the double genitive of its grammar. It is at once the subject *matter* or object of theory, and, at the same time, it indicates the act of theorizing itself. This tension, as well as the question as to whether the gap between the theorized subject and the subject that theorizes can be closed, is apparent in Kant's *Critique of Pure Reason*. This question notwithstanding, Kant insists that the freedom of the subject lies in its autonomy.

In his 1781 preface to the *Critique*, Kant claims that his age is one of feigned disinterest toward metaphysical questions in light of the irresolvable contestations and dogmatisms of metaphysical systems as compared to the real advances made by the sciences:

> And now, after all methods, so it is believed, have been tried and found wanting the prevailing mood is that of weariness and complete *indifferentism* — the mother, in all sciences, of chaos and night, but happily in this case the source, or at least the prelude, of their approaching reform and restoration.[2]

For Kant, this mood of 'indifferentism' is a sign that metaphysics has reached the turning point between exhaustion and renewal. Continued indifferentism would mean losing what is essential to the subject: its demand for unconditioned knowledge, arising from its own surpassing of everything empirical. But because the human subject is also the subject of reason, indifference toward metaphysics can only be 'feigned', because the interest of reason drives us toward the unconditioned whether we acknowledge it or not.

Reason, for Kant, is a power of synthesis, an activity of bringing manifolds into unity, and its demand for unconditioned knowledge is a reflection of its own unconditioned unity in act (see *CPR*, p. 137: 'For the mind could never think its identity in the manifestation of its representations, and indeed think this identity *a priori*, if it did not have before its eyes the identity of its act'). In this regard, it is free and autonomous, and this Kant discovers in himself, for, as he says: 'I have to deal with nothing save reason itself and its pure thinking; and to obtain complete knowledge of these, there is no need to go far afield, since I come upon them in my own self' (*CPR*, p. 10). Kant thus becomes the subject of his own thinking, and he attempts to enact the autonomy and unconditionality he ascribes to reason. Reason, he says, represents the unconditioned conditions for the possibility of a thinking being (*CPR*, p. 366), and thus the soul 'knows in itself' the following:

(1) *The unconditioned unity of relation* (the soul is self-subsistent);
(2) *The unconditioned unity of quality* (the soul is simple, not a 'whole' or unity of parts);
(3) *The unconditioned unity in the plurality of time* (the soul is always one and the same subject);
(4) *The unconditioned unity of existence in space* (the soul is conscious of its own existence only, and of other things merely as its representations).

These unities are the basis for philosophical concepts of the subject that extend beyond Kant and into the nineteenth century. But already in Kant, the transcendental subject proves to be a problematic notion.

Kant informs us that his inquiry aims for completeness and certainty. That means the objective validity of a priori concepts must be affirmed in empirical intuition, i.e. their certainty is guaranteed by the presentation of examples in sensory experience. However, because these concepts are not derived from experience but have their origin in the understanding, completeness requires further inquiry into this subjective ground (reason). Here, the question is 'what and how much can the understanding and reason know apart from all experience?' (*CPR*, p. 12). In the *Critique*, the difference between these two inquiries becomes problematical, for the account of the subjective ground is not objectively certain, and the account of objective certainty is, considered by itself, incomplete.

This difficulty arises because Kant denies 'intellectual intuition', which would be the subject's intuition of its act of giving itself *to* itself, or bringing itself into existence, rather than being affected by or *appearing* to itself (*CPR*, p. 88). Kant's solution to this problem is an appeal to the unity of consciousness, or the 'transcendental unity of apperception', which he says could not be possible unless there were already a synthesis of the manifold of representations. As he remarks, 'the mind could never think its identity in the manifoldness of its representations, and indeed think this unity *a priori*, if it did not have before its eyes the identity of its act' (*CPR*, p. 137). Hence, he 'deduces' the original synthesis as the ground of the unity of his own consciousness, and thereby deduces reason as the ground of the identity of the self. However, the nature of this synthesis is a matter of subsequent dispute. Kant himself attributes this act first to productive imagination, and then to the spontaneity of the understanding. The reason, apparently, is that productive imagination is a synthesis of activity and receptivity in the same act, prior to apperception (consciousness), while the understanding is the unity of apperception *in relation to* the synthesis of imagination. The originality of productive imagination would undermine his appeal to the unity of consciousness as the basis for deducing the unity of the original synthesis, since there would be no guarantee that the unity of apperception, which is active only, mirrors or reflects a unity that is also the difference between passivity and activity (or between sensibility and understanding). In the 'B' Deduction, Kant relegates imagination to a faculty of receptivity and distinguishes the understanding as the *only* faculty of spontaneity and synthesis in relation to the manifold of intuitions, thus restoring consciousness as the mind's unity 'before its own eyes', and securing this unity in objective certainty.

In regard to the cognition of objects, therefore, the subject is not fully autonomous, relying as it does upon the given-ness of these objects to begin with, a given-ness that leads Kant to posit the existence of 'things in themselves' beyond all cognition and experience. On the other hand, Kant insists upon the complete autonomy of reason in the moral sphere, where the moral law (our sense of what 'ought' to be) is given by reason without the mediation of anything empirical. The sense of the 'ought' also presupposes the freedom of the subject insofar as our responsibility to the 'ought' would be contradictory and impossible if our actions in the world were merely events of nature and therefore determined by nature's causal mechanisms. It is noteworthy that Kant refuses to identify moral freedom with the spontaneity of the understanding, but he raises the question of a common ground between them. This presumption of a common, subjective, ground for knowledge and morality (i.e. for what 'is' and what 'ought' to be) is taken up by Kant's idealist successors.

Fichte, for example, attempts to think out a system of knowledge (*Wissenschaftslehre*) in which the intellect and the moral will are one and the same act, a *Tathandlung*, in which the subject gives itself to itself in intellectual intuition, Kant's dismissal of the notion notwithstanding. For Fichte, objective given-ness is not grounded in the positing of an unknowable thing in itself, but is simply a representation accompanied by a feeling of necessity, just as other representations might be accompanied by a feeling of freedom. Both of these feelings are nothing more than modifications of the 'I', the subject who is the ground and basis of any experience whatsoever. However, because the I is the explanatory ground for all experience, it must be posited as lying outside of all experience, and thus it can only be *posited* by consciousness as the first principle (*Grundsatz*) of knowledge. Furthermore, the freedom of the I as the original act has its correlate in the freedom of empirical consciousness to posit it. Such a positing cannot be forced by proof or argumentation: it must be a free and spontaneous act. However, once posited, the concept forces consciousness to think according to its own necessity, and this thinking constitutes the system of idealism. Thus, the *Wissenschaftslehre* proceeds as follows: 'It summons the listener or reader to think freely of a certain concept. If he indeed does this, he will discover that he is obliged to proceed in a certain way'.[3] In other words, once the concept is freely posited, its inner necessity will lead consciousness through its series of grounds and conditions until their systematic completeness has been worked out.

Empirically, however, the identity between the freedom of the conscious subject and the necessity of nature cannot be completely realized. It can only be approximated in practical action, under the command of reason to realize its own unconditionality. But, since consciousness and its relations to nature are conditioned by time, the identity between the absolute as pure act (outside of time) and human action (which can only occur in time) will remain, as Kant would say, a regulative idea and an infinite task. The thinking subject will never attain complete identity with the world.

For the early Schelling, on the other hand, the freedom of the I is absolute from the very beginning. It is not empirical consciousness that posits the I, but the I that is the ground of consciousness posits itself. The absolute I is not a subject, according to Schelling, because a subject is always a unity of consciousness in relation to an object, and it can become an object itself through conscious reflection. Consciousness, including reflective consciousness, is always conditioned, and therefore never absolute, but the freedom of the I, as pure act, is unconditioned, and therefore it is *not* an act of consciousness. '*The essence of the I is freedom*,' declares Schelling, 'it is not thinkable except inasmuch as it posits itself by its own absolute power... Freedom *is* only through itself'.[4] Conscious self-awareness, on the other hand, 'is not a free act of the immutable but an unfree urge that induces the mutable I, conditioned by the not-I, to strive to maintain its identity and to reassert itself in the undertow of endless change' (*IPP*, p. 76). Such striving would never occur, says Schelling, if the unconditioned identity of the absolute I were not the unconscious ground of the empirical I from the beginning. But because the conscious I is temporal and changeable, just as in Fichte, its identity with the pure I can never be objectively known. However, this identity can be experienced in feeling, where, in the artwork, conscious intention is joined with unconscious nature, and their synthesis is felt by consciousness as aesthetic enjoyment. Schelling refers to this identity as a 'point of indifference' in which the absolute inheres in itself.

Although Hegel is deeply indebted to Schelling, he finds Schelling's characterization of the absolute I to be a mere *Grundsatz* — an abstraction consciousness posits outside of itself. But to be *real*, the absolute must be experienced by consciousness, not as something external and other, but as arising within the temporality of consciousness as *spirit*. As Hegel puts it, 'What moves itself is spirit (*Geist*); it is the Subject of the movement and equally the *moving* itself, or the substance through which the Subject moves'.[5] Unlike Schelling's point of indifference (which, in the preface to *The Phenomenology of Spirit*, Hegel mocks as 'the night in which all cows are black'), spirit for Hegel 'is the process of self-differentiating, the positing of distinctions'.[6] These distinctions include not only the individually existing subject, but also the universal consciousness that is real as the community of individuals who share a common culture. As Hegel remarks, 'not the individual by himself, but together with the consciousness of the community and what he is for this community, is the complete whole of the individual as spirit' (*PS*, p. 462).

This bond between individual and community is religion, which in previous ages expressed itself in outward forms of art and cultic practices. But in these forms, spirit is the substance of a consciousness that does not yet reflect into itself, and therefore has not come into its true shape as subjectivity. Only Christian Protestantism, the religion of inwardness, brings this culture to an end and inaugurates a new one. For Hegel, this is the meaning of the Crucifixion and Resurrection: the God on the cross was the absolute appearing in the world as a temporally existing, mortal individual, and in the death of this individual 'death becomes transfigured from its immediate meaning, viz. the non-being of this *particular* individual, into the *universality* of the Spirit who dwells in His community, dies every day, and is daily resurrected' (*PS*, p. 475). But insofar as the community's self-consciousness exists only in the form of 'picture thinking', that is, in the form of non-identity between consciousness and what it represents to itself, the community is not yet perfected. In order to attain its perfection, consciousness must undergo the profound grief that *God Himself is dead*, as expressed in the line of the Lutheran hymn 'O Traurigkeit' (attributed to Johann Rist, 1641): 'O grosse Not! Gott selbst ist Tot' [Oh great distress, God himself is dead!]. Such grief opens the inward depth of spirit, in which the totality of the whole is taken up as something lost, and then resurrected in the inwardness of thinking. As Hegel writes in *Faith and Knowledge*, 'the highest totality can and must achieve its resurrection solely from this harsh consciousness of loss, encompassing everything, and ascending in all its earnestness out of its deepest ground to the most serene freedom of its shape'.[7] This, then, is the impetus of the Hegelian project; a supreme act of recollection in which the lost totality, mourned in religious grief, is resurrected in thought as history, that is, as a substance shattered by the negativity of time and reshaped into the unity of conscious reflection.

This transformation is predicated upon God's appearance in the world as a particular existing human being, for only the human form can represent spirit for a thinking consciousness. This appearance is God's revelation, or God *as* revelation, and it requires the witness of others *for whom* and *to whom* God's truth is revealed. For revelation to take place, it must become the object of history, and can only be experienced as something past by the community in question. It is only for *this* community that the existence and death of a particular individual is the revelation of divine truth, a revelation that *did not* occur contemporaneously with the events historically presented. In other words, this revelation could only come about once the community of 'the faithful' has taken shape (the church).

In this moment, the particular existence of the human being who died is now elevated into singularity (*Einzelheit*), which Hegel describes as being 'exclusively *for others*' (*LPR*, p. 133). This means the community of *faith* is founded only *after* the death of the particular individual has removed his appearance from the temporal sphere. As Hegel remarks: 'It is now the community that is formed and in which the Holy Spirit dwells' (*LPR*, p. 149). This death is a transition into *love*, a shared inwardness binding together many existing individuals above and beyond their worldly interests and attachments. It is also a moment of reconciliation between the human and the divine: absolute spirit has become human, suffered humiliation and death, and is resurrected *as* the community of the faithful, in which infinite subjectivity becomes conscious of itself in shared inwardness.

The fulfilment of this religious transformation occurs in the Reformation, and especially in Lutheranism. However, subsequent to the Reformation, modernity has taken shape as a world mediated by self-conscious spirit, whose true form is conceptual knowledge, i.e. *Wissenschaft*, or 'science', and whose systematic consummation is philosophy. Where the Enlightenment subjected religious representations to the critical activity of the understanding and its oppositions (e.g. God is either one or not one, but not both), true philosophy is a function of reason, which reconciles the apparent contradictions of the understanding by elevating them into dialectical development (God is *one movement* through moments of difference and negation). Instead of suffering critical destruction, says Hegel, 'Religion must take refuge in philosophy' (*LPR*, p. 162), which is to say, the philosophical community.

But, contrary to those who find in Hegel the announcement of the end of history, he declares that spirit's reconciliation with itself is only partial, for it remains sequestered in philosophy as 'a sanctuary apart', whose members 'constitute an isolated order of priests' (*LPR*, p. 162, n. 259). The external world, on the other hand, remains rife with dispute and disorder. How the empirical present is to find its way out of its own discord, says Hegel, is 'not the immediate practical business and affair of philosophy' (*LPR*, p. 162, n. 259). This is to say that philosophy's grasp of the history of spirit is no predictor of what will empirically happen in the world today or tomorrow. Instead, philosophy is a continuous labour to enact, in thought, the reconciliation of reason with itself as the substance and subject of the world.

Hegel's temporalization of the absolute closes the gap between the absolute and consciousness, as well as the difference between the subject and its world. As he insists, 'the world is in the subject; it is there as the impulse toward nature, toward social life, toward art and science [...] monkish withdrawal means that the heart is not concretely developed' (*LPR*, p. 340). However, this Hegelian reconciliation between subject and world is challenged by Søren Kierkegaard, for whom religious faith is a moment of inwardness in which the subject relates itself to a God who has no worldly being. Hence, for him, Christianity is founded upon a logical absurdity. As he writes in *Concluding Unscientific Postscript*: 'The eternal truth has come into being in time: this is the paradox'.[8] In Kierkegaard's view there is no substantive continuity between God and the world, or between God and man. 'God does not think, he creates; God does not exist, He is eternal,' he declares, 'Man thinks and exists, and existence separates thought and being, holding them apart from one another in succession' (*CUP*, p. 296). Faith, however, is precisely the belief that God *has existed* (*CUP*, p. 291) and this is the paradox philosophy cannot resolve into conceptual knowledge.

Nor can philosophy bring the subject into complete knowledge of itself. In a famous journal entry, Kierkegaard addresses his fundamental difference with Hegel on the relationship between existing and knowing:

> Philosophy is perfectly right in saying that life must be understood backward. But then one forgets the other clause — that it must be lived forward. The more one thinks through this clause, the more one concludes that life in temporality never becomes properly understandable, simply because never at any time does one get perfect repose to take a stance — backward.[9]

In other words, the consciousness that Hegel says recollects and interiorizes the lost totality in religious grief cannot recollect and unify *itself*, because it is always out ahead of itself in existence. This is certainly a statement Hegel would agree with in reference to empirically existing subjects, but for him it would not apply to spirit as *reason*, whose being must be conceived from its own concept. However, Kierkegaard insists that existence or being is radically *incommensurable* with its concept; it is that which thought can never take up into itself and 'know'.

This is what Kierkegaard calls the paradox of all thought, the collision of reason with the unknown, which, in relation to reason, is the absolutely different.[10] Insofar as thought 'is', it cannot think its own coming into being in the moment, for the moment is a discontinuity and a breach between being and non-being, a breach that can only be crossed by a leap that reason and consciousness cannot render into self-identity. As Kierkegaard says, 'In the *Moment* man becomes conscious that he is born: for his antecedent state, to which he may not cling, was one of non-being' (PF, p. 25). This coming into being in the moment is not knowledge; it is a suffering, an undergoing, and a passion, and this is the meaning of the Christian paradox that God himself *has been* (PF, p. 107): that God suffered coming into existence, underwent the passion of temporality, and 'died'. But the nature of this incarnation and death is quite other than that conceived by Hegel.

In *Philosophical Fragments*, Kierkegaard describes the passage from non-being into being as an event of difference, a breach in the continuity of the substance of the actual. 'The elusiveness pertaining to an event,' he writes, 'consists in its having happened, in which fact lies the transition from nothing, from non-being' (PF, p. 101). Hence, this 'having happened' is only something that can be believed, but not objectively presented. As he remarks: 'Faith believes what it does not see; it does not believe the star is there, for that it sees, but it believes that the star has come into existence' (PF, p. 101). This holds, as well, for the belief that God has become actual, 'revealed' himself in the world, and this is the paradox of the God-man. The man who appears is 'there', but the God whose coming into existence *was* the event of this appearing, is *not* there.

In opposition to Hegel, Kierkegaard maintains that Christianity is precisely faith in the paradox that God came into existence in the appearance of a human being while remaining wholly other to human beings. As he writes in *The Sickness Unto Death*: 'Christendom's basic trouble is really Christianity, that the teaching about the God-man [...] is profaned by being preached day in and day out, that the qualitative difference between God and man is abolished'.[11] Hegel's community of the faithful is thus Kierkegaard's 'Christendom', a reduction of the event to something that appears to and for 'others' who are never a single individual, but 'humanity in general', represented by the concept 'man'.

For Kierkegaard, if there is reconciliation between God and man, it is *not* God's revelation as an appearance to and for a community, but God's forgiveness of the sinner. As he says: 'The category of sin is the category of individuality [...]. The individual human being lies beneath the concept; an individual human being cannot be thought, but only the concept "man" [...] just as one individual person cannot be thought, neither can one individual sinner' (*SD*, p. 119). If there is reconciliation, it can only be between God and the individual, and the individual only in relation to God. Faith, therefore, does not belong to the category of the ethical, but is a suspension of the ethical in a moment of transcendence. This moment is one of irreducible difference between the individual and God: 'As sinner, man is separated from God by the most chasmal qualitative abyss. In turn, of course, God is separated from man by the same chasmal qualitative abyss when he forgives sins' (*SD*, p. 122). In this regard, the abyss between God and the existing individual is not only the event of having been born, but also that of death.

As Kierkegaard writes, 'Christianly understood, death itself is a passing into life' (*SD*, p. 17), meaning that death is not the worldly end of life, but is dying *to* the world in the withdrawal of the event. The death of the individual, then, is a passing into the eternity of God. But this death is no natural occurrence that appears to 'others'; it is the death of the self, the subject, who relates itself to itself in its own inwardness, and who must find salvation in relating itself to God as the forgiver of sins. In other words, the self must 'die' to itself, and to temporality, and relate itself instead to God, whose existence (coming into being) can only be believed in. Faith, therefore, is not knowledge, but a passion that intensifies the subject's awareness of its own existence to the highest degree.

The figure who could be said to bring philosophical thinking on the subject to a critical 'end' is, of course, Friedrich Nietzsche. It is Nietzsche who writes in *Twilight of the Idols* that the concept of the I is the fundamental error of Western metaphysics. Here, he states that the notion of the I as *that* which wills, or thinks, is merely an illusion of grammar:

> We find ourselves in the midst of a rude fetishism when we call to mind the basic presuppositions of the metaphysics of language — which is to say, of *reason*. It is *this* which sees everywhere deed and doer; this which believes in will as cause in general; this which believes in the 'ego', the ego as being, in the ego as substance, and which *projects* its belief in the ego-substance on to all things.[12]

Our notion of the subject is thus the effect of linguistic practices and conventions, particularly the grammatical requirement of a 'subject' for every verb. But for Nietzsche, the subject is itself a performative 'effect' of language: language 'speaks' the subject, not the other way around. For this reason, Nietzsche says in *On the Genealogy of Morals* 'there is no "being" behind doing, effecting, becoming; "the doer" is merely a fiction added to the deed — the deed is everything'.[13]

In this respect, we can better understand the sense of his perhaps most infamous statement, 'God is dead', in *The Gay Science*. While Nietzsche is not the first to risk this hard saying, he adds the coda: '*We have killed him* — you and I!'[14] The atheists of the marketplace who ridicule the madman for saying this are themselves unaware of the import of the message, that *they,* all of them, and all of us, are God's murderers. This is not an announcement of God's revelation coming into existence, but the declaration of an act that falls upon us as our own, or, rather, an act we must make our own. In contrast to Hegel, Nietzsche's pronouncement is not addressed to a community of the faithful; it is an opening to the future and the possibility of a community that does not yet exist.

The point would be that the notion of God no longer has any effective force in the world, regardless of personal professions of religious belief. Such belief belongs to the psychology of feelings and representations, and it is often provoked by an underlying sense of loss. For Nietzsche, expressions of personal religiosity confirm the very thing they deny. The practices and mechanisms of the modern world, shared by believers and non-believers alike, have denied to the notion of God any functional reality. In this sense 'we' have killed God, 'we' with our modernity, our science and technology, and our mundane sensibilities. The atheists of the marketplace have missed the crucial insight: with the death of God the foundation of their own standpoint (the non-existence of God as a fact) collapses as well. Without God, there is no such 'fact' to be determined because facts themselves are no longer grounded upon a bedrock of unquestionable truth.

For Nietzsche the death of God is not a fact, but an event. In the words of the madman of *The Gay Science*: 'This tremendous event is still on its way, still wandering; it has not yet reached the ears of men. Lightning and thunder require time; the light of the stars requires time; deeds, though done, still require time to be seen and heard' (GS, p. 125). Just as many of the stars we see at night burned out eons ago, their demise is invisible because the event is still on its way to us. Hence, where Kierkegaard remarks that we see the star, but we *believe* it came into being, Nietzsche would say we see the star, but we intimate its death. Furthermore, for Nietzsche the temporality of the event is not so much of the past (it has happened) but of the future (it is on its way). In this regard, Nietzsche distinguishes himself from both Kierkegaard and Hegel, and this difference becomes most acute in *Thus Spoke Zarathustra*.

'"All 'it was' is a fragment," says Zarathustra, "a dreadful accident — until the creative will says to it, 'But thus I willed it' ... thus I shall will it"'.[15] This is an exhortation to overcome the greatest burden of existence: that 'it was' has suffered coming into being in the first place. For Nietzsche, the philosophical and religious underpinnings of the West have harboured a resentment toward existence and life. In essence, it is the sense that all that comes to be perishes, and all that perishes *deserves* not to be. It is, in other words, a metaphysics of guilt and punishment. 'And where there was suffering,' says Zarathustra, 'one always wanted punishment too' (Z, p. 140). Hence Nietzsche's diagnosis of a secret *ressentiment,* the presumption that all coming into being is *guilty.* This is the burden to be shouldered, and creatively transformed into affirmation.

For Nietzsche, this can only mean a projection toward the future, for, as Zarathustra declares: 'man is a bridge and no end' (Z, p. 198), and:

> I taught them to work on the future and redeem with their creation all that *has been*. To redeem what is past in man and to re-create all 'it was' until the will says, 'Thus I willed it! Thus I shall will it'. (*Z*, p. 198)

Here the concept of the subject founders, not only upon the gap of the moment, but upon the freedom that opens in the breach of the future, dissolving the substance of the 'it was' and its seeming irrevocability. Openness to the future means shattering identity, for identity can only be a repetition of the 'it was'. But in *Zarathustra* Nietzsche denies the closure and circularity that such repetition requires, as evident in the famous section entitled 'On the Vision and the Riddle', where he gives his most extensive iteration of the notion of 'eternal return'.

To attentive readers, Nietzsche is clear that eternal return does not mean a literal repetition of the past. When Zarathustra stands at the gateway whose name is 'Moment', he is at the intersection of the paths of past and future. He asks the dwarf (the spirit of gravity) if the two paths must contradict one another eternally, to which the dwarf responds, 'All that is straight lies [...]. All truth is crooked; time itself is a circle' (*Z*, p. 158). But Zarathustra replies, 'do not make things too easy for yourself!' and then asks:

> What do you think, dwarf, of this moment? Must not this gateway too have been there before? And are not all things knotted together so firmly that his moment draws after it *all* that is to come? Therefore — itself too? (*Z*, p. 158)

The question is whether the moment is an endless repetition of the 'it was' and its unbearable density, or is, perhaps, a breach, a cut in time's substance that opens the possibility of the new.

The latter possibility is suggested by what follows in the text. The dwarf disappears, and Zarathustra is startled by the sight of a shepherd with a black snake stuck in his throat. 'Then it cried out of me,' he says, 'Bite! Bite its head off!' (*Z*, p. 159). The shepherd bites and spews out the head of the snake, and then jumps up. 'No longer shepherd,' says Zarathustra, 'no longer human — one changed, radiant, *laughing!* Never yet on earth has a human being laughed as he laughed!' (*Z*, p. 160). Nietzsche's image recalls the figure of the ouroboros, the image of time as a snake, coiled in a circle, swallowing its own tail. The shepherd's bite severs the closure of the circle and elicits a laughter not yet heard on earth, in other words, a laughter that is *new*.

Nietzsche's text has elicited innumerable interpretations, perhaps precisely because of its literary qualities. Nonetheless, he makes an undeniable connection between the riddle of time and the question of the subject. '*What* did I see then in a parable?' asks Zarathustra, 'And *who* is it who must yet come one day? *Who* is the shepherd into whose throat the snake crawled thus?' (*Z*, p. 160). Is it Nietzsche himself? Zarathustra? The Overman? Or perhaps someone yet to be imagined?

It is no accident that nineteenth-century reflections on the subject come to a crucial turn in writing that is intensely literary as much as it is philosophical, and this literary turn continues into the later twentieth century, and now the twenty-first. It is especially subjects (now in the plural) entwined with literary-philosophical texts that Christina Howells refers to as 'mortal'. As she writes in the epilogue to *Mortal Subjects*: 'Mortality is the very condition of possibility of subjectivity in the modern sense. It is precisely because I am *not* self-sufficient or self-identical or immortal that my subjectivity comes into being in its self-division and diaspora [...] or *différance*' (*MS*, p. 220). But contrary to Kant's conception, here the non-self-sufficiency of the subject, *not* its autonomy, constitutes its freedom. Howells remarks: 'It is precisely our failure to achieve self-identity that allows us to be free: our non-self-coincidence, our *pour soi* which is riven by self-division and is never *soi*, our "diasporic" subjectivity provide the key to our ability to change, and to choose who we want to be' (*MS*, p. 218). We could say the same for *theorizing* the subject as well, since theory is an enactment of the subject as much as it is about the subject, and therefore structured by the same non-identity.

As this excursion through nineteenth-century thought has shown, when it comes to the subject, we theorize because we do not know, and we do not know because we theorize. It is another iteration of the difference that makes possible the very thing that becomes impossible at the same time. The 'subject of theory' does not name a determinate self or subject-matter, but a movement of thinking driven by its own irresolution. By the logic of 'loser wins', this irresolution is the freedom of thinking as it wanders on its way, returning us ever anew to the question: 'who?'

Notes to Chapter 1

1. Christina Howells, *Mortal Subjects: Passions of the Soul in Late Twentieth-Century French Thought* (Cambridge: Polity Press, 2011), p. 2; subsequently referred to as *MS* in the main text.
2. Immanuel Kant, *Critique of Pure Reason*, trans. by Norman Kemp Smith (New York: St. Martin's Press, 1964), p. 8; subsequently referred to as *CPR* in the main text.
3. J. G. Fichte, *Introductions to the Wissenschaftslehre and Other Writings*, trans. by Daniel Breazeale (Indianapolis: Hackett, 1994), pp. 30–31.
4. Friedrich Schelling, 'Of the I as the Principle of Philosophy', in *German Idealism*, ed. by Brian O'Connor and Georg Mohr (Chicago, IL: University of Chicago Press, 2006), p. 75; subsequently referred to as *IPP* in the main text.
5. G. W. F. Hegel, *Phenomenology of Spirit*, trans. by A. V. Miller (Oxford: Oxford University Press, 1977), p. 477; subsequently referred to as *PS* in the main text.
6. G. W. F. Hegel, *Lectures on the Philosophy of Religion, Volume III: The Consummate Religion*, trans. by R. F. Brown, P. C. Hodgson and J. M. Stewart (Berkeley: University of California Press, 1985), p. 311; subsequently referred to as *LPR* in the main text.
7. G. W. F. Hegel, *Faith and Knowledge*, trans. by Walter Cerf and H. S. Harris (Albany, NY: SUNY Press, 1977), p. 191.
8. Søren Kierkegaard, *Concluding Unscientific Postscript*, trans. by David F. Swenson and Walter Lowrie (Princeton, NJ: Princeton University Press, 1941), p. 187; subsequently referred to as *CUP* in the main text.
9. Søren Kierkegaard, *The Essential Kierkegaard*, ed. by Howard and Edna Hong (Princeton, NJ: Princeton University Press, 2000), p. 12.
10. Søren Kierkegaard, *Philosophical Fragments; or, A Fragment of Philosophy*, trans. by David Swenson and Howard Hong (Princeton, NJ: Princeton University Press, 1936), p. 55; subsequently referred to as *PF* in the main text.
11. Søren Kierkegaard, *The Sickness unto Death: A Christian Psychological Exposition for Upbuilding and Awakening*, trans. by Howard and Edna Hong (Princeton, NJ: Princeton University Press, 1980), p. 117; subsequently referred to as *SD* in the main text.
12. Friedrich Nietzsche, *Twilight of the Idols* and *The Anti-Christ*, trans. by R. J. Hollingdale (Baltimore, MD: Viking Penguin, 1968), p. 138.

13. Friedrich Nietzsche, *On the Genealogy of Morals*, trans. by Walter Kaufmann (New York: Random House, 1967), p. 13.

14. Friedrich Nietzsche, *The Gay Science*, trans. by Walter Kaufmann (New York: Random House, 1974), p. 181; subsequently referred to as *GS* in the main text.

15. Friedrich Nietzsche, *Thus Spoke Zarathustra: A Book for All and None*, trans. by Walter Kaufmann (Baltimore, MD: Viking Penguin, 1966), p. 141; subsequently referred to as *Z* in the main text.

PART I

Freedom and the Subject in Jean-Paul Sartre

CHAPTER 2

Iterable Praxis: Theory and Sartre's Concept of the Practico-inert

Patrick Chambers

In this chapter I shall consider the subject's potential to theorize when acting in a shared material environment governed by the Sartrean 'practico-inert'. I shall approach the difficult concept of 'theory' here from a broad, phenomenological perspective: by theory, I mean the creative totalization of structures in the world, whether in the thrust of practical engagement or abstraction.

I shall begin by outlining the basic structure of the practico-inert, as developed in *Critique de la raison dialectique* [Critique of Dialectical Reason] (1960), before discussing the powerful influence that this 'secteur' plays in directing, shaping, and redefining the subject's activity in the world. I shall draw on Derrida's concept of iteration to explore the idea of the practico-inert as a space in which supposedly discrete contexts, not the least that of the human, are deconstructed by the iterable inscriptions of praxis. Finally, I shall consider what remains of 'pro-jection' — the motion by which embodied consciousness defines itself through its engagement in the world — and what freedom the subject, as project, has to theorize in the fragmented, distorted world of the practico-inert.

The Practico-inert — in a Game of Football

The practico-inert, as Sartre presents it, emerges from the ceaseless crystallization of human activity in a shared material field. The material environment is the page onto which any human project must write itself; pro-jection can only exist as inscription.[1] All such acts of inscription — all attempts at meaningful reorganizations of the material field — are firstly limited and then recorded, combined and endlessly redefined by the shifting material structures of the practico-inert. Infused with human creativity, material takes on a life of its own and enters into a dialectic with our efforts to act upon it.

The practico-inert limits our field of possible actions through 'exigences' [demands] that the environment lays upon us. When we act, both in the moment of action and its aftermath, the practico-inert exerts a distorting influence on our praxis that Sartre names 'la contre-finalité' [counterfinality]. This distorting practico-inert mediation leads to the experience of reorganizing a material field and achieving an unexpected, alienating outcome — an experience referred to as 'la nécessité' [necessity]. To approach the complex reality of practico-inert mediation in a shared environment, let us to turn to a sporting metaphor that takes on great significance over the course of the *Critique*.

In a game of football, the way play develops and the formation of the players on the pitch at any given moment are the product of a series of totalizations of totalizations — that is to say, the players must keep responding creatively to their opponents' use of the space around them. Each team pro-jects beyond their opponents' strategy, anticipating their moves and trying to lure them into error. The football metaphor is, on close inspection, a highly sophisticated one, for it shows intersubjective conflict played out simultaneously on two levels: inter-group and inter-individual. Here, however, it is on the shared material field — the pitch — that our focus lies.

Over the course of the game, each totalization of totalizations, each move and counter-move, is structured by the trace that the collective activity of a multiplicity of groups and individuals has left on the pitch (*CRD*, I, 569; 473). Say, for example, the groundsman has marked out a narrow pitch to protect a damaged area of the sports ground. The game is then likely to be congested with a lack of space on the wings, and the teams will be forced to alter their tactics and team-selection accordingly. If there have been several games over the weekend, the pitch could be badly torn up in important strategic areas. This damage might mean a certain body position is called for at a given moment for a player to avoid a costly slip; in another situation, the ball might become bogged down, transforming a defensive pass into a chance for the opposition. In short, the praxis of the players is constrained at all moments by demands that the pitch makes upon them in the context of the game.

An inert material sector, the pitch has absorbed a range of human praxes over time in a way that is likely to be beyond the immediate understanding of any of the players. Synthesizing 'l'indéfini sériel des actes humains' ('the serial infinity of human acts') (*CRD*, I, 329; 219), it takes on a life of its own, developing into what Sartre might call 'un être étrange et vivant' ('a strange and living being') (*CRD*, I, 279; 169), and becomes an active element in the game. Though the players may not always be conscious of it or fully understand it, the material link that enables their intersubjective conflict is not neutral; whilst enabling the different projects to mediate one another, the pitch exerts its own force of mediation through a set of demands. The intersubjective mediation between projects is itself mediated, and so transformed, by a practico-inert influence which is the material context of the game itself and which, therefore, the players are powerless to pro-ject beyond.

Counterfinality: The Destructive Power of the Practico-inert

Needless to say, in other real-world contexts, the mediation of the practico-inert can manifest itself in far more profound and destructive ways. Sartre, for example, considers the case of the deforestation and flooding caused by widespread subsistence farming in China (*CRD*, I, 271–74; 161–64).

Here, we are shown the impossibility for remote individuals or groups to operate in genuine isolation within a shared material environment. When the floods strike, the farmers are united in their impotence, faced with a common destiny towards which all have contributed but which none could have prevented. The very form of the landscape, shaping their mutual remoteness and basic way of life over generations, made them blind to the collective impact of their relative praxes and led them inexorably towards their own destruction. There is no sense, it must be emphasized, in which the farmers are the victims of some supernatural force beyond the realms of human influence. Over centuries, the farmers acted positively on the landscape, reorganizing it through their praxis to cultivate a means of survival, and the floods that followed were an example of *counterfinality*: the negative product of positive human reorganization (*CRD*, I, 275; 164). Nevertheless, the joint factors of landscape, multiplicity, time, and space do make for an equation in which any given farmer is effectively powerless to alter the course of events.

The farmer experiences a form of practical destiny constituted by the demands of the 'champ magique de contre-finalité' ('magical field of counterfinality') (*CRD*, I, 333; 224). Infused with praxis, the environment has the power, as passive activity, to trap him within the confines of an 'avenir indépassable' ('future which cannot be surpassed') (*CRD*, I, 344; 235, translation modified); in effect, the farmer's project finds itself surpassed by a counterfinality that is precisely the negation of human pro-jection. As in Sartre's favourite military analogy, the project has been drawn into an ambush, yet, in this instance, the enemy is disinterested, intangible, and unbeatable.

The basic motion of the farmer's pro-jection has not been obstructed, yet the result of his praxis is entirely other than he intended. We have here the fundamental experience of *necessity*:

> La première expérience pratique de la nécessité doit se faire dans l'activité sans contrainte de l'individu et dans la mesure où le résultat final, bien que conforme à celui qu'on escomptait, se révèle en même temps comme radicalement Autre.
>
> [The first practical experience of necessity occurs in the unconstrained activity of the individual to the extent that the final result, though conforming to the one anticipated, also appears as radically Other.] (*CRD*, I, 332; 223)

We begin to see that there can be multiple 'avenirs indépassables' at play within any given intersubjective conflict. In the case of a seemingly straightforward, binary conflict between groups, one group can outwit another, harnessing its freedom against it, yet, as we saw with the game of football, the conflict as a whole is inevitably surpassed by the mediation of the practico-inert. Ultimately, both groups are working towards ends that the practico-inert field has defined.

To add still more complexity, the situation of the conflict is not static; on the contrary, it too is in ceaseless dialectical motion. The groups are not only mediated by the practico-inert but constantly feed this mediation through their actions, entangling themselves further. As it crystallizes, each act of praxis brings a subtle modification to the whole of the shifting quasi-totality of 'matière ouvrée' ('worked-on material') and creates the possibility of a new kind of counterfinality (*CRD*, I, 334; 225).

At the very moment of its inscription, praxis is rendered other than itself. Always within a fluid network of dialectical relations and limited to a certain position in time and space, there is no possibility for a project to account for the movement of the practico-inert. It is in this sense that a single farmer's act of land clearance defines itself beyond him, becoming 'deforestation' and, ultimately, 'self-destruction' (*CRD*, I, 334; 225).

The practico-inert emerges, then, as a shifting and transformative quasi-totality. It is *real*, surrounding and conditioning us (*CRD*, I, 429; 324); yet it has no straightforward presence or identity. The mediation of the practico-inert, we can argue, denies any stable foundation for totalization. It follows that, as an individual, my pro-jection rests on a delusion of sameness in a world defined by difference and alterity. Within the 'champ magique', faced with the tyranny of the practico-inert, I would seem to have little hope of achieving meaningful reorganization of my environment.

Iterable Praxis: *Itération* and the Practico-inert

To appreciate the distorting mediation of the practico-inert, we might usefully draw on the Derridean notion of *itération*. My aim in introducing Derridean thought and terminology here, it must be stressed, is neither to 'existentialize' Derrida nor to establish the *Critique* as a work of deconstruction *avant la lettre*; rather, it is a matter of borrowing certain concepts put forward by Derrida to help us explore the depth and subtleties of Sartre's theory.

In the well-known essay, 'Signature événement contexte' [Signature Event Context] (1971), Derrida argues that, in order to function, any form of communication must be iterable, repeatable, outside the immediate context of its production. It must, that is to say, continue to act in the absence of both the communicator and the recipient. Decipherability to a third party in a wholly separate time, place, or context is the condition of possibility of communicative acts.[2] Severance from the context of production, then, is not merely possible but inevitable; in the moment of its inscription or emission, the iterable form of my communication begins to act independently of my 'intentions'.

Over the course of 'Signature événement contexte', the idea of the iterability of communicative acts develops into a vehicle for a broader, radically transgressive conception of human experience. The movement of iteration fragments the idea of contained, determinable contexts; rather than depending on a given context for its signification, communication is precisely that which exceeds contextual boundaries:

> Tout signe, linguistique ou non linguistique, parlé ou écrit (au sens courant de cette opposition) [...] peut être cité, mis entre guillemets; par là il peut rompre avec tout contexte donné, engendrer à l'infini de nouveaux contextes, de façon absolument non saturable.

[Every sign, linguistic or nonlinguistic, spoken or written (in the current sense of this opposition), in a small or large unit, can be cited, put between quotation marks; in so doing it can break with every given context, engendering an infinity of new contexts in a manner which is absolutely illimitable.] (*M*, p. 381; 12)

Once the idea of closed fields of communication has been dispelled, we are left with a field of 'itérabilité générale' ('general iterability') within which different forms of iteration circulate (*M*, p. 389; 18). There is no possibility of absolute ownership over one's acts of communication within the field of general iterability, for each act is always already structured by iteration. In straightforward terms, a communicative act cannot be created *ex nihilo* but always necessarily contains an element of citation; it cannot be defined by a pure, self-present intention on the part of the communicator.

It is not merely communicative acts that are structured by iteration in Derrida's view; he locates the whole of human experience within the field of iterability:

Cette possibilité structurelle d'être sevré du référent ou du signifié (donc de la communication et de son contexte) me paraît faire de toute marque [...] la *restance* non-présente d'une marque différentielle coupée de sa prétendue 'production' ou origine. Et j'étendrai même cette loi à toute 'expérience' en général s'il est acquis qu'il n'y a pas d'expérience de *pure* présence mais seulement des chaînes de marques différentielles.

[This structural possibility of being weaned from the referent or from the signified (hence from communication and from its context) seems to me to make every mark [...] the non-present remainder [*restance*] of a differential mark cut off from its putative 'production' or origin. And I shall even extend this law to all 'experience' in general if it is conceded that there is no experience consisting of pure presence but only of chains of differential marks.] (*M*, p. 378; 10)

The implications of this position are numerous and far-reaching. Presence is only possible in spectral form, as presence-absence. There can be no secure subjectivity; the subjective context is certainly not rendered irrelevant, no more than any other, but its boundary disintegrates. Temporality is left 'out of joint' as the presence of the present moment is ruptured and future, past and present invade one another's domains.[3] Here, however, our focus must remain on the relationship between individuals and their environment.

Derrida's concept of iteration, it can be said, offers us a powerful tool for understanding the fluid quasi-totality of the Sartrean practico-inert and the way in which it relates to praxis. In short, the practico-inert can be thought of as a field of iterability and its motion as that of iteration.

Derrida's analysis centres on acts of communicative inscription, and he would no doubt accept that the 'marques' an individual inscribes through his work upon the material environment fall into this category. Working on material is certainly communicative in the Sartrean model: reorganization through praxis is the project's representation of itself in the material field. Furthermore, the pro-jection of an individual or group is decipherable according to Sartre; indeed, offering the tools needed to uncover projects is the central aim behind the dialectical approach to anthropology he develops in the *Critique* (*CRD*, i, 157–58; 40–41).

Following Derrida's reasoning, the decipherability of pro-jection must entail iterability: a project can be comprehended because it is embedded within the iterating structures of the world. In the example of window-opening that Sartre gives in *Questions de méthode* [Search for a Method], an example which highlights the communicative value of action in the world, the speaker is able to grasp the meaning of his friend's efforts to reach and open the window only on the basis of pre-existing instrumental structures: 'Dans la pièce, portes et fenêtres ne sont jamais tout à fait des réalités passives: le travail des autres leur a donné leur sens, en a fait des instruments, des possibilités *pour un autre* (quelconque)' ('In the room, doors and windows are never entirely passive realities; other people's work has given them their meaning, has made instruments and possibilities out of them *for another* (any other)').[4] The dynamic between the two is mediated by the presence-absence of a certain alterity, the traces of other signifying acts inscribed in the material world.

Following Derrida's analysis in 'Signature événement contexte', as a 'projet pratique' [practical project] operating in the practico-inert, the inscriptions I make upon the material around me would be defined as part of a differential chain. I would not be fully present to the environment; rather, my relationship with it would be mediated by an endless series of other acts of inscription. My goals or intentions would not be fully my own, for they would carry within them the trace of other iterations.

The above picture, it can be argued, correlates closely with the one which emerges from the pages of the *Critique*. We have seen how the practico-inert acts upon subjective pro-jection to render it other than itself. My reorganization of the material field, the singular signature I inscribe into the world around me in accordance with my project, becomes that which defines my alterity. This material signature carries the trace of otherness in its very conception; my project, emerging into a given socio-material reality, must be a reaction to a multitude of material traces crystallized in the quasi-totality of the practico-inert. As an act of signification, my reorganization of the world instantly exceeds and fragments the context of my own singular intentions, taking on a life of its own within the 'champ *magique*' [*magical* field] (my emphasis), or the field of iterability, that is the practico-inert.

If the practico-inert is understood as a field of iterability and praxis within that field as a form of iteration, it follows that the specificity of human activity must be deconstructed by a crossing of contextual borders. Indeed, as we shall see, the *Critique* does portray the human context bleeding into various material contexts, not least that of the machine, as individuals invest themselves in inert structures in the world around them.

Intérêt: A Merger Between the Human and Material Contexts

Even at the most basic level, individuals in the world of the *Critique* live in a state of symbiosis with the material objects onto which their projects are inscribed. These 'objets-vampires' ('vampire-objects') soak up the lifeblood that is praxis (*CRD*, i, 280; 169). Having to pro-ject across a material field, my only option is to invest my creative power in material structures; I must make myself into a tool in order to act within the world: 'Le sens du travail humain, c'est que l'homme se réduit à la matérialité inorganique pour agir matériellement sur la matière et changer sa vie matérielle' ('The meaning of human labour is that man is reduced to inorganic materiality in order to act materially on matter and to change his material life') (*CRD*, i, 289; 178). A remarkable process of transubstantiation occurs, whereby inert material becomes truly, dialectically active within (and yet beyond) the original context of its materiality.

Sartre's gothic metaphor, notable as a rare moment of stylistic flair in the text of the *Critique*, should alert us to the sinister aspect of the relationship between humans and objects. For the 'projet pratique', the investment of itself into material soon gives way to various complex forms of servitude. One such form is defined by Sartre as *intérêt* [interest]. *Intérêt* emerges when subjects attempt to escape their iterability by rediscovering an unmediated relationship with material (*CRD*, i, 328; 219). This attempt rests on a belief in the firm borders of private property.

Sartre gives the example of home ownership. As a proprietor, I use my house as a receptacle for my most intimate identity; each room stands as a monument to certain memories of the life I have lived (*CRD*, i, 308; 198). Of course, this process of self-reification within the house is ill-founded, for the objects that decorate the space each carry the mark of alterity. More significant, however, is the influence that the house as a whole proceeds to exert over me. I may own a property, yet that does not make it exempt from the governance of the practico-inert; its status is inevitably affected by external series that are beyond my control. Most fundamentally, my ownership itself and the rights which give it substance are expressions of the law. The right to exclude others absolutely from my space, for example, though it may seem essential to my identity as 'owner', is a legal reality — one that emerged in the nineteenth century thanks to an increasing insistence on property ownership as a right of absolute enjoyment. More visibly, the example of the housing market shows the property's power to influence my behaviour. Fear of declining value, for example, directs my praxis as I struggle to raise the stock of my property and so preserve my own standing (*CRD*, i, 309; 198–99). I might react by refitting my bathroom and kitchen, not for reasons of free self-expression but because that is what the market demands to safeguard my assets, my self. The house, furthermore, demands to be lived in (*CRD*, i, 280; 169). I must heat it and maintain it, and I must do so according to a series of processes that I do not define.

In short, the work I do to organize and maintain my home protects neither the freedom nor the singularity of my project; on the contrary, it brackets me as a 'homeowner', heightening my iterability and subjugating me to the will of the practico-inert.

My house, then, is sustained by my praxis, offering an image of myself inscribed onto the material field; at the same time, it is a monstrosity with a will which incorporates and surpasses my own:

> Chacun de nous passe sa vie à graver sur les choses son image maléfique qui le fascine et l'égare s'il veut se comprendre *par elle*, encore qu'il ne soit pas autre chose que le mouvement totalisant qui aboutit à *cette* objectivation.

> [All of us spend our lives engraving our maleficent image into things, and this image fascinates and bewilders us if we try to understand ourselves through it, even though we are nothing other than the totalising movement which results in this particular objectification.] (*CRD*, I, 336; 227, translation modified)

In an industrial setting, a machine can represent a factory owner's *intérêt* (*CRD*, I, 310–11; 200–01). Once installed, it becomes an embodiment of his project; all his praxis is directed at preserving and fulfilling its functionality. That same industrial setting throws up a yet more troubling example of human praxis losing itself in material. For the worker, the machine represents the impossibility of self-reification in the form of *intérêt*; in the state of semi-automatism required for efficient operation of the machine, she becomes the embodiment of its project (*CRD*, I, 316; 207).

For the worker, there is no private realm of personhood to which she can retreat. Any retreat constitutes a subjective realization of her objectivity (*CRD*, I, 342; 233). To demonstrate this absence of self-intimacy, Sartre offers the example of female factory workers falling into sexual reveries as they operate their machines. On the face of it, such reveries would seem a straightforward form of subjective escapism. In reality, however, they are entirely a response to the demands of the machine: 'Mais c'est la machine en elle[s] qui rêvait de caresses [...] la machine exige et crée dans l'homme un semi-automatisme inversé qui la complète' ('But it was the machine in them which was dreaming of caresses [...] The machine demands and creates in the worker an inverted semi-automatism which complements it') (*CRD*, I, 342; 233, translation modified). We see here how the machine and the worker form a relationship of perfect symbiosis, each hosting the other.

The worker *is* a machine of the machine, yet she is so through the free movement of her project. She brings to the machine the experience and creativity, even the fantasy, which its mechanisms demand. The machine then dialectically shapes the experience she invests within it.

Crucially, this dialectic between machine and worker is one the worker engages in actively; over time, she works to develop her relationship with the machine, to help merge their realities further. In short, she works to bring about the sentence the machine has imposed upon her (*CRD*, I, 431; 326). Her fantasies are a way to relieve the boredom of the work, but they are equally a conscious effort to maximize its output (*CRD*, I, 343; 234).

The worker *is* her societal role but in a non-essentialist sense, without falling into *mauvaise foi*. In so far as she must constantly *be*, in her body, the site of her own regulation by the practico-inert, she is simultaneously hosted by and a host of socio-material demands. Her project is in full motion, but she is only able to fashion herself in the machine's image.

Decentring the Body: The Emergence of the 'homme-machine'

The worker's condition, along with that of all beings in the practico-inert, is one of bodily servitude: 'le champ practico-inert est le champ de notre servitude [...] cela veut dire que tout homme lutte contre un ordre qui l'écrase réellement et matériellement dans son corps' ('The practico-inert field is the field of our servitude [...]. This means that everyone struggles against an order which really and materially crushes his body') (*CRD*, I, 437; 332).

The body is the site of practico-inert mediation. Crucially, the theory of corporeality given in *L'Être et le néant* [Being and Nothingness] (1943) is deconstructed by the *Critique*. In the earlier text, Sartre locates the body at the centre of the world (where 'world' refers to the whole fluid, synthetic network of tools at a subject's disposal); it is 'un centre absolu d'instrumentalité' ('an absolute centre of instrumentality').[5] We are told that it is only through the body, as an undetectable point of reference, ceaselessly redefined by the movement of the project, that the world can exist at any given moment. Without the body, there would be no end to the play of instrumentality; any action, that is, would be impossible which is not itself acted upon, with every tool requiring a further tool to leverage it (*EN*, p. 365; 326).

The body in *L'Être et le néant* is the one tool I do not use but which lends all others their use value; it is the tool I *am* (*EN*, p. 363; 324). It functions as a core of sense and purpose within the world — albeit flickering as it is endlessly renewed by the motion of the project — and anchors the complex sets of differential relations which give the objects around me their identity. This core, it is important to note, is always beyond the reach of (thetic) consciousness; invisible and ungraspable, the body can only be lived (*vécu*) in the moment of 'dépassement' [surpassing], that is, in action. When I wield a tool to act in the world — Sartre gives the example of writing with a pen — it becomes an extension of my body, and my body retreats from sight (*EN*, p. 363; 324).

In the *Critique*, on the other hand, the subject's body is no longer the anchor for an otherwise limitless network of tools. Now, that central point which gave form to the world (even if only in the instant of the subject's pro-jection), is displaced and fragmented. The practico-inert acts as a shared field of instrumentality and governs the bodies within it, bringing together a multiplicity of projects in kaleidoscopic fashion within its shifting structures.

The world of *L'Être et le néant* was not stable; indeed, it was as spectral as the project which gave it meaning. It was, at least, whole. Now, the *Critique* offers us a world that is always already fragmented, even in the moments of its renewal. At its most complete, it only has the present-absent form of a quasi-totality. In an important sense, the *Critique* puts forward the very reality that *L'Être et le néant* attempts to dispel: the practico-inert does not regulate the world according to a unified (if fleeting) project but rather passive-actively hosts a fluid network of tools. This mediated and mediating world is precisely a space in which one cannot act without also being acted upon.

The body constitutes the very situation of the human in *L'Être et le néant* (*EN*, p.

348; 309). It is thanks to the body, we can say, that the human context can survive in closed, determinable form. The *Critique*, on the other hand, shows the body to be iterable and the human context to be open. The human context is not, however, eliminated by the theory of the *Critique*; we should not see the worker's condition as one of straightforward inhumanity. Rather, the worker's human context flows beyond itself into the mechanical and vice versa. The reverse side of this fragmentation of contextual boundaries, it is important to note, is that the machine takes on a human form. The machine acts, organizes its environment, creates its workers and even dreams.

From the dialectical mediation of the practico-inert, then, emerges a hybrid form of being, one that is definitively non-human but not inhuman: the 'homme-machine' ('man-machine') (*CRD*, 1, 301; 191). Sartre offers a sketch of this new being from his favourite Cartesian viewpoint:

> Le champ [pratico-inerte] existe: pour tout dire, c'est lui qui nous entoure et nous conditionne; je n'ai qu'à jeter un coup d'œil par la fenêtre: je verrai des autos qui sont des hommes et des conducteurs qui sont des autos [...]. Tous ces êtres — ni choses ni hommes, unités pratiques de l'homme et de la chose inerte.

> [The [practico-inert] field exists: in short, it is what surrounds and conditions us. I need only glance out of the window: I will be able to see cars which are men and drivers who are cars [...]. All these beings — neither things nor men, but practical unities made up of man and inert things.] (*CRD*, 1, 429; 324)

This remarkable image of urban life conveys the full transformative power of the practico-inert. It must be emphasized that the project remains intact within the practical unity that is the 'homme-machine'. Without the energy of free activity, the dialectic between the 'homme' and the 'contre-homme' would come to a halt.

It might seem an obvious contradiction to unite freedom and mechanism, but it is vital to understand that freedom, in this context, does not refer to the possibility of choice but the necessity of totalization and praxis in response to demands: 'En d'autres termes, liberté, ici, ne veut pas dire possibilité d'option mais nécessité de vivre la contrainte sous forme d'exigence à remplir par une *praxis*' ('In other words, freedom, in this context, does not mean the possibility of choice but the necessity of living these constraints in the form of demands which must be fulfilled by a praxis') (*CRD*, 1, 432; 327, translation modified). Freedom, ironically, is the prerequisite of oppression.

The 'homme-machine', we can say, is not an ontological category; the practico-inert has not wrought a fundamental metamorphosis of man, as project, into material. Given, however, that a member of a society is, practically speaking, always already mediated by the practico-inert, the lack of change on an ontological level arguably has little direct relevance. As a practical unity, the 'homme-machine' is real, operative, and inescapable.

Incorporated within a hybrid being, the project retains its original motion but is surpassed and alienated to the point where, effectively, it has been transformed.

In the context of the 'homme-machine', praxis can no longer be understood as free organization of the practical field. In real terms, such a notion of praxis is wholly abstract: '[la praxis] n'est plus la libre organisation du champ pratique mais la réorganisation d'un secteur de matérialité inerte en fonction des exigences d'un autre secteur de matérialité' ('[praxis] ceases to be the free organisation of the practical field and becomes the re-organisation of one sector of inert materiality in accordance with the demands of another sector of materiality') (*CRD*, I, 301; 191, translation modified). The motion of pro-jection finds itself fully immersed within materiality.

Conclusion: Pro-jection and the Theorizing Subject in the Practico-inert

For Sartre, the world governed by the practico-inert is a realm of alterity where human being itself is an abstraction. Powerless to reorganize meaningfully through praxis, a person must face 'l'impossibilité réelle de vivre humainement' ('the real impossibility of living humanly') (*CRD*, I, 434; 330). This impossibility is itself impossible, however, from the perspective of a praxis defined by the irrepressible motion of pro-jection (*CRD*, I, 435; 330).

As pure, abstract motion, the project sustains a person's sense of freedom. There is neither a goal here nor the means to achieve one; this is not motion towards. Directionless, we might say that is motion in the form of dislocation, a certain instability that offers possibility in the realm of the impossible. This disruptive motion exists in the moment of praxis, on the level of unreflective or non-thetic consciousness. Sartre uses the term 'mystification' to describe this inability of praxis to grasp human impossibility as its own (*CRD*, I, 430; 325).

Drawing on Derrida's ideas in 'Signature événement contexte' to read the practico-inert as a field of iterability, we have seen the boundaries of the human become difficult to locate. The socio-material reality presented by the *Critique* reveals itself to be one of shifting, mutually transgressive contexts. Within the being of the 'homme-machine' lurk the spectres of endless contexts. In the broadest terms, this being exists to challenge any straightforward differentiation between humanity and the worked-upon material that surrounds it in the practical field. As such, it radically questions the specificity and possibility of human identity in the world. It would seem that praxes, like words, 'vivent de la mort des hommes' ('live off the death of men') (*CRD*, I, 211; 98).

What, then, of the subject who theorizes? As a subject within the iterating structures of the practico-inert, I am defined by impotence and alterity. Beyond the shelter of *mystification*, my being constitutes the fulfilment of the reality dictated to me by the demands of the practico-inert. My only space for creativity lies within that small degree of singularity which marks my particular way of *being* what I have been *made* (*CRD*, I, 435; 330). In Derridean terms, I am akin to a signature: I am expected in a certain place and have an assigned functionality, yet there is inevitably a certain play in the movement by which I fulfil these demands.

On an individual level, this play can preserve a sense of freedom, but it cannot support the free, creative reorganization of the world that theory, as we have approached it, requires. Arguably, we are left with two possibilities regarding the nature of theory. Theory might be understood as its own set of iterating structures, one whose motion is dependent on the spontaneity of human consciousness but which is beyond the control of any subject to shape or define. This view, however, threatens to bind theory to the cold, arbitrary regulation of the practico-inert. Alternatively, the *Critique* does offer the hint of a more optimistic possibility in an area I have not touched upon in this essay. Given the right circumstances, the singularity subjects retain can allow for a new, albeit highly unstable, form of co-operative pro-jection, one which asserts itself against the practico-inert. Perhaps, finally, we can only find space for theory through the fleeting protection of what Sartre labels 'mediated reciprocity' — that is, in the rupture brought about by the formation of a *group*.

Notes to Chapter 2

1. Jean-Paul Sartre, *Critique de la raison dialectique précédé de Questions de méthode*, 2 vols (Paris: Gallimard, 1985), I, 288; *Critique of Dialectical Reason*, ed. by Jonathan Rée, trans. by Alan Sheridan-Smith, 2 vols (London: Verso, 2004–06), I, 178; this work subsequently referred to as *CRD* in the main text.
2. Jacques Derrida, *Marges de la philosophie* [1972] (Paris: Minuit, 1975), pp. 374–76; *Limited Inc*, trans. by Samuel Weber and Jeffrey Mehlman (Evanston, IL: Northwest University Press, 1988), pp. 6–8; this work subsequently referred to as *M* in the main text.
3. Jacques Derrida, *Spectres de Marx* (Paris: Gallimard, 1993), p. 41.
4. *CRD*, I, 115; the translation is adapted from *Search for a Method*, trans. by Hazel Barnes (New York: Vintage Books, 1968), p. 153.
5. Jean-Paul Sartre, *L'Être et le néant: essai d'ontologie phénoménologique* [1943] (Paris: Gallimard, 1972), p. 364; *Being and Nothingness: An Essay on Phenomenological Ontology*, trans. by Hazel Barnes (London: Routledge, 1969), p. 324; this work subsequently referred to as *EN* in the main text.

CHAPTER 3

Sartre and the (un-)Freedom
of the Reading Subject

Marieke Mueller

The phenomenon of reading has become a vast field of enquiry which stretches across many disciplines, including philosophy, literature, education studies, and cognitive science and has given rise to a number of its own journals. In French theory, attention famously shifted from the author to the reader in the 1960s and 70s, a move perhaps most frequently identified with Barthes's *S/Z*. This coincided with the falling out of fashion of Sartre and appeared to seek liberation from a reverential conception of the author which Sartre, the 'intellectuel total' in Bourdieu's words, seemed to embody. The implicit association of Sartre with an unqualified adherence to a conception of the author as a coherent, indivisible, and authoritative entity is as false as is the assumption of a supposedly unproblematic and 'whole' Sartrean subject, shown to be an illusion by Christina Howells, Nik Farrel Fox, and others.[1]

Despite the now infamous appeals to the responsibility of the writer in *Qu'est-ce que la littérature?* (1948), Sartre's literary theory is from the outset interested in advancing a nuanced and precise understanding of the nature of the activity of reading.[2] In the following, I shall consider the development of Sartre's approach to reading through a comparison of *Qu'est-ce que la littérature?* and his biography of Flaubert, *L'Idiot de la famille* (1971–72).[3] It will be suggested that Sartre's literary theory accords more and more importance to the figure of the reader and seeks to elucidate the possibility of the reader's freedom with increasing precision. In this sense, Sartre's theory of reading is viewed as a contribution to debates about the freedom and unfreedom of the subject. At the same time Sartre's literary theory will be considered in relation to a thriving field of research concerned with reading from a variety of angles. The approach to reading advanced in *L'Idiot de la famille* not only speaks to more recent theorizations such as Michel Picard's view of reading as *jeu* (both 'play' and 'game'), but also represents an original contribution to the field of reception theory by integrating an experiential and a sociological account of reading.[4] The comparison with Picard demonstrates the relevance of Sartre's thought not only with regard to his structuralist and post-structuralist contemporaries, but also for approaches that seek to go beyond theories of the reader developed in the 1960s and 70s.[5]

The Reader in *Qu'est-ce que la littérature?*

Qu'est-ce que la littérature?, although often associated with the idea of the committed author, already views the writer in conjunction with the reader. The long history of the different situations in which various generations of authors found themselves is entirely constructed around their respective readerships. Famously, Sartre categorizes the different kinds of reading public with which the author can be confronted: a dual reality of a real and a virtual (or potential) readership in some historical situations; a readership felt as unavailable (such as the bourgeois readership in the second half of the nineteenth century); or a hypothetical ideal or free readership that would exist in a utopian society in permanent flux. If the reader is omnipresent throughout the text, this is primarily the case in the sense of a moral demand placed upon the author. Moreover, the theoretical justification for the emphasis on the reading public is the assumption that the figure of the reader plays a crucial part in the functioning of literature itself: 'c'est l'effort conjugué de l'auteur et du lecteur qui fait surgir cet objet concret et imaginaire qu'est l'ouvrage de l'esprit. Il n'y a d'art que pour et par autrui' ('It is the joint effort of author and reader which brings upon the scene that concrete and imaginary object which is the work of the mind. There is no art except for and by others') (*QL*, p. 50; 51–52). Thus, from the 1940s, Sartre theorizes reading not as simple reception of a message in an act of communication, but as active creation.

Michel Picard's approach, which views reading as a playful activity, provides a fruitful comparison to Sartre's account, in both *Qu'est-ce que la littérature?* and *L'Idiot de la famille*. His *La Lecture comme jeu* (1986) draws on psychoanalysis in order to go beyond what he identifies as abstract and functional conceptions of the reader developed at the end of the 1960s by Riffaterre, Althusser, Iser, and others (*LJ*, p. 147). Picard also includes Sartre in this group, citing the famous formulation from *Qu'est-ce que la littérature?* according to which literary works always contain the image of the reader whom they address (*LJ*, p. 146). For Picard, such abstract notions of the reader need to be accompanied by a concrete account of the 'rapport individuel *réel* à la lecture' (*LJ*, p. 301). Picard's interpretation of *Qu'est-ce que la littérature?* as reducing the reader to merely an abstract function of the text is perhaps testament to how widespread selective readings of Sartre's text are; particularly because Picard in fact shares with Sartre an attitude that views reading primarily as an activity characterized by freedom. The reader invests her own history in the text and thereby produces it creatively (*LJ*, p. 52); reading is 'play' insofar as it mobilizes the imagination, but it is also a 'game', subject to specific rules and codes that need to be learned (*LJ*, p. 162). The result is a process which, in the ideal case, has a beneficial 'modelling' effect on the formation of the subject:

> Ce qui nous arrive dans la lecture nous arrive en effet pour de bon. Les péripéties de l'histoire [...] la progression vers le réel et la découverte conjointe de l'altérité [...] tout donc nous offre une sorte d'apprentissage particulier et, comme tel, irremplaçable. (*LJ*, p. 161)

> [What happens to us when we read happens to us for good. The twists of the story [...] the progression towards the real and the associated discovery of

alterity [...] all this offers us a kind of learning which is particular and therefore irreplaceable.]

Qu'est-ce que la littérature? is similarly keen to consider reading processes in a concrete manner, and similarly optimistic about the benefits of the encounter with the literary text. Firstly, if the reader brings the text into existence, it is because she animates it with her own subjectivity in mobilizing her own feelings: 'L'attente de Raskolnikoff, c'est *mon* attente, que je lui prête; sans cette impatience du lecteur il ne demeurerait que des signes languissants' ('Raskolnikoff's waiting is *my* waiting which I lend him. Without this impatience of the reader he would remain only a collection of signs') (*QL*, p. 52; 53). For this reason, Sartre optimistically concludes that reading is operated by 'la liberté du lecteur en ce que cette liberté a de plus pur' ('the freedom of the reader, and by what is purest in that freedom') (*QL*, p. 55; 54). Because reading is a process that engages freedom, the reader cannot be manipulated into a certain sentiment, or rather, only an alienated freedom could be. Secondly however, reading is a 'création dirigée' ('directed creation') (*QL*, p. 52; 53), i.e. an act that is on the one hand creative and on the other hand guided by the text (and, perhaps less convincingly, by the author).

Thirdly, this particular exercise of freedom is described as bringing astonishing benefits to the subject overall: according to *Qu'est-ce que la littérature?*, the act of reading involves the imagination in an enterprise that is not distinct from engagement in the real world. It makes possible a modulation of our freedom via the imaginary and thus, by addressing our freedom in a uniquely direct manner, opens up a world of 'possibles' in front of us. Insofar as reading implies momentary captivity, a dialectic between passivity and activity takes place:

> Comme l'activité s'est faite passive pour mieux créer l'objet, réciproquement la passivité devient acte, l'homme qui lit s'est élevé au plus haut. C'est pourquoi l'on voit des gens réputés pour leur dureté verser des larmes au récit d'infortunes imaginaires; ils étaient devenus pour un moment ce qu'ils auraient été s'ils n'avaient passé leur vie à se masquer leur liberté.

> [And just as activity has rendered itself passive in order for it better to create the object, conversely, passiveness becomes an act; the person who is reading has raised herself to the highest degree. That is why we see people who are known for their toughness shed tears at the recital of imaginary misfortunes; for the moment they have become what they would have been if they had not spent their lives hiding their freedom from themselves.] (*QL*, p. 58; 58, translation modified)

When compared to Sartre's previous writings on the imaginary, these passages express an extraordinary faith in the imagination to produce a beneficial, if only vaguely defined, effect on the real world.[6] At the same time, Sartre admits that the reading process outlined is an ideal case and that readers in reality are in various states of alienation. This brings Sartre on to the lengthy chapter 'Pour qui écrit-on' [For Whom does One Write?], in which he traces the different kinds of audiences for whom authors since the seventeenth century have written. This literary history, however, describes the reader of each epoch in rather general socio-political terms and does not develop the implications for the freedom of the reading subject.

In *Qu'est-ce que la littérature?* there is thus a discrepancy between the historicized consideration of the author and the abstract analysis of the figure of the reader. *L'Idiot de la famille*, published over twenty years later in an intellectual climate in which the reader had taken centre-stage over the author, pays considerably more attention to reading processes in their phenomenological and historical dimensions.

'Passive' and 'Neurotic' Reading in *L'Idiot de la famille*

In *L'Idiot de la famille*, three cases of readers are analyzed in detail: Gustave Flaubert himself, his classmates, often referred to as the 'Rouen schoolboys', and the reading public during the Second Empire. In all three cases, reading is characterized by a high degree of passivity, turning *L'Idiot*'s readers into counter-examples of the optimistic stress on the reader's activity in *Qu'est-ce que la littérature?*. Jean-François Louette points out that Sartre's portraits of reading could be approached pheno-menologically and in a chronological perspective (i.e. concerning the acquisition of the skill of reading).[7] The first reader presented by Sartre is the young Flaubert himself, and in his case Louette's distinction is far from straightforward. Sartre identifies the young Flaubert as a 'passive agent' who consequently has difficulties with language acquisition which in turn foreshadow his passive attitude to the written word. A bad interpreter of spoken language, Gustave's capacity to under-stand the written text is equally insufficient. For example, the text portrays Gustave's attitude in front of his law books as a student in the early 1840s. His engagement with his law books is mere pretence, an 'imaginary action' in that it is almost entirely passive (*IF*, II, 1711; III, 583). A first definition of reading is provided negatively at this point, i.e. as that which Gustave refuses to accomplish, namely the act of synthesizing and recomposing the text. Instead, Flaubert places himself 'au plus bas' [at the lowest end] of the different levels of reading, at that of a proof-reader who does not synthesize the text beyond isolated sentences. Sartre identifies this form of reading as 'quasiment passive', and, although the passage strictly refers to Gustave's passive reading of the *Code civil*, this observation is generalized by adding that 'la lecture d'une œuvre littéraire, chez Flaubert, n'est jamais *agressive*, elle ne se réduit pas aux significations abstraites: celles-ci lui parviennent à travers l'activité de sa passivité' ('The reading of a literary work, for Flaubert, is never aggressive, it does not reduce itself to abstract meanings: these come to him through the activity of his passivity') (*IF*, II, 1713; III, 584). Implied in this passage are thus already two forms of passive reading: the lowest form of purely 'material' reading applied by Flaubert to his law books, and a second kind of passive reading, in which the meaning of the text is apprehended passively and not by 'aggressively' transcending sentences towards their 'signification rigoureuse' ('strict meaning') (*IF*, II, 1713; III, 585). While the opposition between 'aggressive' and 'passive' resembles Roman Ingarden's categorization of active and passive reading (the latter activity involving 'no intellectual attempt to progress from the sentences read to the objects appropriate to them and projected by them'), Sartre's version of passive reading does seem to imply a form of cognition close to comprehension, as is evident from the formulation, quoted above, '[les] significations abstraites [...] lui parviennent à travers l'activité de sa passivité' (*IF*, II, 1713; III, 584).[8]

A second case of imperfect reading processes is presented in the context of Gustave's classmates. Having staged a thwarted rebellion in the school, the boys feel excluded from historical agency and resort to nocturnal readings of Romantic poets. As a result of their failure, a 'passage à l'imaginaire' ('passage to the imaginary') takes place (*IF*, II, 1367; III, 252). Although less permanently than Gustave, his classmates too are in a state of passivity, which turns them into 'rêveurs en puissance' ('potential dreamers') (*IF*, II, 1377; III, 262). Their reading is also characterized by a 'postulation onirique' ('oneiric postulation') (*IF*, II, 1378; III, 263). Temporarily constituted as passive by the historical situation, the Romantic reader relinquishes the freedom to produce images, and is instead 'mobilisé à produire celles [les images] qu'on lui propose' ('mobilized to produce those images proposed to him') (*IF*, II, 1382; III, 266). Much like Gustave, the children are temporarily swallowed up by the imaginary: 'l'imaginaire *écrit*, torride, impitoyable, est une image totale d'un bout à l'autre virulente, qui exclut toute liberté de concevoir autre chose qu'elle' ('the *written* imaginary, torrid, pitiless, is a total image, and utterly virulent. It excludes all freedom to conceive something other than it') (*IF*, II, 1382; III, 266–67). The adjectives with which Sartre describes the imaginary ('torride', 'impitoyable', 'virulente') emphatically underline the forcefulness of this encounter with the written text.[9]

In some ways, the schoolboys' reading echoes the situation in *Qu'est-ce que la littérature?*, where the reader is equally in a state of passivity, belief, and dream during the act of reading. In the text from 1948, however, passivity is the result of a constantly renewed exercise of freedom: 'le lecteur se fait crédule [...] le propre de la croyance esthétique c'est d'être croyance par engagement [...]. A chaque instant je puis m'éveiller et je le sais; mais je ne le veux pas: la lecture est un rêve libre' ('The reader renders himself credulous [...] the characteristic of aesthetic consciousness is to be a belief by means of commitment [...]. I can awaken at any moment, and I know it; but I do not want to; reading is a free dream') (*QL*, pp. 56–58; 57). The schoolboys too, says Sartre, could 'in principle' abandon the book, and wake up, but this possibility is far more distant in the Romantic variant of reading (*IF*, II, 1383; III, 268). This heightened captivity by the imaginary is primarily conditioned by their particular situation, which pushes them increasingly towards an imaginary version of their struggle. The reader's 'agreed' passivity is less free because it is provoked by an external factor, the historical situation. *L'Idiot de la famille* therefore unites a historical and a phenomenological account of reading, two aspects that were present but unrelated in *Qu'est-ce que la littérature?*.[10]

The differences between Romantic 'oneiric' reading and the ideal reader in *Qu'est-ce que la littérature?* are particularly illuminating if we consider the respective ways in which the reader is invested in the text. As already mentioned, in 1948 Sartre insists that the subjectivity of the reader animates the fictional world. The relationship between character and reader, which in *Qu'est-ce que la littérature?* is dominated by the latter, is inverted in the case of Romantic reading. In the

Romantic hero the schoolboys find an imaginary version of the ideals that proved to be 'irréalisable' as a result of their 'political' failure (IF, II, 1377–78; III, 262–63). During their nocturnal reading sessions, they revive those ideas by 'incarnating' themselves in the text. They project their ego into the third-person character and (imaginarily) adopt the character's *moi* as the product of their own reflexive consciousness (IF, II, 1381; III, 266).

Further, the descriptions of the reading processes in *Qu'est-ce que la littérature?* and in *L'Idiot de la famille* manifest differing relationships between the reader and what could be termed the 'possible' and the 'necessary'. In *Qu'est-ce que la littérature?* the reader is said to progress through the text 'dans la sécurité', since she knowingly follows a path created by the author (QL, p. 60; 60). Despite this voluntary passivity, however, Sartre argues that the ideal text allows an 'engagement imaginaire dans l'action' ('imaginary participation in the action') (QL, p. 67; 66). Therefore, as we have seen, freedom may render itself passive, but the action in which the reader engages on the level of the imaginary reverses this passivity into activity and even works against bad faith. To rephrase the situation in terms borrowed from *L'Idiot*, the engagement with fictional 'necessity' (the rigidity of the plot) opens up a *real* field of 'possibles' [possibilities]. Logically, this is only conceivable if the 'possibles' are 'réalisables'. In *L'Idiot*, the effect of the schoolboys' reading is the exact opposite of this positive outcome in *Qu'est-ce que la littérature?*: due to the reader's passivity, reading does not provoke an 'engagement dans l'imaginaire', but 'le triomphe de l'engagement imaginaire sur le libre jeu de l'action' ('the triumph of imaginary engagement over the free play of imagination') (IF, II, 1382; III, 267). The schoolboys' incarnation in the character increases their absorption by the 'necessity' of the plot.

Any fictional world, Sartre insists in *L'Imaginaire* and in *L'Idiot de la famille*, fundamentally excludes the 'possible', which belongs to the realm of activity in the real world. For the school students, however, fictional necessity and real possibility become indistinguishable, and, upon 'awakening' from their dream-like reading, they remain 'vampirisé[s]' by the character, seeking to make the fictional imperative a reality (IF, II, 1416–18; III, 300–01). The 'necessity' of fiction, transposed into the real world, however, reveals itself, once more, to be 'irréalisable': 'rien ne va plus quand [...] ils tentent de *réaliser* pendant la veille [...] le personnage funèbre qui les vampirise' ('but nothing works anymore when [...] they try to *realize* during their waking hours [...] the funereal character who vampirizes them') (IF, II, 1419; III, 303). The situation could hardly be any more different from the one laid out in *Qu'est-ce que la littérature?*: there, the reader's understanding of the 'possible', a category of the real, is enhanced as a result of reading, whereas the schoolboys' consumption of Romantic texts enduringly damages their connection with the real.

While different processes of reading are described throughout *L'Idiot de la famille*, the third volume seeks to analyze the literary situation during the Second Empire in a systematic manner. The success of *Madame Bovary*, which might be seen as a rather banal fact, or as a mere sign of its 'quality', is of capital importance to Sartre. Flaubert's first successful novel, according to Sartre, is *the* novel of the Second Empire because its author's subjective neurosis corresponds to the 'objective neurosis' and to a desire for 'lecture-névrose' ('reading-neurosis') (*IF*, III, 418; V, 389). The reading of *Madame Bovary* at the time of its publication, then, pertains to a third variant of imperfect reading, namely 'neurotic reading'. Sartre's argument here draws on a historical analysis of the bourgeoisie: as a class in power the bourgeoisie has lost its claim to be the defender of universal values, and it has moreover experienced its own otherness in the conflict with the working class in 1848. As a result, Sartre argues, the bourgeoisie refuses to know itself and produces an ideology of 'false ideas' (*IF*, III, 37; V, 29). During the Second Empire, society is, according to Sartre, characterized by an 'objective neurosis'. This corresponds to Flaubert's 'subjective' neurosis; thoroughly relativizing any notion of literary success, the public's own neurosis is identified as conferring a status of 'false objectivity' upon the text (*IF*, III, 27–37; V, 20–29). Moreover, the affinity between Flaubert and his public is lived during the reading process: the public is able to experience a moment of misanthropy which it senses in Flaubert's work, whilst being able to pretend that *Madame Bovary*'s supposed Realism expresses their own positivist faith in scientific progress, itself part of the bourgeoisie's 'false ideology' for Sartre.

Sartre maintains that post-Romantic literature aims at 'derealizing' the readers, forcing them to 'incarnate themselves' in the character or to identify with the author (*IF*, III, 328; V, 305). Post-Romantic reading thus mirrors aspects of reading processes by which the young Flaubert and his classmates were conditioned, and it is equally characterized by an intense 'envoûtement onirique' ('oneiric spell') (*IF*, III, 323; V, 299, translation modified). The reader, in this process, transposes a real hatred for humanity onto the level of the imaginary, and, while reading, discovers his (or her) own misanthropy in a moment of short and provoked neurosis (*IF*, III, 327; V, 303). Post-Romantic reading does not lead to any 'prise de conscience', or a renewed appreciation of reality, but is largely characterized by passivity and the quest for a perpetuated dream-like state. While *Qu'est-ce que la littérature?* stressed the potential of the imagination to open up new, real, possibilities for our freedom, post-Romantic readers are described as desiring to be as unfree as possible. Nevertheless, the reader acquires a non-verbal sense of his own experience, or, as Roland Barthes phrases it, Flaubert's writing touches a 'sixième sens' [sixth sense].[11]

The three reading processes with which we are concerned in this chapter, namely Gustave's reading, the schoolboys' Romantic reading, and 'neurotic reading' practised by the bourgeoisie during the Second Empire are not identical, but in all cases the reader is relatively passive, identifies with the author or 'incarnates himself' in the character, and enters a dream-like state dominated by the imaginary. Sartre's emphasis on Romantic reading and the post-Romantic reading public as 'nocturnal' expresses the particular gap between the reader and reality. Through these descriptions Sartre establishes a panorama of passive and fundamentally uncritical forms of reading. Despite the obvious differences in approach, scope, and style that exist between *L'Idiot de la famille* and Barthes's *Le Plaisir du texte* (1973), the form of reading practised by Flaubert's readership at times resembles Barthes's category of 'plaisir', which he opposes to 'jouissance'.[12] Similar to Sartre's emphasis on the reader's 'incarnation' in the text, Barthes stresses the physical aspect of reading. His formulation of the pleasure of the text as the moment 'où mon corps va suivre ses propres idées' ('when my body pursues its own ideas') could well describe the self-abandonment experienced by the readers presented to us in *L'Idiot*.[13] Their reading is further close to the 'pleasure of the text' in the imaginarizing moment; the alternative, for Barthes, is a form of 'jouissance' which 'retire le texte des imaginaires du langage' ('withdraws the text from the image-systems of language').[14]

While *L'Idiot de la famille* here invites the comparison with its immediate contemporaries, it is helpful to turn again to Picard who is also concerned to delineate 'passive' and thus unsuccessful forms of reading. While the engagement with literary texts, in the ideal case, takes the shape of a playful creativity that is simultaneously cognizant of the game's rules, the negative case is introduced early on in the text when Picard concedes that reading is a game in which the player can 'cheat'. This is the case for example when we destroy the 'hermeneutic code' of the text by skipping passages or even jump to the end, a movement in which the reader 'se soustrairait à l'altérité' [would remove herself from otherness], thus withdrawing from the beneficial effects of literature (*LJ*, p. 169). Moreover, 'une bonne lecture' for Picard depends on a productive interplay between three components of reading which he terms the 'liseur', the 'lu', and the 'lectant'. The 'liseur', the physical reader whose hands are holding the book, remains attached to the real to a certain extent, while the 'lu' gives in to the imaginary world in an act of sublimation *(LJ*, p. 112). The 'lectant' fulfils a reflective function and establishes a distance to what is being read (*LJ*, pp. 213–14).[15] One case of what Picard calls 'alienated' reading is a passive relationship with the text in which the reading process is dominated by the 'lu': in 'false reading', the 'texte ne [...] sert que de tremplin, de piste d'envol [...] c'est une fuite' [the text is only a trampoline, a spring-board [...] it is a form of escape] (*LJ*, p. 117). In such cases, the illusion seems almost real and the reader is in a passive state (*LJ*, p. 118). Both Sartre and Picard thus identify passive reading as particularly unsuccessful and both use a pathologizing vocabulary to do so. Picard's approach of differentiating between three components of the reading process is particularly helpful in that it opens up a possibility for a change in reading practices. The idea that playful and active reading depends on a certain awareness and knowledge which is brought into play by the 'lectant' leads Picard to reflect on changes to the education system that would be necessary in order to help readers develop the faculty of the 'lectant'. Picard's approach could at times be accused of bordering on elitism, since he comes close to making 'successful' reading overly dependent on classical education and, contrary to Sartre, overlooks the beneficial effects of the instance of the 'lu'. It nevertheless provides a useful corrective to Sartre's theory which is less interested in possible future changes in reading practices. Sartre's account of passive reading, at the same time, provides two important moments of nuance, which will be considered in the following: firstly, it identifies an element of activity in the most passive form of reading, and secondly, it adds a socio-historical dimension to an experiential account of reading.

What Happens to the Responsibility of the Reader?

If *L'Idiot de la famille* shares with critics such as Barthes or Picard the recognition of imperfect and passive reading processes, Sartre's account stands out in that it nevertheless refuses to paint a picture which excludes all activity. Paradoxically, it is because of the generalization of his dream-like state that the post-Romantic reader is led to activity:

> L'envoûtement onirique, quand il est le but de la lecture, ne s'obtient et ne se maintient que par des *opérations* incessantes du lecteur, qui, loin de se borner à un simple décodage, tente de prévoir à l'intérieur de la fiction, et constitue, pour chaque personnage et pour tous, un avenir en *inventant* les intentions futures de l'auteur, c'est-à-dire en transformant à la limite le lecteur en auteur [...] par un libre dépassement du donné [...]. A quelque époque que se situe le livre [...] l'écrivain [...] doit [...] nous abandonner tôt ou tard [...] et nous laisser faire seuls le travail.

> [The oneiric spell, when it is the purpose of reading, is obtained and maintained only through the incessant *operations* of the reader, who, far from limiting himself to a simple decoding, tries to foresee the interior of the fiction, and constitutes a future for every character by *inventing* the author's future intentions. This implicitly transforms the reader into the author [...] through a free surpassing of the given [...]. Whatever the period in which the work is situated [...] the writer [...] must abandon us sooner or later [...] and let us do the work alone.] (*IF*, III, 323; V, 299–300, translation modified)

Importantly, this passage reinforces the creativity of the reader. The latter no longer only participates in the creative act, lending his or her subjectivity to the character, but takes over completely. *Qu'est-ce que la littérature?* suggested not very convincingly that the author continues to guide the reader throughout the text. *L'Idiot de la famille*, on the other hand, posits a cut between reader and author, reducing the latter to an intention the reading subject imagines. In a rather Foucaldian move, Sartre reduces the author to a specific function in the process of reading. The reader is thereby liberated from the author, and, this is Sartre's conclusion, is as responsible for the historical situation as are the authors: 'nos capables sont aussi criminels que les chevaliers du Néant' ('our professionals are as criminal as the Knights of Nothingness') (*IF*, III, 324; V, 300).

By highlighting the 'inventive' component of the reader's own creation of the character's trajectory, Sartre outlines a situation that is at least different from, if not in contradiction to, his account of the schoolboys' Romantic reading. He is closer at this point to critics who view the novel as an organization of 'possibles' instead of pure fictional 'necessity'. We might add, with Picard, that the dimension of the 'possible' in the novel is a category that depends on the reader's concrete capacity to actualize it. Flaubert's readers are *both* 'possessed' *and* engaged in the act of freely inventing the misanthropy they find in the text.

Moreover, historicization replaces the category of morality to a large extent. The Second Empire was the particular milieu in which Flaubert thrived. *Madame Bovary* is a masterpiece because it corresponds to the objective neurosis of its readers, without which it would be seen as a pathological text (*IF*, III, 29; V, 22). Hence, there is a decidedly relativist component to Sartre's reading of Flaubert. In *Qu'est-ce que la littérature?* Sartre establishes the opposition between the 'real' public ('le public réel') and the 'virtual' public ('le public virtuel'), the currently existing public available to an author and the potential public that is beginning to appear on the horizon (*QL*, pp. 158–59; 136–37). Although this distinction remains relevant throughout Sartre's texts, the third volume of *L'Idiot de la famille* introduces a further specification by opposing the 'real' to the 'natural' public. In this distinction, the 'natural' public is a subcategory of the real public that is particularly favourable to the type of literature in question. While the 'real' public, similar to its definition in *Qu'est-ce que la littérature?*, is constituted by the bourgeoisie during the Second Empire, the 'natural' readership of *Madame Bovary* is a more narrowly defined group, the *capables* or *capacités*, the professional parts of the middle classes who, according to Sartre, elaborate bourgeois ideology in the 1850s.

Sartre argues that the bourgeoisie entertains a 'fausse conscience' of itself, seeking to conceal its own class-being. The group whom Sartre identifies as *capables* are tasked with the elaboration of this ideology. Their affinity with neurosis–literature is particularly intense, for they themselves are at the heart of the creation of an ideology that responds to a social neurosis. Without following Sartre through his entire account of the bourgeoisie under the Second Empire, this model is interesting with regard to the analysis of the reading public. By identifying the *capables* as being especially attracted to the misanthropy of post-Romantic literature, Sartre is able to explain the contradictory reception of *Madame Bovary*: while the 'natural public' accepts the texts unequivocally, the wider 'real public' is initially scandalized and puts Flaubert on trial.[16] Eventually, however, the text convinces the larger readership: 'c'est pourtant l'art qui leur convient' ('this is nonetheless the art that suits them') (*IF*, III, 311; V, 288). Sartre's account thus combines a sociological and historical understanding of reading with a phenomenological description of the precise reading process pertaining to a given period of (literary) history. A combined reading of *Qu'est-ce que la littérature?* and *L'Idiot de la famille* suggests thus that, similarly to Picard's text, Sartre's work defines the relative benefit that the subject draws from reading by the degree of activity and thus freedom involved. The extent to which active reading is possible, though, depends on a multiplicity of factors such as the historical situation of the reader as well as the disposition of the text itself.

The theory of a correspondence between author and readership is certainly a consistent one, although its validity should perhaps be ascertained by applying it to other situations. Sartre, for example, does not explain the lasting success of *Madame Bovary*, well beyond the end of the Second Empire. In this respect, the debate about Flaubert's grammatical mistakes that emerged at the beginning of the twentieth century could be mobilized as evidence in favour of Sartre's argument that the society of the Second Empire entertained a special affinity with Flaubert's writing.[17] The Sartre critic Traugott König also reflects on this question, hypothesizing that it follows from *Madame Bovary*'s continued success that the social conditions described in *L'Idiot de la famille* are still in place.[18] While this question is not addressed directly by Sartre, Picard, who also uses *Madame Bovary* as an example of different reading practices, is concerned by this problem too. His analysis of the text points towards elements that can encourage either a 'mystifying' or a 'de-mystifying' reading. The narrative's central occupation with Emma Bovary, her 'charm', or various 'effets de réalité' can all be mobilized in a reading in which the 'lectant' plays no great role and which simply allows the 'lu' to be absorbed by imaginary adventures (*LJ*, pp. 267–69). At the same time, elements such as montage, dissonance, and parody invite a highly active, and de-mystifying, reading of *Madame Bovary*. The text thus becomes a tool which the reader needs to know how to use: 'Si le lecteur se perd avec l'instrument de la libération, c'est simplement qu'il ne l'utilise pas, qu'il ne sait pas jouer avec le jeu qui lui est offert' [If the reader loses him or herself in the presence of an instrument of liberation, this is simply because he or she does not use it, because he or she does not know how to play the game that is being proposed] (*LJ*, p. 276).

For Picard, the reason why a reader might perform one reading of *Madame Bovary* rather than another is largely to do with access to education: 'chaque joueur joue selon la couche sociale à laquelle il appartient' [every player plays according to his or her social position] (*LJ*, p. 297). At the same time, although in a less developed way than Sartre, Picard is also interested in the use that an entire epoch makes of a certain text. He therefore notes the contemporary predominance of television and film adaptations of *Madame Bovary* which contribute, according to him, to a reading that perpetuates a simplistic reading in which the intrigue dominates. Picard, much like König in his reflection on *L'Idiot de la famille*, ends up suggesting that 'nous vivons dans l'univers d'Emma' [we live in Emma's universe] (*LJ*, p. 299), a world in which books are fetishized rather than read critically. Whether or not one agrees with Picard's here rather bleak outlook, his reading of *Madame Bovary* certainly provides a helpful addition to Sartre's notion of a correspondence between a text and an epoch or society. Picard's focus on the polysemy of the text and the different readings it allows adds a degree of nuance, as it accounts for the coexistence of a multiplicity of readings. What Sartre's multifaceted framework of text, historical reader, and phenomenology of reading can bring to this discussion is perhaps a reminder that behind the discussion of the technicalities of reading also lies the uncomfortable question of freedom, sometimes in the most adverse of circumstances.

Notes to Chapter 3

1. Christina Howells, 'Sartre and the Deconstruction of the Subject', in *The Cambridge Companion to Sartre*, ed. by Christina Howells (Cambridge: Cambridge University Press, 1992), pp. 318–52; Nik Farrel Fox, *The New Sartre* (London: Continuum, 2004).
2. Jean-Paul Sartre, *Qu'est-ce que la littérature?* (Paris: Gallimard, 1948); *'What is literature?' and Other Essays*, trans. by Steven Ungar (Cambridge, MA: Harvard University Press, 1988); this work subsequently referred to as *QL* in the main text.
3. Jean-Paul Sartre, *L'Idiot de la famille*, 3 vols [1971–72] (Paris: Gallimard, 1988); *The Family Idiot*, trans. by Carol Cosmans, 5 vols (Chicago, IL: Chicago University Press, 1981–93); this work subsequently referred to as *IF* in the main text.

4. Michel Picard, *La Lecture comme jeu* (Paris: Minuit, 1986); this work subsequently referred to as *LJ* in the main text. Translations are my own.

5. For a comprehensive account of the development of Sartre's theory of literature see Christina Howells, *Sartre's Theory of Literature* (London: MHRA, 1979).

6. Jean-Paul Sartre, *L'Imaginaire* (Paris: Gallimard, 1940).

7. Jean-François Louette, 'Petite tératologie de la lecture selon Sartre', in *L'Écriture et la lecture: des phénomènes miroir? L'exemple de Sartre*, ed. by Natalie Depraz and Noémie Parant, Rencontres philosophiques 2 (Mont-Saint-Aignan: Publications des Universités de Rouen et du Havre, 2011), pp. 83–95 (p. 83).

8. Roman Ingarden, *The Cognition of the Literary Work of Art* (Evanston, IL: Northwestern University Press, 1973), p. 38.

9. For a discussion of the relationship between the imaginary and reading in Sartre see Christina Howells, 'Sartre: esquisse d'une théorie de la lecture', in *Études Sartriennes*, 2–3, ed. by Michel Rybalka and Geneviève Idt, Cahiers de sémiotique textuelle 5–6 (Paris: Université Paris X-Nanterre, 1986), pp. 159–70.

10. Incidentally, it would seem that Edward Casey's claim, to the effect that *L'Idiot* is part of Sartre's Marxist and therefore non-phenomenological phase, is only tenable if one discounts the attempt made in *L'Idiot* to historicize phenomenology. See Edward S. Casey, 'Introduction', in Mickel Dufrenne, *The Phenomenology of Aesthetic Experience*, trans. by Edward S. Casey, 1st edn (Evanston, IL: Northwestern University Press, 1973), p. xvi, n. 2.

11. Roland Barthes, *Le Degré zéro de l'écriture*, (Paris: Seuil, 1973), p. 52.

12. The two categories are neither entirely distinct nor clearly defined; broadly speaking one could define the pleasure-provoking text as being far less challenging to the reader than the bliss-provoking text. The two categories evolve out of the distinction between the readerly and the writerly text established in *S/Z*.

13. Roland Barthes, *Le Plaisir du texte*, (Paris: Seuil, 1973), p. 27; *The Pleasure of the Text*, trans. by Richard Miller (New York: Hills and Wang, 1975), p. 17.

14. Ibid., p. 47; p. 33.

15. As mentioned previously, Picard's model relies heavily on psychoanalysis; the three instances are thus also explained in terms of their respective relationship with the ego, the id and the superego.

16. Sartre produces no empirical evidence for the adoption of the text by its natural public at this stage, but he intended to study the relationship between *Madame Bovary* and its first readers in the fourth volume. A study of the early reception of Flaubert's writings would certainly be a fascinating test of Sartre's theory of the spreading of a text through layers of society.

17. See Gilles Philippe, 'La Querelle sur le style de Flaubert', in *Sujet, verbe, complément: le moment grammatical de la littérature française, 1890–1940* (Paris: Gallimard, 2002), pp. 47–66.

18. Traugott König, *Sartres Flaubert lesen* (Hamburg: Rohwolt, 1990).

CHAPTER 4

Sartre and Lacan:
Reading *Qui Perd Gagne*
alongside *Les Non-Dupes Errent*

Sinan Richards

In this chapter, I engage with Christina Howells's analysis of *qui perd gagne* [loser wins] in *Sartre: The Necessity of Freedom*.[1] I agree that *qui perd gagne* is the most convincing shorthand for the strategy that Jean-Paul Sartre employs concerning subjectivity in *L'Être et le néant* [Being and Nothingness].[2] Further, I am convinced by Howells's argument, which ties Jacques Derrida to a similar strategy in his work. My chapter aims to re-articulate Howells's intellectual gesture expressed in her analysis of *qui perd gagne* in relation to Jacques Lacan's psychoanalysis by demonstrating its repeatability in the late Lacan. Lacan's early work is, in many ways, indebted to Sartre's existential philosophy, as Clotilde Leguil demonstrated in *Sartre avec Lacan*.[3] However, Lacan sees his later work as enacting a 'déviation fatale' [fatal deviation] away from Sartre.[4] Contrary to Lacan's self-representation, I argue that his later engagement with *les non-dupes errent* [the undeceived are mistaken] closely resembles *qui perd gagne*.[5] I begin by sketching the Lacanian framework to build an account of typical subject development by comparing it to psychotic subject development, thereby demonstrating Lacan's ontological discovery about subjectivity. Then, I discuss *qui perd gagne* in relation to disavowal; I show how the 'recuperative transformation' of *qui perd gagne* is a form of fetishistic disavowal if viewed in Lacanian terms (*NF*, p. 198). I finish by arguing that, if considered in this way, Lacan has effectively morphed *qui perd gagne* into *les non-dupes errent*. The central argument is, therefore, to realign, after a brief complication, the notion of *qui perd gagne* with *les non-dupes errent*. I argue that Lacan reconnects the recuperative transformation expressed in *qui perd gagne* to the heart of subjective understanding. *Qui perd gagne* settles, in some way, the impasse of subjectivity expressed in the symbolic triad: *le nom-du-père* / le non du père / *les non-dupes errent* [The name of the father / The no of the father / the undeceived are mistaken].[6]

Lacan's Ontological Discovery

Psychosis and foreclosure are fundamental concepts in Lacan's scheme and are central to understanding Lacanian subjectivity. I will begin by discussing foreclosure. It is precisely the absence of phallic meaning in psychosis that informs my understanding of Lacan's view of sexual difference, love, and subjectivity, all of which are key to understanding how the 'recuperative transformation' of *qui perd gagne* operates in its Lacanian conception. This reconstruction of Lacanian theory is located at the level of the Symbolic Order, which is to say the level of intersubjective structures overseen by Master Signifiers.

Though we encounter the Symbolic Order at the original level of naming, and so language, we are only properly inculcated into the Symbolic Order from later childhood onwards. It is during this process that subjects are either properly oedipalized or not, as Howells argues: 'entry into the Symbolic Order is conditional on the initial renunciation of *jouissance* in the castration complex; because the signifier creates and splits the subject'.[7] Subjects are exposed to certain signifiers, for example *le nom-du-père,* and these are either recognized or misidentified, which results in a structuring or mis-structuring of a subject's relationship with the Symbolic Order. And according to Lacan, this has serious consequences for subject development. Much like the interrelated concept of language, the Symbolic Order is both beyond all comprehension and the mechanism by which all comprehension is apprehended. This is why Lacan refers to the big Other as something of which we know nothing: 'l'Autre en tant qu'il n'est pas connu' ('the Other in as much as it is not known').[8] The big Other is of the register of the Symbolic, and, in crude terms, it is the mis-structuring of this relationship which leads to psychosis.

Lacan aims to show how the subject experiences foreclosure by studying the clues offered by psychotic subjects and their manifestation in psychotic breakdowns. Foreclosure is a specific operation located at the origin of psychosis and predicated on the subject's rejection of certain foundational signifiers.[9] Lacan's analysis attempts to exemplify foreclosure by undertaking a close reading of Daniel Schreber's *Memoirs of my Nervous Illness.*[10] Lacan argues that Schreber was not properly inculcated into the Symbolic Order at the Oedipal stage. In simple terms, Schreber experienced foreclosure, a rejection of the primordial signifiers, which resulted in delusions and dysfunctional intra-human relationships. Schreber's psychosis, according to Lacan, was prompted by an improper inculcation into the Symbolic Order, a schism which only appears at a later moment in the subject's development. Psychosis and foreclosure do not indicate that Schreber did not identify with *a* Symbolic Order; Lacan insists on this point. Lacan interprets Schreber's delusions from the perspective of Schreber's unique identification with God, and this relationship reveals his connection with *a* Symbolic Order. Schreber's psychotic delusions, Lacan argues, are comprehensible from within the triadic schema: Real, Symbolic, Imaginary (RSI), precisely because Schreber's delusions signify that his inculcation is a fractured symbolic articulation, capable of being translated into comprehension.

In typical subject development, the subject's symbolic castration offers them the chance to form normal libidinal relations with others. For this to happen the subject must renounce the mother's unregulated desire, or in other words, the subject 'gives up some jouissance'.[11] If it does not, it risks being faced with the big Other's *jouissance* which is totally incomprehensible from the subject's standpoint. Lacan shows the normal structuring of desire and the phallus economy produces exemplary libidinal relations between subjects and others. In the case of the psychotic, the foreclosure of *le nom-du-père* indicates an absence of phallic meaning which results in forming dysfunctional libidinal relations.

Le père, the signifier that structures *la vérité de la chose* [the truth of the thing], is defective in the pre-psychotic, which precipitates the pre-psychotic's descent into psychosis. However, what happens to the subject when *le père*, qua actual empirical being, is himself missing or defective? 'Que se passe-t-il' [What happens], Lacan asks, 'quand la vérité de la chose manque, *quand il n'y a plus rien pour la représenter dans sa vérité,* quand par exemple le registre du père est en défaut?' ('when the truth of the thing is lacking, *when there is nothing left to represent it in its truth,* when for example the register of the father defaults') (*P,* p. 230; 204, my emphasis). Lacan disassociates the signifiers from actual empirical beings, individuals, or for example one's father. Reading the paternal function in relation to empirical beings, or understanding 'the phallus' literally, for example, would be to have missed the point of Lacan's argument.[12] Lacan argues that the process of oedipalization, symbolic castration, and the general inculcation into the symbolic by way of the signifiers, can be achieved (or forfeited) simply by exposure to the image of the signifier itself: *Un-père.* Lacan argues: 'Supposons que cette situation comporte précisément pour le sujet l'impossibilité d'assumer la réalisation du signifiant père au niveau symbolique. Que lui reste-t-il? Il lui reste l'image à quoi se réduit la fonction paternelle' ('Let's suppose that this situation entails for the subject the impossibility of assuming the realisation of the signifier *father* at the symbolic level. What's he left with? He's left with the image the paternal function is reduced to') (*P,* p. 230; 207). The image of the signifier (*Un-père*) is more important than the empirical person who assumes the position of the signifier in the Symbolic Order. The centrality of *le père* is the key to my argument, because it is around the signifier 'father' that the Symbolic Order is organized and, as we will see, this signifier is a fake.

Lacan develops the Master Signifier argument by first relating the father's role as that of the name-giver and thus the signifier that inaugurates a subject's entry into the Symbolic Order. We had said that the symbolic exists at the original level of naming; this highlights the importance Lacan places on the father since this signifier creates the symbolic space by naming the subject. Lacan's linguistic dexterity is evident: *le nom-du-père* is a Master Signifier whose role is to act as a regulative principle, but it also contains the injunction le non-du-père [the No of the Father]. Lacan's neat linguistic formulations capture the core characteristics of the Symbolic Order: the Symbolic Order places restrictions on named subjects, hence the *nom/non* homophony. Lacan develops the homophony further in Seminar XXI (1973–74) where he morphs it from *le nom-du-père* to *les non-dupes errent* [the undeceived are mistaken]. The idea, though I will flesh this out a bit later, is for us to accept that we must be dupes of the Symbolic Order. I will argue that this is the 'recuperative transformation' of *qui perd gagne*, par excellence (*NF*, p. 198). Furthermore, *les non-dupes errant* could also be understood as elevating the necessary lie into a regulative principle for truth. In short, this means we need certain untruths for truth itself to function since truth can only be *mi-dit* [half-said]:

> Je sais bien qu'il y a *cette sacrée question de la vérité* [...]. Mais nous n'allons pas comme ça, après ce que je vous en ai dit, et combien de fois... et y revenant et y retournant, nous mettre à y coller sans savoir que *c'est un choix*, puisqu'elle ne peut que se *mi-dire*. (*NDE*, p. 19)

> [I am aware that there remains this *holy question of the truth* [...]. However, we won't approach it directly like that. Not after what I have told you about it, and how many times, returning and labouring it. We'll pin ourselves to the truth not knowing *it's a choice* since it can only be half-said.]

Truth, if it exists, is only half-said (*mi-dit*): this is because we are unable to express the unconscious in speech. *Les dupes qui errent* [the undeceived who are mistaken] are those who refuse to recognize this fact; and so, *qui perd gagne* [the loser wins], since we must be dupes to gain some truth in language.

Before further expanding on the relationship between *qui perd gagne* and *les non-dupes errent*, let us return to the image of the signifier. A subject's defective identification could mean that the subject forecloses, by misperceiving the captivating image that is without limits and so manifests himself 'dans l'ordre de la puissance et non dans celui du pacte' ('in the order of strength and not in that of the pact') (*P*, p. 230; 205). The pact with the father is the normal resolution of the Oedipus complex: the child would be said to have been properly castrated. The subject's exposure to, and subsequent realization of, a father who had rightful possession of the mother is central to the subject's resolution of the Oedipus complex, the son having ascended to the standard model of virility (*P*, pp. 230–31; 205). Conversely, the subject who forecloses would not be able to model themselves against a more complete Other (the father) and therefore relates to a Symbolic Order characterized by an absent core. This problem, the original mis-structuring of the Symbolic Order, is carried forth throughout the subject's life until prompted into psychosis by certain key triggers in their life.

The psychotic subject forecloses and annihilates himself through a misidentification with the Other's desire. However, the pre-psychotic subject descends into madness only after a traumatic moment that triggers the underlying psychosis in the subject's life, which had been a life of normal functioning until the onset of delusions. Since the pre-psychotic, Schreber for example, is plainly in *a* Symbolic Order, not *the* Symbolic Order, any attempt to resolve the question of the father or the problems of his sexual identity is being undertaken at the wrong level. And so, it takes an encounter with *le nom-du-père* for a psychotic, like Schreber, to break down.[13] *Le nom-du-père* summons the subject to recognize their confrontation with the symbolic. The sheer weight of this summoning causes the subject to become decompensated. This actualization, brought on by exposure to the signifier uncovers the absence and demonstrates the lack of sexual identity. In Schreber's case, the absence of a primordial male signifier was hidden for a long time, 'il avait l'air de tenir son rôle d'homme, et d'être quelqu'un, comme tout le monde' [he looked as if he, like everyone else, were upholding his role as a man and of being somebody] (*P*, p. 286; 252). And since virility signified something essential for Schreber, it is no surprise that the onset of his psychosis was triggered by having discovered that his wife was newly pregnant and that his ascension to the local judiciary was complete, igniting in him the fear of castration. This meant that the missing signifier, in Schreber's case, came to light in the guise of his desire to be a woman experiencing sexual intercourse. Schreber's delusion was that he could only construct the realities of the world, the cosmos, according to the idea that he must be the universal God's wife (*P*, p. 286; 252). The decompensation that Schreber suffered occurred because he realized that he couldn't become a 'Father': the phallus economy had not been properly installed in him (*P*, p. 360; 320).

The 'typical' subject is not more complete than a 'psychotic' simply because they are named at birth, and so initiated into a relationship with the Symbolic Order; Schreber, too, was named. Rather, it is the process of castration and a subject's relationship with the big Other which structures the typical functioning of the Symbolic Order. The clinical tools, such as foreclosure, which Lacan develops from case studies of psychotics like Schreber, are not inserted to wedge a distinction between 'normal' and 'abnormal,' as if only psychotics were abnormal through their identification with a symptom. Hence Lacan makes both an ontological and a clinical point. Subjects are initially inculcated into the symbolic at the original level of naming. We are spoken to, thus interpellated, and so initiated into a relationship with the various processes governing the Symbolic dimension. However, it is important to note that even though this may be 'typical', it does not follow that it is successful. This is Lacan's ontological discovery. As Žižek argues, our typical inculcation into the Symbolic Order represents a necessary failure:

> The subject *is* the retroactive effect of the failure of its representation. It is because of this failure that the subject is divided — not into something and something else, but into something (its symbolic representation) and nothing, and fantasy fills the void of this nothingness. And the catch is that this symbolic representation of the subject is primordially *not its own*. [...] The speaking subject persists in this in-between: prior to nomination, there is no subject, but once it is named, it already disappears in its signifier — the subject never is, it always *will have been*.[14]

This is because, ultimately, and Lacan is unequivocal on this point, the Master Signifier is not something that we can possess or know. Recall how we identified that symbolic articulations could be established without the presence of a physical signifier, but by relying solely on the image of the signifier. Lacan illustrates the concept of the phallus-as-signifier with reference to the celestial sphere ('Le Phallus et le météore' ('The Phallus and the Meteor'), *P*, pp. 349–63; 310–23). The Master Signifier is spectral, denoting nothing but a glimpse of the Symbolic Order itself — as the manifestation of 'the law' in a symbol *le nom-du-père*. This is why the Symbolic Order, as governed by the spectral Master Signifier, is a *mi-dire* [half-saying] of the truth: it is necessary for us to get to the truth via the medium of the lie. The lie states that *le nom-du-père* is real and organizes our relations, but it is a nonexistent fraud of which we must be dupes, *qui perd gagne*. Nevertheless, it still structures our actions.

The signifier is distanced from the signified, and Lacan emphasizes that this Master Signifier is the *quilting point* (*le point de capiton*) in the construction of the Symbolic Order. In such a paradigm, the fulcrum that binds the set together does not need to be real, and crucially it need not be true either. In order for a community of people to communicate on a shared topic, the shared Master Signifier does not need to exist. Moreover, Lacan suggests that the Master Signifier does not require meaning:

> Il s'agit de la transmission de quelque chose de vide, qui lasse et épuise le sujet. À leur naissance, ces phénomènes se situent à la limite de la signification, mais ils deviennent bientôt tout le contraire — résidus, déchets, corps vides.

> [It's a question of the transmission of something empty that wearies and exhausts the subject. At their first appearance, these phenomena are situated at the limit of meaning, but they soon turn into quite the contrary — residue, refuse, empty bodies.] (*P*, p. 294; 259).

This Master Signifier guarantees the big Other but is an empty signifier without a signified:

> La crainte de Dieu est un signifiant qui ne traîne pas partout. Il a fallu quelqu'un pour l'inventer, et proposer aux hommes, comme remède à un monde fait de terreurs multiples [...]. Remplacer les craintes innombrables par la crainte d'un être unique qui n'a d'autre moyen de manifester sa puissance que par ce qui est craint derrière ces innombrables craintes, c'est fort.

> [The fear of God isn't a signifier that is found everywhere. Someone had to invent it and propose to men, as the remedy for a world made up of manifold terrors [...]. To have replaced these innumerable fears by the fear of a unique being who has no other means of manifesting his power than through what is feared behind these innumerable fears is quite an accomplishment.] (*P*, p. 302; 267).

Slavoj Žižek argues that the quilting point is the first serious qualification to the structure of the big Other that Lacan effectuates in the mid-1950s during his work on psychosis.[15] The second revision that Lacan makes concerning the big Other is in Seminar XX in the 1970s, where he uses the logic of the 'not-all' and the 'exception constitutive of the universal'.[16] Lacan argues that in order to invent a system structure with a Master Signifier like that of the *fear-of-God* for example, one must be either a prophet or poet, 'au moins par la grâce de Racine, qu'il peut user comme il le fait de ce signifiant majeur et primordial' ('at least by the grace of Racine, that he can use as he does this major and primordial signifier') (*P*, p. 302; 267). For Lacan, Racine effectuates a sleight-of-hand that transmutes normal fear into a faith *in* God, which guarantees an end to standard fear by supplanting it with the Master Signifier: the *fear-of-God*. This equips the subject with enough faith to confront standard fear; however, Lacan points out that the Master Signifier (*fear-of-God*) is a fabrication. God signifying nothing, it is an empty container.

The central feature of the quilting point is that signifiers hardly need to be real to function as signifiers. The *fear-of-God* is not founded on a real fear; *fear-of-God* doesn't signify anything in reality. Lacan maintains that God is merely an imagined construction of poets and prophets, and yet, he does not mean to suggest that faith should be ridiculed or ignored. On the contrary, faith is a foundational signifier which governs human actions. Faith operates under the same conditions as *le nom-du-père* in the Symbolic Order; God is its Master Signifier. The pious refer to God, and what binds them together is their shared *ignorance* of what constitutes God as Master Signifier, or as the big Other. This is why we argued earlier that the speaking subject persists in this in-between. I showed how: 'prior to nomination, there is no subject, but once it is named, it already disappeared in its signifier — the subject never is, it always *will have been*' (*D*, p. 211). We know why the subject is not, because the signifier is not, too. It is a failure of representation. And yet, this failure should not be taken as the impossible thing-in-itself or the celebration of failure, as Žižek puts it, 'the idea that every act ultimately misfires and that the proper ethical stance is [to] heroically accept this failure'.[17] It could be said that this idea underlines the argument of *qui perd gagne*. However, I argue we can better understand this heroic celebration of failure if we view it as a form of fetishistic disavowal.

Oui, mais quand même...

In *Clefs pour l'imaginaire ou l'Autre Scène*, Octave Mannoni explains fetishistic dis-avowal as '*je sais bien, mais quand même!*' [I know well, but all the same!]. Mannoni argues that, although Freud did not explicitly deal with belief, he always had it in his line of sight. Mannoni claims that Freud tied the problem of belief to disavowal, as early as his 1927 essay on fetishism. Disavowal, according to Mannoni's reading of Freud, is the moment that the child recognizes the feminine anatomy of his mother as the absence of the phallus. However, the child's immediate reaction is to repudiate this fact:

> Il désavoue ou répudie le démenti que lui inflige la réalité afin de conserver sa croyance à l'existence du phallus maternel. Seulement il ne pourra la conserver qu'au prix d'une transformation radicale (dont Freud a tendance à faire surtout une modification du Moi). 'Ce n'est pas vrai, dit-il, que l'enfant, après avoir pris connaissance de l'anatomie féminine, conserve intacte sa croyance dans l'existence du phallus maternel. Sans doute il la conserve, mais aussi il l'abandonne. Quelque chose a joué qui n'est possible que selon la loi du processus primaire. Il a maintenant à l'égard de cette croyance une attitude divisée.' C'est cette attitude divisée qui, dans l'article de 1938, deviendra le *clivage* du Moi.

> [He disavows or repudiates the refutation of his belief that is imposed by reality. Yet he can retain this belief only at the price of a radical transformation (which Freud tends to treat, first and foremost, as a modification of the ego). 'It is not true,' says Freud, 'that, after the child has made his observation of the woman, he has preserved unaltered his belief that women have a phallus. He has retained that belief, but he has also given it up ... [*sic*] a compromise has been reached, as is only possible under the dominance of the ... [*sic*] primary processes. The child has maintained a divided attitude towards that belief'. This 'divided attitude' becomes, in the 1938 text, the *splitting* of the ego.][18]

Mannoni's argument is that at the core of the split subject, in Freudian psycho-analysis, we find a disavowal of belief. The fetishist does not allow experience to repudiate the belief that women do not possess a phallus, yet the fetishist, according to Freud, conserves their fetish precisely because they do not possess one: 'Il conserve un fétiche *parce* qu'elles n'en ont pas. Non seulement l'expérience n'est pas effacée, mais elle devient à jamais ineffaçable, elle laisse un *stigma indélébile* dont le fétichiste est marqué à jamais. C'est le souvenir qui est effacé' ('He cultivates a fetish because they *do not* have one. Not only is the experience not eradicated, it is ineradicable. It leaves an *indelible mark* on the fetishist, one he bears forever. What is eradicated is the *memory* of the experience') (*CI*, p. 11; 69–70). This is not employed by the fetishist in terms of sexual perversions. Mannoni is not suggesting that in Freud's work the fetishist *wishes* a phallus for the mother — they know she does not possess one. This is not what is at stake in disavowal. Clearly one could not say about perversion: 'je sais bien' that the mother does not possess a phallus, 'mais quand même...'. However, what we can say is that we are attempting to locate, as Mannoni does, something between strangeness and banality. Mannoni argues 'that belief in the presence of the maternal phallus is the first belief that one disavows and the paradigm for all other acts of disavowal' (*CI*, p. 10; 76). Fetishistic disavowal is the paradigm for very 'puzzling phenomena that can easily escape our attention' (*CI*, p. 12; 71).

What escapes our attention in the logic of *qui perd gagne* is, I would argue, the false sense of heroism it contains, that I mentioned at the end of the previous section. The false sense of heroism is especially evident if placed in relation to Lacan's conceptual schema. Howells exemplifies the heroism of *qui perd gagne*:

> It becomes clear that there are in Sartre's view two versions of success through failure or *qui perd gagne*. The one, condemned, tries to recuperate failure as success in another dimension, i.e. in the future or on a different level of attainment. The other, his own version of salvation through defeat, sees the possibility of failure as proof of the freedom of human consciousness from the deterministic process. (*NF*, p. 199)

Although both versions show the heroism at work in *qui perd gagne* it is more evident in the second variant, 'salvation through defeat'. Sartre, Howells argues, sees the potential for failure as an opportunity for freedom, the resultant freedom thereby liberates us from determinism.[19] Sartre is effectively accepting the desolation of the human condition, while nonetheless replying 'oui, mais quand même...!'[20] However, my preliminary argument is that the logic of *qui perd gagne* should include the rigid determinism of the structures of *les non-dupes errent*, which is to say the structures of the Symbolic Order itself. Although these structures might be bound together by a lie, as we have seen the Master Signifier need not exist, we nevertheless act as though the Master Signifier is real, and all our actions are mediated by this belief, which makes *qui perd gagne* a kind of fiction that points to a truth which is only *mi-dit* [half-said]. This is the *stigma indélébile* [indelible mark] that is the result of the fetishistic disavowal in Sartre's philosophy in relation to *qui perd gagne*.

Les Non-Dupes Errent

Lacan's 'de-centred' subject has been broadly conceived in two ways. On the one hand, the argument goes that 'my subjective experience is regulated by objective unconscious mechanisms that are de-centred with regard to my self-experience and, as such, beyond my control' (*D*, p. 222). This is the reading that says that Lacan places the subject as 'always-already displaced, decentred, pluralized' (*FTK*, p. xvi). Rather, as Žižek puts it in *Disparities*, 'something much more unsettling' is meant by Lacan's de-centred subject:

> I am deprived of even my most intimate subjective experience, the way things 'really seem to me,' that of the fundamental fantasy that constitutes and guarantees the core of my being, since I can never consciously experience it and assume it. (*D*, p. 222).

That the 'subject "as such" is the name for a certain radical displacement, a certain wound, cut, in the texture of the universe, and all its identifications are ultimately just *so many failed attempts to heal this wound*' (*FTK*, p. xvi, my emphasis). The core Lacanian thesis is the idea that we are alone, irremediably lost to ourselves, and unable to understand even the most basic features of our existence. The unconscious is an incoherent jumble, Žižek continues:

> This is what Lacan means by '*il n'y a pas de rapport sexuel*': there is no deep instinctual formula of the harmony between the sexes which should be uncovered, the Unconscious is not a deep-seated wisdom but a big mess, a bricolage of symptoms and fantasies which deal with or cover up this deadlock. (*D*, p. 218)

The crucial distinction between the Symbolic and the Real is the radical incoherence of the subject in the Symbolic versus the equally incoherent antagonisms in the Real. And it is this radical inconsistency that *les non-dupes errent* adds to *le nom-du-père*. Lacan says:

> Dans ces deux termes mis en mots, des *Noms du Père* et des *non-dupes qui errent*, c'est le même savoir. Dans les deux. C'est le même savoir au sens où l'inconscient c'est un savoir dont le sujet peut se déchiffrer. C'est la définition du sujet, qu'ici je donne, du sujet tel que le constitue l'inconscient. (*NDE*, p. 5)

> [Both terms, put into words, the name of the father, and the undeceived are mistaken, contain the same knowledge. In both. It's the same knowledge in the sense that the unconscious is knowledge from which the subject can be deciphered. What I'm giving you here is the definition of the subject, the subject as the unconscious constitutes it.]

Lacan is associating *le nom-du-père* and *les non-dupes errent* in the same logic; they both contain the same knowledge (*savoir*). However, the knowledge gained is analogous to the relationship between the knowledge the subject can obtain from the unconscious, which is a facetious point since the subject is unable to learn much from the unconscious as it is an incoherent jumble. Lacan argues that this is the definition of the subject, a subject is one who has been constituted by the unconscious. However, Lacan further complicates the account:

C'est à savoir que cet inconscient, par rapport à ce qui couplerait si bien le moi au monde... le corps à ce qui l'entoure, ce qui l'ordonnerait sous cette sorte de rapport qu'on s'obstine à vouloir considérer comme naturel ...c'est que par rapport à lui, cet inconscient se présente comme essentiellement différent de cette harmonie — disons le mot — *dysharmonique*. (*NDE*, p. 263)

[That is to say that this unconscious, in relation to what would couple so well the ego to the world ... the body to what surrounds it, which would order it under this kind of relationship that we persist in wanting to consider natural ... it is that in relation to the ego, this unconscious is presented as essentially different from this harmony — say the word — *dysharmony*.]

That is the central truth of the fantasy; the unconscious, though it might be structured like a language, is also characterized by *dysharmony*. The subject might be drawn from the unconscious, but this means that it is formed from within the chaos of the Real. *Le nom-du-père* is a synecdoche for the rules which govern the Symbolic Order. However, Lacan's point in Seminar XXI is that we must not forget the impact of the Real and the *savoir du Réel* [knowledge of the Real]. *Qui perd gagne* without this knowledge is just another one of the 'bricolage of symptoms and fantasies' which is heroically deployed to deal with the deadlock of the de-centred subject. There will always be a baseline level of incoherence which cannot be subsumed into *qui perd gagne*.

The fact that we hide from the deadlock of the de-centred subject is itself a form of fetishistic disavowal. It could be formulated thus: 'Je sais bien que je suis perdu. Mais, quand même...' [I know very well that I am lost, but all the same...]. This is *qui perd gagne* par excellence. A lie we tell ourselves to stave off the hopelessness inscribed in our human condition, it is a form of self-deception. However, what one receives from such a lie is not *la morale,* as though one should not lie. What one gets instead is the basic positive value of the lie. The lie which is the sincerest demonstration of love itself. Shakespeare captured this impulse clearly in Sonnet 138:

> When my love swears that she is made of truth,
> I do believe her, though I know she lies,
> That she might think me some untutored youth,
> Unlearnèd in the world's false subtleties.
>
> Thus vainly thinking that she thinks me young,
> Although she knows my days are past the best,
> Simply I credit her false-speaking tongue:
> On both sides thus is simple truth suppressed.
>
> But wherefore says she not she is unjust?
> And wherefore say not I that I am old?
> Oh, love's best habit is in seeming trust,
> And age in love loves not to have years told.
>
> Therefore I lie with her and she with me,
> And in our faults by lies we flattered be.

'When my love swears that she is made of truth | I do believe her, though I know she lies': she lies because the truth is only ever *mi-dit* [half-said]. We are all 'untutored youth'. We are 'unlearnèd in the world's false subtleties' since we are privy only to conscious knowledge not the knowledge of the Real in the unconscious. All our tongues are 'false-speaking'. It is the 'seeming trust' that is key; we seemingly trust symbolic appearances. The Bard first theorized *les non-dupes errent*: 'On both sides thus is simple truth suppressed | But wherefore says she not she is unjust?' The underlying value of the lie is finally redeemed: 'Therefore I lie with her and she with me | And in our faults by lies we flattered be'. Lacan says: 'Dites n'importe quoi, ça touchera toujours au vrai' [Say anything, it will always touch the truth] (*NDE*, p. 178).

This is the crucial tragedy that we confront. I have argued that it's not quite *qui perd gagne*; we don't necessarily win. According to Lacan, we simply persist incoherently. Therefore, either we admit that we don't know, or we lie earnestly. However, we must be dupes to these lies, dupes to, for example, the *nom-du-père*. Gaining something from being duped is the reason why *les non-dupes errent* is closely related to *qui perd gagne*. And, although Lacan tried to distance himself from Sartre in his later work, the Sartrean concept of *qui perd gagne* as articulated by Howells has returned in a different form. It remains a manner of 'recuperative transformation', however, the key difference concerns the (fake) Master Signifier which governs the symbolic dimension. We must be aware of its deceit and choose to be dupes to *qui perd gagne*; however, this is a necessary choice, and so ultimately a false choice. The false choice of the Master Signifier's deceit *is* the little piece of the real, the essential antagonism, included in *les non-dupes errent* which is missing from *qui perd gagne*.

Regardless of the differences between *qui perd gagne* and *les non-dupes errent*, one thing is certain: 'On both sides thus is simple truth suppressed'.

Notes to Chapter 4

1. Christina Howells, *Sartre: The Necessity of Freedom* (Cambridge: Cambridge University Press, 1988); this work subsequently referred to as *NF* in the main text.
2. Jean-Paul Sartre, *L'Être et le néant: essai d'ontologie phénoménologique* (Paris: Gallimard, 1943).
3. Clotilde Leguil, *Sartre avec Lacan: corrélation antinomique, liaison dangereuse* (Paris: Navarin, Le Champ freudien, 2012).
4. Jacques Lacan, *Autres écrits* (Paris: Champ Freudien/Seuil, 2001), p. 179; English translation is my own.
5. Jacques Lacan, *Séminaire XXI, Les Non-dupes errent 1973–74*, ebook, <http://www.valas.fr/IMG/pdf/S21_NON-DUPES---.pdf> [accessed 23 January 2019]; this work subsequently referred to as *NDE* in the main text. *Seminaire XXI* has not been officially published by Seuil, nor is there an available official English translation. Throughout I cite Patrick Valas's transcription of Lacan's spoken word; all translations are my own. *Les non-dupes errent* could be translated as 'the non-dupes err', however, for clarity I follow Fredric Jameson's 'the undeceived are mistaken'; see Fredric Jameson, 'First Impressions', *London Review of Books*, 7 September 2006, pp. 7–8.
6. I am very grateful for the perspicacious comments I received from Christina Howells in Venice, which transformed my entire argument and led me to *les non-dupes errent* in the first place.
7. Christina Howells, *Mortal Subjects: Passions of the Soul in Late Twentieth-century French Thought* (Cambridge: Polity Press, 2011), p. 137.
8. Jacques Lacan, *Le Séminaire de Jacques Lacan, Livre III, Les Psychoses (1955–1956)* (Paris: Champ Freudien/Seuil, 1981), p. 51; *Book III, The Psychoses 1955–1956*, trans. by Russell Grigg (London & New York: W. W. Norton, 1993), p. 40); this work subsequently referred to as *P* in the main text.

9. J. Laplanche and J. B. Pontalis, *Vocabulaire de la psychanalyse* (Paris: PUF, 2014), p. 163.

10. Daniel Paul Schreber, *Memoirs of My Nervous Illness,* trans. and ed. by Ida Macalpine and Richard A. Hunter (Cambridge, MA: Harvard University Press, 2000).

11. Bruce Fink, *The Lacanian Subject* (Princeton, NJ: Princeton University Press, 1995), p. 99.

12. It is interesting to note that Bruce Fink argues that Lacan's point is that phallic *jouissance* should also be viewed as fallible (Fink, *Lacan to the Letter: Reading Écrits Closely* (Minneapolis: University of Minnesota Press, 2004), p. 159).

13. Jacques Lacan, *Écrits,* (Paris: Champ Freudien/Seuil, 1966), p. 577.

14. Slavoj Žižek, *Disparities* (London: Bloomsbury, 2016), p. 210); this work subsequently referred to as *D* in the main text.

15. Slavoj Žižek, 'The Real of Sexual Difference', in *Reading Seminar XX: Lacan's Major Work on Love Knowledge, and Feminine Sexuality*, ed. by Susanne Barnard and Bruce Fink (New York: State University of New York Press, 2002), pp. 57–75 (p. 58).

16. Ibid, p. 58.

17. Slavoj Žižek, *For They Know Not What They Do: Enjoyment as a Political Factor* (London & New York: Verso, 1991), p. xii); this work subsequently referred to as *FTK* in the main text.

18. Octave Mannoni, *Clefs pour l'Imaginaire ou l'Autre Scène* (Paris: Seuil, 1969) p. 10; 'I Know Well, But All the Same...', in *Perversion and the Social Relation,* ed. by Molly Anne Rothenberg, Dennis Foster and Slavoj Žižek, trans. by G. M. Goshgarian (Durham, NC, & London: Duke University Press, 2003), pp. 69–70; this work subsequently referred to as *CI* in the main text.

19. I discuss this at greater length in my DPhil thesis.

20. Sartre calls the desolation of the human condition 'une maladie' in *L'Être et le néant*, p. 669.

PART II

Freedom and Necessity in
Jacques Derrida

CHAPTER 5

Stylistic Liberties:
Derrida, Rhetoric, Style

Paul Earlie

In his comprehensive *A New History of Western Philosophy*, published in four volumes between 2004 and 2007, the Oxford philosopher Anthony Kenny makes a surprising omission.[1] Although the 1088-page synopsis of European thought devotes considerable space to Bertrand Russell's contribution to philosophy, no mention is made of Russell's 1945 bestseller, *A History of Western Philosophy*, to which the title of Kenny's book is a clear allusion.[2] Shortly after the publication of the book's final volume, Kenny gave an interview to the popular philosophy podcast, *Philosophy Bites*, in which he touched on this omission. As he told the podcast's producers, although he was a 'great admirer' of Russell's tome, in particular of its stylistic qualities (it is 'wonderfully written', 'exciting'), the persuasive qualities of Russell's writing could at times be deceptive. Russell's *History* was sometimes 'wildly inaccurate and extremely unfair' to figures such as Aristotle and Kant.[3] More commendable was Frederick Copleston's *History of Philosophy*, which was 'more accurate' but unfortunately less exciting to students.[4] Weighing up the merits and shortcomings of both books, Kenny wanted his 'new' history of Western philosophy to avoid the Scylla of Russell's seductive style and the Charybdis of Copleston's overly dry presentation — to be, as he put it, 'more entertaining' than the latter but 'more accurate' than the former.

Should philosophy be entertaining? To what degree should style inform a philosopher's practice of writing? How much freedom should philosophers have to diverge from stylistic conventions, as determined by the usual gatekeepers of academic research? Such questions have a curiously timeless quality, having formed the mainstay of philosophical debate since Socrates's defining battle with the sophists. Russell's latter-day sophist adversary was the French philosopher Henri Bergson, whose influence the analytic philosopher condemns in an aggressive but powerful chapter of his *History*. Bergson's seductive writing style is here synonymous with 'Bergsonian irrationalism'. If clever analogies, similes, and metaphors abound in his prose, they amount to little more than 'the charm of an excellent style' (*HWP*, p. 719). What lean argumentation Russell does glean from Bergson's writing is found to be specious or trivial. Ultimately Bergsonism is an 'anti-intellectual philosophy [which] thrives upon the errors and confusions of the intellect' (*HWP*, p. 720) and its founder is more a poet than a philosopher:

> His imaginative picture of the world, regarded as a poetic effort, is in the main not capable of either proof or disproof. Shakespeare says life's but a walking shadow, Shelley says it is like a dome of many-coloured glass, Bergson says it is a shell which bursts into parts that are again shells. If you like Bergson's image better, it is just as legitimate. (*HWP*, p. 722)

Reading these remarks today one is struck not so much by their hostility as by their disinterest in what Bergson himself has to say on the subject of style and its role in philosophy. In singling out Bergson's writing, however, Russell is not targeting the mere presence of style in philosophy. In texts such as 'How I Write', Russell takes delight in the formal beauty of a well-balanced sentence or in the ingenuity of an adeptly chosen metaphor.[5] But he remains uninterested in Bergson's own reflections on the closeness of dream imagery to the mutability of inner experience ('durée'), or to what this might tell us about the stylistic patterning of Bergson's own image-laden prose. In effect, Russell denies any philosophical underpinning to the stylistic verve of Bergson's texts.

A belief in the extraneousness of style to argument likely motivates this indifference to Bergson's account of the relationship between language, rhetoric, and philosophy, or of his discussion of the limitations of the classical opposition of *morphe* (form) and *hyle* (content). As Kenny's comments in his *Philosophy Bites* interview suggest, this opposition is not simply classical; it is also profoundly contemporary. Indeed, it is one of the most operative distinctions in Kenny's *New History of Western Philosophy*. The book's 'General Introduction' concludes that patient textual analysis, or what is here called 'internal exegesis', is the most important tool at the disposal of the historian of philosophy: 'In internal exegesis the interpreter tries to make the text coherent and consistent, employing the principle of charity in interpretation'. 'External exegesis', on the other hand, involves 'comparing' and 'contrasting' a text with other texts (*NHWP*, p. xv). The centrality of this exegetical method to Kenny's book, and the form-content opposition which underpins it, is clear from his treatment of one of the most notorious of modern 'philosophical' stylists: Jacques Derrida. A chapter entitled 'From Freud to Derrida' returns repeatedly to a cluster of themes which are also central to Plato's *agon* with the sophists and Russell's tussle with Bergson. Highlighting the superficiality of this modish thinker (in 2007, at least), Kenny puts Derrida's writing at the heart of his critique of deconstruction, holding Derrida's 'later' literary or poetic style responsible for the divergence of Continental and 'Anglophone' philosophy. Things had, he argues, appeared more hopeful in Derrida's pre-1967 writings, where the latter's early interest in the linguistic philosopher J. L. Austin pointed to a temporary bridging of this divide. Even in this case, however, where both thinkers address the 'same topic' (performativity), their approaches are wildly different. Although both have a fondness for neologisms, Austin's lexical idiom is 'defined in lucid terms and [...] illuminated by examples'; Derrida, by contrast, multiplies technical terms ('gram', 'reserve', 'incision', 'pharmakon') without definition, thereby confusing 'ideas that are perfectly distinct' (*NHWP*, p. 826). Derrida takes enormous formal liberties but he does so without assuming the requisite stylistic responsibility that 'serious' philosophy requires:

> His philosophical weapons are the pun, the bawdy, the sneer, and the snigger. [...] there are no doctrines to present [...] it is unsurprising that [Derrida's] fame has been less in philosophy departments than in departments of literature, whose members have had less practice in discerning genuine from counterfeit philosophy. (*NHWP*, p. 828)

Style, in other words, is the vehicle of content, an expressive detour en route to the *telos* of the Idea.

Is a different approach to Derrida's style — and perhaps to style more generally — possible? What might it look like? One approach might consist in trying to work backwards from Derrida's stylistic experimentations to the content of his arguments. This was, and indeed remains, a relatively common strategy amongst partisans of deconstruction; but it has led, I think, to an unfortunate divide between those who would rehabilitate Derrida as a hyper-philosophical rationalist and those for whom deconstruction can only ever be found between the cracks of rational discourse. This will not be my approach here, for reasons I hope will become progressively clear. As Derrida himself noted, stylistically speaking, his most charitable readers were sometimes his most critical, and uncharitable readers (such as Kenny) could even be his most perceptive.[6] A simultaneous blindness and insight towards style on the part of Derrida's critics, then, accompanied by a flippancy with regard to style on the part of many of his defenders, has left something of a scholarly vacuum which it is the ambition of this essay to fill.

The Drug of Rhetoric

In commenting on Derrida's influential early essay on Plato, 'La Pharmacie de Platon' [Plato's Pharmacy], Kenny rebukes the French thinker for a wilful inattentiveness to Plato's rhetoric: 'Derrida's charge of phonocentrism has to be based on a number of eccentric texts starting with an ironic passage in Plato's *Phaedrus*' (*NHWP*, p. 825). The 'ironic passage' in question needs no introduction: the '*procès de l'écriture*' [trial of writing] recounted by Socrates in Plato's *Phaedrus*, in which the Egyptian King Thamus condemns writing as a poison (*pharmakon*) for memory after its inventor, Theuth, had presented it as a cure (*pharmakon*) for forgetfulness.[7] Probably because this legendary scene exemplifies so many abiding concerns of deconstruction — most notably phonocentrism, the privilege metaphysics accords to speech over writing — it has provided much fertile ground for readers both sympathetic and hostile to Derrida's mode of reading. My focus here, however, will be on an aspect of 'La Pharmacie de Platon' that has received relatively less attention: its dramatization of the relationship not of speech to writing but of philosophy to rhetoric.

'La Pharmacie de Platon' is in fact concerned less with a speech-writing hierarchy than with hierarchy in general. No matter how rigorous or detailed one's commentary or analysis, Derrida claims, it is impossible to establish an unimpeachable hierarchy of themes in Plato's dialogue. What he calls 'platonisme' [Platonism] refers to is a vast network of *un*hierarchical, interlocking binaries, in which the speech-writing opposition, for example, cannot be divorced from Plato's distinction between the living remembrance of Forms (*anamnesis*) and the counterfeit memory of note-taking (*hypomnesis*), just as both oppositions in turn intersect with Socrates's distinction between philosophical dialectic and sophistic rhetoric. Within this constantly evolving spider's web, no single point is more important or more central than another other; and it is by virtue of this differential structure of meaning (*différance*) that every textual point can be linked at every moment to every other point.

At their most general level, all approaches to textual commentary — from Kenny's 'internal exegesis' to the kind of *explication de texte* targeted by Derrida in 'La Pharmacie de Platon' (*D*, p. 79; 69) — work by establishing a hierarchy of what is and is not rhetorically important in the interpretation of a text.[8] In the opening pages of 'La Pharmacie de Platon', Derrida recalls that ancient commentators on the *Phaedrus* had considered it an inferior dialogue. According to Diogenes Laertius, the dialogue was said to be Plato's first since it 'manifested a certain juvenile quality' (*D*, p. 83; 72). Evidence of this youthfulness can be found in the exegetical difficulties one faces when trying to extract a larger argument or theme. The dialogue contains too many heterogeneous and unbalanced elements, the most jarring of which is the sudden shift in setting to ancient Egypt when Socrates recites the myth of the origin of writing. In both its style and structure, it is simply too incoherent to sustain a comprehensive internal exegesis of the type proposed by Kenny.[9]

Here we begin to touch on the problem of irony, for while Plato's dialogue takes aim at rhetoric as the corrupting invention (*technē*) of the sophists, the *Phaedrus* is nonetheless constructed according to rhetorical strictures of 'good' writing, in which unity of theme, for example, corresponds closely to unity of setting. It seems no accident that the background to Socrates's exchange with the orator Lysias is the place where Orithyia had once played before her abduction by the god Boreas — a little fountain dedicated to Pharmacia:

> Les *topoi* du dialogue ne sont pas indifférents. Les thèmes, les lieux, au sens de la rhétorique, sont étroitement inscrits, compris dans des sites chaque fois signifiants, ils sont mis en scène; et dans cette géographie théâtrale, l'unité de lieu obéit à un calcul ou à une nécessité infaillibles.

> [The *topoi* of the dialogue are never indifferent. The themes, the topics, the (common-)places, in a rhetorical sense, are strictly inscribed, comprehended each time within a significant site. They are dramatically staged, and in this theatrical geography, unity of place corresponds to an infallible calculation or necessity.] (*D*, pp. 85–86; 74)

Already in its setting, the calculating rhetoric of Plato's dialogue sets the stage for an attack on rhetoric as *pharmakon*, a poisonous influence on the youth of Athens.

Given his attack on sophistic rhetoric, in the *Phaedrus* and elsewhere, is Plato's attentiveness to the dialogue's *topoi* a deliberate form of irony? If so, what effect is it seeking to produce? Careful, logically consistent commentary might be in a position to answer such questions, but as 'La Pharmacie de Platon' reminds us, twenty-five centuries of philological commentary culminated in the conclusion that the text was 'mal composé' ('badly composed') (*D*, p. 82; 72). The originality of Derrida's strategy of reading is that while it rejects traditional commentary as based on a naive distinction between figural and literal, internal and external, it can still capture the immense richness of Plato's writing: 'Elle découvre de nouveaux accords, les surprend dans un minutieux contrepoint, dans une organisation plus secrète des thèmes, des noms, des mots' ('it discovers new chords, new concordances; it surprises them in minutely fashioned counterpoint, within a more secret organization of themes, of names, of words') (*D*, p. 83; 72).

The strengths of this strategy of reading are exemplified in Derrida's account of the *pharmakon*, whose occurrence at a pivotal point in the *procès* of writing presents an otherwise perplexing challenge to commentators. It is often asserted that for Derrida the problem with Plato's use of the word φαρμακός is that it simultaneously signifies 'cure' *and* 'poison'. This structural indeterminacy is what is alleged to flummox even the most rhetorically-attuned of readers. In fact, the meaning of the *pharmakon*-metaphor in 'La Pharmacie de Platon' is more than a simple problem of translation; it concerns the structural impossibility of ever fully meaning what one says (*vouloir-dire*). To say that the *pharmakon* simply 'means' (*veut dire*) 'cure' *or* 'poison' in the trial of writing passage is to trap oneself within the same logical categories (non-contradiction) and metaphysical oppositions (form-content, style-matter, and so) which Derrida's reading works to subvert. What is most threatening in the signifier *pharmakon*, he points out, is its continual merging with a vast and ever-expanding spider's web of signifiers (remedy, recipe, poison, drug, philter, and so on) which no manual of rhetoric, however rigorous or detailed, could ever hope to master. To affirm this slipperiness in the meaning of the term is not to say of Plato's text that 'il fait eau de toute part' ('is leaking on all sides') (*D*, p. 161; 130). It is rather to say that one cannot assert that the term has a single 'proper' or 'literal' meaning which could be returned to it *after* its metaphorical displacements have been fully interpreted.[10]

In teasing out a network of lexical associations linked to but not explicitly mentioned in Plato's text — the relationship between the figure of the *pharmakeus* (scapegoat) and the *pharmakon* itself, for example — 'La Pharmacie de Platon' moves beyond the classical binaries on which the exercise of commentary-writing depends (literal/figurative, latent/manifest, voluntary/involuntary, conscious/unconscious, etc.). At stake in Derrida's essay is less the destruction of metaphysically charged modes of rhetorical commentary (from *explication de texte* to internal and external exegesis) than a reflection on its conditions of possibility and impossibility, the possibility, that is, of a rule-based passage from A (e.g. literal or proper meaning) to B (e.g. metaphorical or allegorical meaning) and back again. A certain syntactical structure of play (*jeu*) — *différance*, *dissémination*, etc. — allows non-hierarchical or lateral movement between words and concepts which, within the terms of the text, may not have any immediately obvious association, such as the 'metaphorical' *pharmakon* Thamus refers to in the *Phaedrus* or the 'literal' *pharmakon* Socrates consumes in the *Apologia*. In this way, Derrida's mode of reading reveals a rhetoric hidden beneath Plato's rhetoric, an infinite (re)networking of the term *pharmakon* that is 'rigoureusement appelée d'un bout à l'autre du *Phèdre*. Toujours avec ironie' ('rigorously called for from one end of the *Phaedrus* to the other. Always with irony') (*D*, p. 83; 72).

What, then, are we to make of Plato's rhetoric of irony? It seems clear what Kenny means when he accuses Derrida of taking this 'ironic passage' too seriously. But if irony is not meant to be taken seriously, what is the purpose of Socrates's condemnation of writing as a poison (quite apart from his apparently calculated use of irony in his exchanges with Lysias)? In Kenny's view, supported as it is by a classical form-content or style-content distinction, Plato makes use of irony as a discrete rhetorical device that is decipherable according to a logical schema in which *either* he is being ironic *or* he is not. Irony, in this understanding, involves stating the contrary of what one actually means ('sure, because *that* sounds like fun', 'yeah, because writing is *such* a poison'), with the final aim of underscoring one's literal or proper meaning. As Claire Colebrook has argued, however, the persuasive power of irony cannot be derived from this either-or, true-false, literal-figurative structure since it involves an essentially 'complex dissimulation' which constantly raises larger epistemological questions: 'how do we know what others really mean, and on what basis can we secure the sincerity and authenticity of speech?'.[11] Socrates uses irony to biting effect in the dialogues, often appearing to feign ignorance, for example, as a way of bringing out the ignorance of his sophist interlocutors. Throughout Plato's dialogues, Socrates's opinions and motives are occluded rather than clarified by his use of this technique. They are thus always questionable in some minimal way, all the better to question the opinions and motives of those around him.[12]

This semantic instability of Socratic irony clearly rubs against the grain of traditional approaches to textual commentary. A long tradition of reading the *Phaedrus*, up to and including Kenny, has tried to reduce the problem of Plato's metaphorization of writing as *pharmakon* to the conventional philosophical logic of non-contradiction (writing is *either* a poison *or* a cure). For Derrida, by contrast, the syntactical play of the *pharmakon* enables its communication with 'la totalité du lexique' [the totality of the lexicon] and even with the subunits of each word, a de-hierarchized structure which overwhelms any form-content-based commentary. If Derrida's own reading cannot be reduced to the latter, his aim is not to dismantle this approach; it is rather to put in question the possibility that one can impose limits on it. This non-hierarchical structure of meaning explains why he begins to use the *pharmakon* as yet another word for the syntactical play he elsewhere terms *différance*, *dissémination*, etc. This play is not unrelated to Socrates's use of irony:

> [L'ironie socratique] ne consiste pas à démonter l'assurance charlatanesque d'un *pharmakeus* depuis l'instance obstinée d'une raison transparente et d'un *logos* innocent. L'ironie socratique précipite un *pharmakon* au contact d'un autre *pharmakon*. Plutôt, elle renverse le pouvoir et retourne la surface du *pharmakon*. Prenant ainsi effet, acte et date, en le classant, de ce que le propre du *pharmakon* consiste en une certaine inconsistance, une certaine impropriété, cette non-identité à soi lui permettant toujours d'être contre soi retourné.

> Irony [...] does not consist in undoing the charlatanesque confidence of a *pharmakeus* [magician, poisoner] from the vantage point of some obstinate instance of transparent reason or innocent *logos*. Socratic irony precipitates out one *pharmakon* by bringing it in contact with another *pharmakon*. Or rather, it reverses the *pharmakon*'s powers and turns its surface over — thus taking effect, being recorded and dated, in the act of classing the *pharmakon*, through the fact that the *pharmakon* properly consists in a certain inconsistency, a certain impropriety, this nonidentity-with-itself always allowing it to be turned against itself. (*D*, p. 148; 121).

One can try to stop this play by appealing to Plato's conscious intention, for instance, or to the internal rhetorical or logical coherence of his dialogue or *œuvre*. Yet the structure of irony is such that it continually displaces all such theses as soon as they occupy, or appear to occupy, a position of security. Irony thus exemplifies a structural doubleness at the heart of rhetoric. On the one hand, rhetorical reading can be shown to be underpinned by an infrastructure of philosophical concepts (*platonisme*) from the classical distinction between form and content to the interior-exterior duality.[13] While these rhetorical philosophemes call into question the oppositional logic of Plato's philosophy-sophistry, reality-appearance, sensibility-intelligibility distinctions, rhetoric also imposes irreducible limits on the commentary form. These limits are imposed by an originary rhetoricity exemplified by the syntactical play of the *pharmakon*: an irreducible structure of expropriation that prevents logic from hierarchizing the 'proper' meaning of a text. In doing so this structure liberates a mode of reading more attuned to the aleatory movements of textuality.

Styles of Philosophy

That the deconstruction of the metaphysical binaries underpinning the commentary form (signifier-signified, form-content, figurative-literal, style-matter, etc.) might entail the collapse of these distinctions is a point often made. Marian Hobson, to take one example, advances such an argument in a discussion of the formal texture of Derrida's writing, which she concludes is the unsummarizable, untranslatable, and irreducible residue of his texts' materiality: 'Can this be called "style"? I think not. Traditionally style has been opposed to "content", which is exactly the divorce Derrida's mode of writing may at points be held to work against'.[14] If Derrida's 'mode of writing' works to undercut the style-content distinction, one of its more interesting effects is that it has given rise to a recognizable set of stylistic gestures which we might loosely call 'deconstructionist' and which for several decades were a source of invigoration within the English-speaking academy. The latter just as soon became the subject of ridicule and pastiche, however, and indeed one pressing question which any treatment of Derrida and style must answer is that of accounting for the difference between the restless innovations of Derrida's complex syntactical and lexical playfulness, and the sometimes stultifying formalism of his imitators.

One way of understanding this difference is by looking very closely at what Derrida himself has to say on the subject of style. One might expect that such a metaphysically charged term would have no place in Derrida's writings; and yet throughout his work, the category of 'style', like that of rhetoric, is curiously intractable. In *L'Écriture et la différence* [*Writing and Difference*], the term features at least thirty times; if not all references allude to 'style' as a practice of writing, the term almost always designates what is individual or peculiar to a thinker or movement. The early lecture on Foucault, 'Cogito et histoire de la folie' [Cogito and the History of Madness], for example, refers to the 'puissant' [powerful] quality of Foucault's 'style' in *Folie et déraison* [History of Madness], by which Derrida seems to mean the book's trenchant or *percutant* ambition.[15] If style here designates the strong assertion of individuality — 'le style est l'homme même' [style is the man himself], as Jacques Lacan (mis)quotes Buffon in the first line of the *Écrits* — it can also entail a 'structure d'expropriation' ('structure of expropriation'), the 'division oblitérante du propre' ('obliterating division of the proper') (*MP*, p. xiii; xix).

In exploring this paradox, it is no accident that Derrida is drawn to the writings of one of philosophy's great stylists: Friedrich Nietzsche. In 'Force et signification' [Force and Signification], he contrasts Flaubert's Apollonian approach to style with Nietzsche's call for a Dionysiac dancing of the pen, 'the ability to dance with feet, with concepts, with words', as Nietzsche puts it (*ED*, p. 48; 34).[16] But even in Nietzsche's case, Derrida notes, a Bacchic style must be restrained or restricted — even Zarathustra must descend from his mountain. In 'Les Fins de l'homme' [The Ends of Man], 'c'est d'un changement de "style", Nietzsche le disait, que nous avons peut-être besoin; et s'il y a du style, Nietzsche nous l'a rappelé, il doit être pluriel' [what we need, as Nietzsche said, is perhaps a change of "style"; and if there is style, Nietzsche reminded us, it must be *plural*] (*MP*, p. 163; 135). What might such a 'plural' style, or styles, entail? One might well wonder, if style is indeed plural, whether the word 'style' can even be justified here, as Derrida's use of scare quotes seems to suggest. Gayatri Chakravorty Spivak's 'Translator's Introduction' to the *Grammatologie* identifies several aspects of Derrida's stylistic plurality, which shifts, she argues, between commentary, interpretation, 'fiction', and the typographical experimentation of texts such as *Glas*.[17] This rather Cartesian approach, which seeks to enumerate the fundamental elements which make up Derrida's singular 'style', seems to betray something essential in his invocation of a 'plural' style; and it does so by distributing Derrida's mode of writing into neat logical compartments which his account of the *pharmakon*, it seems to me, is explicitly designed to displace.

The answer to these and other questions may be found in Derrida's 1978 text, *Éperons: les styles de Nietzsche* [Spurs: Nietzsche's Styles], based on a lecture, 'La Question du style', delivered at Cerisy-la-Salle in July 1972.[18] Here Derrida turns to the most 'literary' of philosophers to explore the question of the relationship between style, philosophy, and, by probing Nietzsche's anti-feminist rhetoric, the 'figure' of woman. The aim of this text is not to valorize a 'literary' style, form, or rhetoric long devalued by logocentrism. In this view, we have seen, a philosopher's use of a given rhetorical device would be a temporary and ultimately extraneous detour en route to the ultimate recuperation of truth.[19] If metaphors are permitted in the philosophical text, it is only to the extent that their use is pedagogical, is never excessive, and does not threaten the final appropriation of 'literal' or 'proper' truth. It is a cliché of deconstruction to say that it consists in showing how proper meaning is always already pre-impressed by the form or style of writing which logically seem derivative and secondary with respect to it. But we must be careful not to misunderstand this reversal as a straightforward valorization of style over content. To do so would be to grant a transcendental status to style and thereby repeat the metaphysical hierarchy, albeit in inverted form. In *Éperons* it is never a case of simply celebrating Nietzsche's stylistic flourishes. The point instead is to show how style itself is underpinned by certain logocentric, and more especially phallocentric, assumptions which are, in their turn, undermined by a more originary, and more disruptive, movement of stylization.

Like rhetoric in 'La Pharmacie de Platon', style in *Éperons* proves to be troublingly undecidable. It is a powerful tool for the philosopher, who uses it for reasons of economy or ornamentation, but it also entails a risk of miscommunication. The former view of style Derrida associates with a certain 'masculinist' or 'phallogocentric' tone in philosophy, which his reading attempts to show is subverted by a prior movement of plurivocity. Playing on the slipperiness of the word 'style', he notes that it always has something to do with an 'examen' [examination], a weighing up or a calculation of 'un objet pointu' [pointed object] (*E*, p. 36). A powerful style, like that of Foucault in *Folie et déraison*, can be aggressive and even invasive, like a *stylet* (a stylus or medical probe), the means by which a philosopher can cut to the heart of a matter, leaving 'une empreinte ou une forme' [an imprint or a form] on his or her subject. Nietzsche's style is famously pointed, even belligerent in its eagerness to mortally wound his perceived adversaries (a 'ferocious attack' or 'onslaught', to cite words used by Kenny to describe Nietzsche's 'poetic and aphoristic' style in his *New History of Western Philosophy*, *NHWP*, pp. 779, 780).

The masculinist tone of Nietzsche's 'style éperonnant' [spurring style] is explored by Derrida through an engagement with Nietzsche's stylistic approach to 'la question de la femme' [the question of woman] (*E*, p. 41). As broached in *L'Écriture et la différence*, Nietzsche's style is governed by a restrained classicism, one that is sometimes more Apollonian than it is Dionysiac. This is what Nietzsche refers to as his *grosse Stil*, his grand or classical style: 'The classical style is essentially a representation of this calm, simplification, abbreviation, concentration — the highest feeling of power is concentrated in the classical type'.[20] The latter is fundamentally opposed to the false 'swagger' and 'dissipatory character' of Wagnerian aesthetics.[21] The aim of this stylistic will to power is the conquest of Truth through the unveiling or de-veiling of the 'feminine' style of cosmetics and concealment. *Beyond Good and Evil* opens with an elaborate metaphor-allegory of the philosophical frustrations of dogmatic metaphysics, which Nietzsche likens to a sexual frustration:

> Supposing that truth is a woman — well? is the suspicion not founded that all philosophers, insofar as they were dogmatists, poorly understood women? that the ghastly earnest and the clumsy obtrusiveness with which they tended to approach truth so far were inept and indecent means for nothing more than charming a female [*Frauenzimmer*: 'terme méprisant, une fille facile' [a term of contempt, an easy woman] in Derrida's gloss, *E*, p. 54] for themselves? What is

certain is that she has not allowed herself to be charmed: — and every kind of dogmatism stands there today with a gloomy and despondent look. *If it stands at all anymore!*[22]

The density of this courtly metaphor suggests a number of shared attributes between woman and Truth, with the pure intelligibility of the latter (as Idea) described through appeal to the material or sensible qualities of the former. Here the 'proper' meaning targeted by Nietzsche's rhetorical conceit seems to be that of Truth as seductive yet coldly distant, and of dogmatic philosophers as eager yet hapless suitors.

The recurrence of this Nietzschean image of the 'philosophe cavalier' [philosopher-knight] (*E*, p. 52) in vain conquest of womanly Truth can be given a feminist reading: Nietzsche's 'woman', we might say, resists the essentialism of dogmatic philosophy, retaining her distance and independence from a suite of opportunistic seducers, like Truth itself. At this point, where tenor and vehicle begin to rotate positions and 'Truth' appears more and more as a metaphor for 'woman', the most immediate question that arises is of how this apparently feminist image can be reconciled with 'l'anti-féminisme acharné de Nietzsche?' [Nietzsche's relentless anti-feminism] (*E*, p. 56). After all, Nietzsche is the author of Zarathustra's notorious imperative: 'You are going to women? Then don't forget the whip!'.[23] Setting aside scholarly debates over the 'proper' meaning of this aphorism and its relationship (or not) to Nietzsche's misogyny (to say nothing of the infamous mountaintop photograph of Lou Andreas-Salomé poised to whip Nietzsche and Paul Rée), the larger point of *Éperons* is somewhat different.[24] For Derrida, it is not that the passage quoted above proves or disproves the existence of a contrary anti-feminist strain in Nietzsche's writings, if only it could be subjected, say, to appropriately rigorous rhetorical commentary. His point is simpler if somewhat less intuitive: the multiplicity of interpretations which this passage engenders in fact *stems from* Nietzsche's famously virulent style, rather than occurring in spite of it, as if style were simply the attempt to limit the undecidability which for Derrida is an irreducible part of meaning's dissemination.

Éperons, in other words, shows how Nietzsche's rhetoricization of woman overflows the calculating strictures of his grand or classical style. In some respects, the performative nature of his style relishes cultivating uncertainty, in a way which resonates with the signature *eironeia* of Nietzsche's adversary-hero Socrates.[25] Like Socrates, Nietzsche plays on the power of the open question ('*Among women.* — "Truth? Oh, you don't know truth, do you! Is it not an outrage on all our *pudeurs* [modesties]?"', *T*, p. 7). His well-known love of italics, while seeming to clarify the distribution of semantic importance in the signifying chain, often has the opposite effect in drawing attention to the multi-layered nature of meaning: '(Progress of the idea: it becomes more refined, more devious, more mystifying — *it becomes woman*, it becomes Christian...)' (*T*, p. 23). This is to say nothing of Nietzsche's use of quotation marks (*E*, p. 106), the hyphen (*E*, p. 48), parentheses (*E*, p. 88) — all of which, for Derrida, resist being reduced to a 'proper' or 'literal' meaning by the 'herméneute' [hermeneut] (*E*, p. 132) or commentator.

The 'nécessité' of Nietzsche's metaphorization of truth as woman, or woman as truth, lies between and beyond that of an 'illustration métaphorique' or 'allégorique' (*E*, p. 86): it is neither a purely extraneous stylistic device nor simply a concept in the dogmatic sense, without any formal materiality. Like irony in the *Phaedrus*, such syntactical features work against the assertion of possession or mastery over the proper meaning of Nietzsche's work — a movement of 'expropriation' which Derrida likens to a structural castration. In classical Freudian theory, castration essentializes the difference between man and woman by mapping it on to the metaphysical opposition of presence and absence ('des effets *ontologiques* de présence ou d'absence' [*ontological* effects of presence or absence], *E*, p. 94). But in *Éperons*, Derrida shows how at least one element of Nietzsche's understanding of castration works against its reduction to a metaphysical opposition of presence or absence. If Nietzsche was critical of the castration of desire represented by the Christian slave morality, he was prudent enough not to counter this discourse with one which simply celebrated a counter-liberation of desire, for to do so would have entailed remaining within the binary logic of castration or decidability (either-or). One way in which this is achieved is through Nietzsche's styles, which allow his texts to avoid a hierarchical reversal of values in which a poison would simply be replaced its remedy, and vice versa: 'Sans parodie discrète, sans stratégie d'écriture [...], sans le style [...], le renversement revient au même dans la déclaration bruyante de l'antithèse' [Without discreet parody, without a strategy of writing, [...] without style, [...] the reversal is nothing more than the noisy declaration of the antithesis] (*E*, p. 94).

By calling into question the possibility of a 'proper' or 'literal' meaning of castration (and thus of 'woman'), the structural castration of style furthermore displaces the classical oppositions of *platonisme* (philosophy-sophistry, philosophy-rhetoric, intelligibility-sensibility, and so on). Nietzsche's styles thus prevent us from extracting a singular 'unité systématique' (*E*, p. 98) with respect to his references to 'woman'. These propositions could only form a systematic unity if *one* style could be extrapolated from competing propositions, if the 'hétérogénéité parodique du style' could be reduced to the content of a single thesis, with the detour of style eventually culminating in the reappropriation of the Idea. One would have to believe, in this case, in the kind of decisive hierarchies which the undecidable play of the *pharmakon* dismantles in advance, starting with substance over style, or content over form. This is why, to return to a question raised earlier, imitation of 'Derrida's style' can only ever amount to a kind of parodic betrayal. In reducing the latter to a 'unité systématique', to one or more key rhetorical effects (use of technical language, allusion, ellipsis, periphrasis, etc.), such stylistic assimilation breaks with what is perhaps the only invariable element of Derrida's style(s): unrepeatability, or the unending search for stylistic plurality.

The 'hétérogénéité parodique' of Nietzsche's style does not mean that meaning is unfindable in his text, only that his rhetorical calculations are always subject to the aleatory nature of undecidability. The difficulty is of conceiving style in a way in which one does not fall back into the same hierarchization of style over substance that Derrida is deliberately trying to undo, for example, by seeing in Nietzsche a kind of extreme parodist. Like irony in the *Phaedrus*, a rhetoric of parody that would be absolutely calculable and decidable in advance would be indistinguishable from a fully transparent or literal confession, or what Derrida likens to writing on a Stone Tablet (*table de la loi*) (*E*, p. 100). Despite the calculations of the sophist-rhetor who designs words and speeches to produce a repeatable effect, a key lesson of *Éperons* is that the *pharmakon* of rhetoric is both threatened and nourished by the undecidability of style. We cannot entirely blame Nietzsche for being inconsistent on 'the question of woman', in other words, because he has always already been caught in a spider's web of which he is never fully in control.

In Derrida's late appreciation of Hélène Cixous's writing, he repeatedly evokes Cixous's genius — like Nietzsche — for the undecidable in language.[26] Commentators on Derrida's style, whether critical or sympathetic, have often alighted on a similar texture of undecidability in his writing. Anthony Kenny, we saw earlier, reserved most of his criticism for the 'profusion' of new and frustratingly undefined terms in Derrida's work (*NHWP*, p. 825). Underpinned by a Platonic distinction between 'good' and 'bad' writing, such rhetorical analyses all too often confuse the undecidability of terms such as the *pharmakon* with their indeterminacy. Indeterminacy entails a philosophical evaluation of style articulated within the horizon of Platonism, with its conventional distinctions between clarity and obscurity, substance and style, speech and writing. Undecidability, by contrast, designates that which no philosophical determination of style can ever fully account for; it is the excess left over when one has tried to decide, naively, if the *pharmakon* is a cure or a poison. It is always tempting to reduce the undecidability of Derrida's styles to the expression of an underlying, 'literal' truth: that language, to take only the most common example, is an inherently unstable phenomenon. To do so, I have argued, is to try to reposition Derrida's thought within a philosophical horizon which it continually questions, whether this is done out of a spirit of critique or out of a desire to set aside the wordplay and get down (at last) to Derrida's underlying arguments. What is most uncomfortable in Derrida's styles is their perceptiveness to the aleatory qualities of language, and their identification of these qualities as a resource which can never quite by contained by our implacable obsession with the substance of style.

Notes to Chapter 5

1. Anthony Kenny, *A New History of Western Philosophy* (Oxford: Clarendon Press, 2010); this work subsequently referred to as *NHWP* in the main text.
2. Bertrand Russell, *A History of Western Philosophy* (London: Routledge, 2004); this work subsequently referred to as *HWP* in the main text.
3. Nigel Warburton and David Edmonds, *Philosophy Bites*, 2017 <http://philosophybites.com/2007/10/anthony-kenny-0.html> [accessed April 2018].
4. Frederick C. Copleston, *A History of Philosophy*, 9 vols (London: Search Press, 1946–75).
5. Bertrand Russell, *The Basic Writings of Bertrand Russell*, ed. by Robert E. Egner and Lester E. Denonn (London: Routledge, 2009), pp. 35–37.
6. Gary A. Olson, 'Jacques Derrida on Rhetoric and Composition: A Conversation', *Journal of Advanced Composition* 10, 1 (1990), 1–21 (p. 20).
7. Jacques Derrida, *La Dissémination* (Paris: Seuil, 1972), p. 83; *Dissemination*, trans. by Barbara Johnson (London: Continuum, 2004), p. 67; this text subsequently referred to as *D* in the main text.

8. Unlike Kenny's internal exegesis, *explication de texte* can appeal to both rhetorical (internal) and contextual (external) evidence. As W. D. Howarth and Charles Leonard Walton show in their 'Introduction' to *Explications: The Technique of French Literary Appreciation* (Oxford: Oxford University Press, 1971), pp. ix–xlvii, while dominating the teaching of literature in *lycées* and universities from the end of the nineteenth century onwards, *explication de texte* was heavily influenced — as Kenny's method of reading is — by Scholastic and Cartesian philosophy. Hence Gustave Lanson's surprising definition of the method of *explication* as 'lire [...] pour acquérir une intelligence claire, précise et distincte des textes' [reading [...] to acquire a clear, precise, and distinct understanding of texts] (*Méthodes de l'histoire littéraire* (Paris: Belles Lettres, 1925), p. 44).

9. A useful summary of these and other arguments concerning the dialogue's composition can be found in Léon Robin's 'Introduction' to the Budé edition: Plato, *Phèdre* (Paris: Budé, 1985). With the kind of irony we will turn to in a moment, the influence of Derrida's essay is such that it is now published as a 'commentaire' to the student edition of the dialogue in France: Plato, *Phèdre: suivi de 'La Pharmacie de Platon' par Jacques Derrida* (Paris: Flammarion, 2006).

10. For an example of rhetorical commentary on Plato's dialogues which reproduces some of these metaphysical presuppositions concerning the primacy of the literal over the figural, see Derrida's remarks on Pierre Louis's *Les Métaphores de Platon* (Paris: Belles Lettres, 1945) in 'La Mythologie blanche: la métaphore dans le texte philosophique', in *Marges — de la philosophie* (Paris: Minuit, 1972), pp. 247–324; trans. by Alan Bass as 'White Mythology: Metaphor in the Text of Philosophy', in *Margins of Philosophy* (Chicago, IL: University of Chicago Press, 1982), pp. 207–72; this work subsequently referred to as *MP* in the main text. As in Kenny's exegetical approach to the *Phaedrus*, in Louis's study, 'on s'aperçoit très vite que l'articulation interne n'est pas celle des métaphores elles-mêmes mais celle des idées "philosophiques", la métaphore jouant exclusivement, quoi qu'en ait l'auteur, le rôle d'ornement pédagogique' ('it can quickly be seen that the internal articulation is not that of the metaphors themselves, but that of the "philosophical" ideas, metaphor playing exclusively the role of a pedagogical ornament') (*MP*, p. 263; 221).

11. Claire Colebrook, *Irony* (London: Routledge, 2004), p. 2.

12. For Paul Allen Miller, Derrida understands Socratic irony as a form of non-coercive and non-violent persuasion; see 'Rhetoric and Deconstruction', in *The Oxford Handbook of Rhetorical Studies*, ed. by Michael J. MacDonald (Oxford: Oxford University Press, 2017), pp. 695–708.

13. As suggested above, a detailed treatment of rhetoric's logocentrism can be found in Derrida's 'La Mythologie blanche'.

14. Marian Hobson, *Jacques Derrida: Opening Lines* (London: Routledge, 1998) pp. 2–3. For an account of Derrida's displacement of the concept of style as it has been variously posed in theory, philosophy, and literature, see Laurent Milesi's wide-ranging 'Style-in-deconstruction', in *Style in Theory: Between Literature and Philosophy*, ed. by Ivan Callus, James Corby, and Gloria Lauri-Lucente (London: Bloomsbury, 2012).

15. Jacques Derrida, *L'Écriture et la différence* (Paris: Seuil, 1967), p. 51; *Writing and Difference*, trans. by Alan Bass (London: Routledge, 2001), p. 34; this work subsequently referred to as *ED* in the main text.

16. Friedrich Nietzsche, *Twilight of the Idols*, trans. by Richard Polt (Cambridge: Hackett, 1997), p. 49; this work subsequently referred to as *T* in the main text.

17. Gayatri Chakravorty Spivak, 'Translator's Introduction', in Jacques Derrida, *Of Grammatology*, trans. by Gayatri Chakravorty Spivak (Baltimore, MD: Johns Hopkins University Press, 1997), p. xlix.

18. Although reference will be to the bilingual edition of Derrida, *Spurs: Nietzsche's Styles / Éperons: les styles de Nietzsche* (Chicago, IL: University of Chicago Press, 1981), all English translations from this text are my own; this work subsequently referred to as *E* in the main text.

19. This is the subject of detailed discussion in 'La Mythologie blanche'.

20. Friedrich Nietzsche, *The Will to Power*, trans. by Michael A. Scarpitti (London: Penguin, 2017), p. 414.

21. The citation from Nietzsche is taken from David Farrell Krell's translation of Martin Heidegger's *Nietzsche*, 4 vols (San Francisco: Harper & Row, 1979–82), I, 124.

22. Friedrich Nietzsche, *Beyond Good and Evil / On the Genealogy of Morality*, trans. by Adrian Del Caro (Stanford, CA: Stanford University Press, 2014), p. 1.
23. Friedrich Nietzsche, *Thus Spoke Zarathustra*, trans. by Graham Parkes (Oxford: Oxford University Press, 2005), p. 58.
24. For a representative view of wider debates on Nietzsche's misogyny, see *Feminist Interpretations of Friedrich Nietzsche*, ed. by Kelly Oliver and Marilyn Pearsall (University Park: Pennsylvania State University Press, 1998).
25. On this ambivalence, see Walter A. Kaufmann, 'Nietzsche's Admiration for Socrates', *Journal of the History of Ideas*, 9, 4 (1948), 472–91.
26. Jacques Derrida, *Genèses, généalogies, genres et le génie: les secrets de l'archive* (Paris: Galilée, 2003); *Geneses, Genealogies, Genres, and Genius: The Secrets of the Archive*, trans. by Beverley Bie Brahic (New York: Columbia University Press, 2006).

CHAPTER 6

❖

Inoperative Governance, or the 'democracy to come': Jacques Derrida's *Voyous: deux essais sur la raison*

Seán Hand

In the charged context of then recent aerial attacks conducted on 11 September 2001 against North American targets in New York City and the Washington, DC, area, now commonly referred to as '9/11', the two lectures that became Jacques Derrida's 2003 *Voyous: deux essais sur la raison* [Rogues: Two Essays on Reason] present a tortured disquisition about the newly exposed foundations of nation-state sovereignty.[1] Taking their distance at key points from the formative influences of Heidegger, Levinas, and Nancy concerning limits on ethical relation which their works are still held to harbour, Derrida's meditations, forming his final major published work prior to his death in 2004, return to grounding texts of Western democracy in Plato and Aristotle, in order to expose their supposedly aporetic emergence of democracy, and so to reflect on premises of international law enforcement. Such a return, elucidated firstly as talks on European soil, has also been tendentiously presented as Derrida's post-9/11 return to 'Europe' in the wake of a claimed late ethical turn in Derrida and that ethics' apparent 'nexus to America'.[2]

With an obsessive disequilibrium and doubling that are made to figure the teetering self-constituting of sovereignty and statehood, and to perform the discursive rehearsals and repetitions that to Derrida are inherent in a post-sovereign unconditionality of true responsibility, the meditations unfold across two texts of unequal length and repeated concern. The ten sections of Part I of the book record Derrida's lectures during a ten-day Cerisy colloquium, 9–18 July 2002, based on the title 'The Democracy to Come (Around Jacques Derrida)'. The second part transcribes Derrida's contribution on 27 August 2002 to an annual *Congrès* at the University of Nice, focusing on 'The Future of Reason, the Development of Rationalities'. Referring to this composition, Derrida's own preface immediately echoes the beginning of Levinas's *Totalité et infini* [Totality and Infinity] in counterpointing morality and violence, force and law. It then clarifies that the text's twin addresses, for different audiences, commonly invoke the unrealized reason of a *democracy to come* (his emphasis) in the age of so-called globalization or *mondialisation*. This specification is the first of many oblique acknowledgements of Jean-Luc Nancy's contemporary work on the subject (*V*, p. 11).[3] However, the historical and global revolutions reviewed in Nancy's *La Création du monde ou la mondialisation* [The Creation of the World or Globalization] here enter a more focused yet suspended circularity of analysis, in which both the contemporary event of the attack on the twin towers of the World Trade Center, and the ramifications for democracy of the pursuit of 'rogue states' to which that event's media-theatricalization has given rise for Derrida, open up a series of governance questions which are sustained through resistance to political or intellectual closure.

This distended questioning exemplifies for Derrida the spatial and differential ethical reception of the event's meaning as being, in his own emphasis, 'une pensée de l'événement *à venir*, de la démocratie *à venir*, de la raison *à venir*' ('a thinking of the event *to come*, of the democracy *to come*, of the reason *to come*'). It is presented here in a way that conjures up the *khōra* of Plato's *Timaeus*, as isolated by Derrida's own 1993 text bearing that name, a feature of *Voyous* being the explicit and constant reframing of Derrida's own earlier works (*V*, p. 15).[4] In this way, Derrida's scrutiny of the logics and economies supporting the demonization of 'rogue states' from the opening rehearses a resistance to the use of deductive reasoning to arrive at a politics or ethics or law from reception of the event, and opens itself to a rebellious and even resistantly 'rogue' mode of welcoming the 'democracy to come'.

Authority and Autoimmunity

In keeping with the theme of dual vision, Derrida's analysis of the phenomenon of the 'rogue state' proceeds in two registers. Framing the notion of global order as a realist issue concerning the reason of the strongest (and evoking his own article on the 'Force of Law' as well as Nancy's analysis of globalization), Derrida ironically registers the obscuring ontotheological justifications for combatting a supposed 'axis of evil' introduced into post-statist security (in obvious reference to the then President George W. Bush's first State of the Union address following the 11 September attacks, on 29 January 2002), and reinforces this by recalling additionally both the biblical phrase 'eye of the needle' to signal the mad wager of a theocratic transposition, and D. H. Lawrence's poem 'Snake', in which the narrative voice calls, in a post-Edenic landscape, for expiation and the snake's return. Recalling with a passing play on words (*serment* and *serpent*) the fundamentalist reptilian imagery traded in propaganda oaths and sermons, Derrida takes it as read that these crude oppositions can only be opposed, or better re-turned, by giving oneself to the hospitality dramatized in Lawrence's poem when the narrator calls for the snake to 'come back' (*V*, p. 23).[5]

After this introduction, the first three sections play on figures of circularity, while interrogating (somewhat doggedly) the key issues of legitimation and effective fulfilment in the contexts of democratic rule, force, and punishment. Derrida isolates theological and dynamic tropes concerning sovereignty in Tocqueville's *De la démocratie en Amérique* [Democracy in America], traces ipsocentric assumptions of sovereignty right back to Aristotle, and locates notions of freedom presupposed by visions of democracy in Plato's *Republic*. Once again alluding ironically to the United States, he underlines that market forces can pertain even to the shaping and interpretation of democracy, given 'la vacance ou l'indétermination sémantique' [semantic vacancy or indetermination] at the heart of its very concept; though simultaneously he claims that the historicity of democracy, and the freedom or play at the heart of its self-understanding, mean that the interpretation of the democratic itself remains democratic, in its 'plasticité intrinsèque et son auto-criticité interminable' [intrinsic plasticity and its interminable self-criticizability] (*V*, pp. 47, 48). For this reason, then, Derrida chooses democracy, precisely because of what he sees as its principled or reasoned maintenance of ethical indetermination.

Asserting next how historically the concept of democracy has become associated uniquely with a European tradition (and for Derrida this tradition effects a form of globalization that is implicitly Christian, as he suggests with the compound neologism 'globalatinizing'), Derrida views such democracy as resisted today rhetorically or actually only by a certain culture of Islam. He therefore now focuses on the 'other' of this democratic injunction, offering the personal example of the 1992 suspension of democratic elections in Algeria, something that was sovereignly enacted in the very name of democracy. Using this example to isolate the tropism of alterity that is internal to democracy, and characterizing it with predictable deconstructive terms such as 'double bind', 'renvoi' (which involves beginning by referring back), 'différance' (which refers to something simultaneously different and deferring) and 'espacement' (or spacing) in a way that once more re-frames his own philosophical grounds, he proposes that paradigmatic to democracy is an *autoimmune pervertibility* that means it generates its own radical and suicidal threats (*V*, pp. 36, 63–64, 59). So the survival of democracy is thought of as resembling deconstruction itself, with the testing of the one read as the self-questioning of the other. More clearly than in some other texts, then, the thinking of the political and the thinking of *différance* are brought into proximity. In this way Derrida really cannot resist recalling that the agents of an 'axis of evil' were trained on US sovereign soil, flew American planes from American airports with the help of American citizens, and benefitted in his view from an autoimmune consent typical of a US administration's relationship to unforeseeability.

This autoimmunity is relevant to certain claims that Derrida's deformalized meta-ethics had previously found more hospitable circumstances in America, including in the contexts of Critical Legal Studies or pragmatist approaches to legal doctrine that are compared superficially to Derridean deconstruction of justice, in an apparent accommodation of flux, untidiness, and theoretical under-construction, so as to then criticize an excessive emphasis on the ethical import of singularity, since that allegedly weakens the status of countervailing identities necessary to adjudicate conflicting claims and their violences. In this light, the autoimmune condition is presented antagonistically in relation to the politically necessary formation of a pluralist ethics.[6] Derrida elaborated on autoimmunity in an interview given a month after 9/11 and published in Borradori's *Philosophy in a Time of Terror*, in a way that links the 'event' of 11 September, and its place in an autoimmunitary logic, negatively to Heideggerian *Ereignis*, the positive world-forming (à la Nancy) of *mondialisation*, and the (implicitly Levinasian) face of the other.[7] In this way, he looked to emphasize how the complex antinomy of a democratic response to terror (and perhaps especially, in his view, of a certain Christian democracy which is supposed to turn the other cheek) brings us to the core of democratism's self-definitions.

Fraternalism or Ferality

In the next sections of *Voyous*, Derrida takes specific issue with Nancy's presentation of freedom in the latter's *L'Expérience de la liberté* [The Experience of Freedom], and more especially with the concept of sharing that is central to Nancy's view of being in both *La Création du monde ou la mondialisation* and *Être singulier pluriel* [Being Singular Plural].[8] Stressing the fraternity inherent in Nancy's vision of freedom and, co-extensively, democracy, Derrida focuses on Nancy's vision of fraternity as equality, complicates the moment of self-postulation of democracy as absolute equality in Aristotle's *Politics*, and then feeds this like a virus back into Nancy's invocation in order to point up the potential dictatorship of *fraternocracy*. He sees Nancy's circumspect recourse to Freudian, Christian, and anthropomorphizing notions of solidarity as related to an internalized mythology about freedom's nativity and legitimated birth. It is this mythology that can then project a figure of the bastard or rogue state which betrays hospitality, as an act of degeneracy or just sin. Warming to this theme (and using Nancy as a scapegoat to denounce certain self-sustaining myths in and of the United States), Derrida radicalizes the autoimmune paradox of democracy, by pointing up how it simultaneously welcomes all 'brothers' (in a gesture that thereby categorizes others as noncitizens or rogues) while none the less offering hospitality to all (which would therefore welcome those excluded). Focusing then on these 'nonbrothers' or rogues, Derrida underlines their necessary performative role in the whole postulation and maintenance of normative democratic rhythms and occupations, to the extent that these rogues must constitute a *countercitizenship*, and indeed a *principle of disorder* that can challenge, and yet thereby confirm, both the hegemony of geo-political alliances such as the United Nations or the G8, and the biopolitical definition of democracy as the sublation of the residual outlaw, or 'loup-garou' [werewolf] (*V*, p. 102).[9]

From Terror to Trauma

The following sections and final 'Envoi' see Derrida repeat such deconstructions, while trying to develop further the taxonomy of the rogue state. More references to historical details, political decisions, and dissenting voices such as Chomsky, Litwak, and Blum, parallel re-categorization of Derrida's own writings from the beginning of the nineties, or put contextually from the advent of George H. W. Bush to the presidency of the USA. Derrida therefore synchronizes earlier critiques with extension of the term *rogue state* into the general discourse and mindset of American foreign policy. Leaving undetailed the way in which he repeats the circular performativity that he isolates as an aporetic discontinuity within the democratic critique of democracy, we note instead that Derrida now chooses to extract from canonic writers the logical necessities of indivisibility, unicity, and incalculability as part of their own efforts to resolve the paradox of democratic foundation. In this way he gives a certain historical grounding to the emergence of the category of 'rogue' within any engendering and attempted placing of what he now evokes here as the 'democracy to come'.

He therefore once more reframes his own texts, and especially 'Force of Law', *Specters of Marx*, and *Politics of Friendship*, in terms now of this insistent call for the democracy to come. They have apparently always therefore been part of a continuous militant political critique. On the basis of this self-appraisal, Derrida then begins to evoke a non-communitarian vision of justice as a radically heterogeneous and therefore relationally *interrupting* messianicity or irreducible futurity (*V*, p. 128). This rather Levinasian prophetism, which Derrida tries to locate in Tocqueville's *De la démocratie en Amérique*, is then linked positively to the very performativity of democracy. So Derrida can predictably advance the deconstructive claim that if a rogue state is, in American political discourse, whatever is designated thus, the most 'rogue state' in the post-Cold War geopolitical scenario is none the less naturally the United States itself. Therefore, 11 September could be seen as marking the emergence of a post-Schmittian non-statist terror, where trauma now becomes properly deterritorialized, and in which simultaneously therefore there are no longer anything *but* rogue states, and at the same time there are no longer *any* rogue states (*V*, p. 150).[10] Concluding provocatively with recollection of the relationship between *Heil* and *Unheil* in Heidegger, as a return to philosophical deconstruction of ontotheologism, Derrida stresses the continuing discursive insecurity of democracy, and signs off with a 'Salut!' that performs a gesture of simultaneous welcome and farewell, health and hope, fraternity and diagnosis.

From Crisis to Unconditionality

Derrida's second collected text, the more conflated 'Le "Monde" des Lumières à venir: (exception, calcul et souveraineté)' [The 'World' of the Enlightenment to Come: (Exception, Calculation, and Sovereignty)], begins with Kantian self-exhortations to save the honour of reason, only to make it plain that this cannot be done, according to Derrida, through desperate imposition of the unity of the regulative Idea in a globalized world (*V*, p. 121). The previous salutation or hint of salvation in 'Salut' has taken on a more melancholy and even mournful air. Tellingly, Derrida considers Husserl's diagnosis of Europe's sickness, *The Crisis of European Sciences and Transcendental Phenomenology: An Introduction to Phenomenological Philosophy* (commonly referred to as the *Crisis*) that was published in 1936 in unfinished form, and is obsessively preoccupied with two world wars. While suggesting both auto-immune irrationalism and temporalization, Husserl's 'crisis' here above all reminds Derrida that the alternative to a heroism of reason is the fall into barbarity, and that the interest of reason must therefore be unconditional. Recalling Plato now, Derrida links this unconditionality to an obligation to the idea of the good. But this leaves unresolved the problem of a political or politicizable upholding of the Good, a problem even reflected for him in Husserl's own desire to grant force to reason. Derrida's second section therefore significantly shifts from Kantian versions of cosmopolitanism or Schmittian sovereignty towards a more undialectizable and obsessive focus on the absolute unconditionality itself of critical exigency. This is an unconditionality that Derrida will claim inheres in deconstruction's principled suspension of all conventions, presuppositions, even conditionalities, including those that themselves found the idea of 'crisis' and the dialectical decisions and judgements to which this idea can then give rise. On the basis of this thought or mood Derrida turns a form of non-irrational thinking of the future back towards 9/11, having first considered (with his contemporary seminars on the beast and the sovereign again in mind) how the limit-cases of the Western ethical axiomatic represented by cloning and zoologism might wholly recontextualize pronouncements about humanity and bestiality (not to mention reflect somewhat uncannily the cloning that the twin towers of the World Trade Center both resembled and encouraged).

So reiterating how post–Cold War globalization effectively ushered in a politics wherein sovereignty could no longer identify, and so counteract, statist threats, Derrida once more comes to isolate the emergence of the rogue state as the ontotheological solution to sovereignty's own delegitimization. In view of this finally unsustainable ploy, which after all itself can generate all sorts of self-serving rationalizations, Derrida concludes by supporting a newly challenged responsibility to sustain the work of a permanently singular 'reasonable' enquiry that remains vigilantly irreducible to the ultimately accommodating and even self-protecting measures of juridical and calculative reason (*V*, pp. 158, 217).

Supplementarity of Evidence

It is worth commenting at this point on the incidental views which *Voyous* employs as support. Derrida ignores contemporary remarks by Agamben or Habermas, just as he marks his distance from Nancy or Levinas. He avoids engagement with the voluminous literature on post-Westphalian politics, and makes no reference to the contemporary and well-known views of Mearsheimer.[11] But he does effectively echo, without direct citation, the ponderously binary postulation of Huntingdon (pre-9/11) that 'while the United States regularly denounces various countries as "rogue states", in the eyes of many countries it is becoming the rogue superpower'.[12] Most remarkably, what he does credit instead are the provocatively dissident North American denunciations of US aggression of the day, represented by Chomsky and Blum, that insistently described the United States as a 'rogue state' in *tu quoque* denunciation of that nation's own activities.[13] Given Derrida's central preoccupation with ethical indecisionism, this avoidance of realist positions, of prescriptive or normative reason, and of even the fraternal sociality or justice for the other developed by Nancy and Levinas, can be considered logical, but to critical ears will evidence clearly a politically useless sophistry. Precisely in part because of these omissions, it does seem merely provocative to present the *serment* of a Chomsky or a Blum at face value — whatever the pertinence of their exposure of US unlawful use of force or (then) general socio-economic sovereignty, or repeated and consistent post-war global destabilizing interventions in other countries, or constant opposition to United Nations resolutions — when the philosophical considerations of Aristotle or Rousseau can be subject to immediate, sustained, and intricate deconstruction.[14]

In defence, it is clear that Derrida's strategic aim is to stage a certain autoimmune bipolarity at the heart of 'rational' reactivity, and so to act almost as an ironic counterperformance to the recapitulations and rationalized plans for protection and retaliation given in a document such as *The 9/11 Commission Report*. Notwithstanding this report's recognition of post-statist developments, we are still at this time presented with a transitional embodiment of a 'catastrophic threat' in the form of the 'Islamist terrorist', whose mindset is precisely ventriloquized as the view that 'America is the font of all evil, the "head of the snake", and it must be converted or destroyed'.[15] Derrida would arguably wish to privilege the counter-voicing of a Chomsky or Blum, then, as part of a general, if sometimes necessarily unknowing, desire to *use* spectacularity against spectacularity; and by engaging performative autoimmunity in this way to reach beyond motivated and controlled support for the rhetoric of 'tolerance, the rule of law, political and economic openness', so as to generate a principled suspension of the opening for heterogeneity.[16]

Both the principles and the problems of this kind of disruptive move are anticipated by Derrida's earlier dialogue with Borradori on 22 October 2001, which is obviously a direct precursor of *Voyous*. While recording in a footnote a different book by Chomsky, entitled *9–11* (published on 4 December 2001), in order to question definitional accuracy and authority, Derrida generally articulates the key concerns repeated in *Voyous*, including in relation to the 'event', traumatism, crisis, singularity, *mondialisation*, democracy to come, and tolerance versus hospitality.[17] But there are two, contradictory, exceptions to this parallelism. The first, responding to a question, is an acknowledgement of the continuing relevance here of a Kierkegaardian uncertainty, of the kind maintained by the 1992 'Force of Law', which turns precisely on a delaying of the regulatory normalizations and groundless violence of law's imposition that stifle the undecidability of full justice. The disappearance of this reference in *Voyous* (and the appearance instead of Blum and the alternative Chomsky text) might suggest a partial acceptance of the need for political traction (or more simply a concern to avoid suggestions of the inappropriate appearance of infinite absolute negativity and sacrificial logic), were it not that the second exception effects the opposite trend. Responding to the question of terrorist ambition, Derrida emphasizes unambiguously that 'such actions and such discourse *open onto no future and, in my view, have no future*'.[18]

This remark, which is also absent from *Voyous,* both goes to the heart of the futurity of unconditional hospitality, and somewhat contradicts the guiding intellectual nurturing of the democracy to come, through its effective echoing of the discursive autoimmunity or normative illocution elsewhere critiqued so radically.[19] This second example may perhaps evidence a contemporary tension towards any qualification of condemnation, in obvious contrast to the more mediated perspectives of *Voyous.* Taken together, though, these subsequently removed remarks further complicate the principled presentation of the democracy to come and its guiding nondeterminative responsibility, through an interesting *chassé-croisé* translation, from dialogue to text, of the extremes of aporia and policing, or ethical deconstruction versus political realism.

Like a Wheel within a Wheel

It is clear, then, that Derrida's injunctions to retain undecidability as the non-determinative precondition for advent of the true democracy to come, must purposely lay thought open to an unending trauma of ethical decision. Such an ultimately morphological approach will therefore antagonize more normative analyses of hegemonic power, propounded by even those, like Laclau, who engage seriously with deconstruction and its purpose here.[20] Whether or not philosophical enquiry is held to be genuinely resisting the pressures of regulatory forces, radical democracy as envisaged by a Laclau must ultimately regard rigorously maintained structural openness in strict terms as being effectively or actually useless. Laclau would therefore insist here on the evident lack of a theory of the decision that must *all the same* be taken in an undecidable scenario, undecidability not being able *itself* to produce such a condition, and therefore not qualifying as 'the necessary source of *any* concrete decision in the ethical or political sphere'.[21] At stake for a Laclau is therefore the primacy of the political, which in Derrida is seemingly made secondary to the ethical demand. Accepting positively the Kierkegaardian madness of this decision, as being precisely the moment of the subject, Laclau still posits such voluntarism as comprehensible, called for, and regulated by the multiplicity of rules and strategies raised by the context.[22] This makes undecidability (just) the generalized logic underpinning *any* action, which will inevitably be an act of hegemonization. Against this attitude, which we can use here as broadly constitutive of a critical reaction to preconditional undecidability, Derrida's insistence on the non-reduction of indetermination can be understood as the foregrounding of the *telos* of decisionism which permeates every one of the Western institutional valorizations of the subject's identity, here activated via the homogenizing identificational reactions to the 'event' of the 'terror', themselves actions that foreclose responsibility by reframing it within 'rational' and 'consensual' moral identifications of a kind left radically unchallenged, even by a Habermas.[23]

For at stake ultimately in Derrida's insistence on the interruptive consciousness of responsibility is both the form and the advent of governance in post-statist politics. In the tense atmosphere of attempts to understand 'what is "happening"' after

9/11, Derrida therefore seeks to demonstrate the logic of true democratic promise wherein effectivity or actuality of the democratic promise must always retain the absolute nature of the undetermined, eschatological relation to the event's futurity, singularity, and unanticipated alterity.[24] This consequently would challenge the regulating designation of 9/11 by a Habermas as 'the first historic world event', an easily accepted designation which is in turn based on prior accepted conceptual definitions of moral and legal universalism that then 'tolerate' new members of an already discursively stable 'moral community'.[25]

Derrida would be rightly wary here of a residual communitarian organicism within this democratic conceptual framework, however much a Habermas would see its formation and maintenance as discursively resistant to visceral assumptions and dedicated earnestly to the continuing elaboration of public space.[26] In other words, Derrida would here isolate an already predetermined goal of confirming a *telos* of mutual understanding by way of a circular logic, which his earliest work had already deconstructed, in the context of Rousseauist myths, as an arche-violence.

By the same token, Derrida's agonistic model of governance will be permanently challenged, as it has already recognized from the beginning, by the fact that the pursuit of undeconstructible justice, as a philosophical spectrality, in a political arena such as that governing the 9/11 'event' must be made to confront both the violence of the rationalization of alterity and the responsive registration of the 'event' which, as Derrida had put it in *De la grammatologie* [Of Grammatology], is itself inevitably a nonethical opening of ethics.[27]

Derrida and Habermas are therefore already in some agreement around what is generally considered a 'cosmopolitan' response to 9/11, in emphasizing at least the need for participatory democracy and global justice.[28] Similarly, Derrida's insistence that radical indetermination subtend moral questions (which can ultimately be appropriated by the gradual normalization of the *rogue* state as a state of 'concern') is also none the less linked willingly by him to the desire to see specific institutions and organizations, such as a modified Security Council, deploy an 'effective intervening force', in the service of a fully operative international institution of law and corresponding court of justice.[29]

Governance, Inoperability, and Cosmopolitanism

However, Derrida is also quite specific that his vision of democracy to come 'would go beyond the limits of cosmopolitanism, that is, of a world citizenship. [...] It would involve, in short, an alliance that goes beyond the "political" as it has been commonly defined'.[30] The Derridean dynamic of governance, suspended by the vision of the democracy to come, therefore differs crucially from cosmopolitan models of democracy, since Derrida's resistance to consciously or subliminally enforced coherence — including in terms of more embedded philosophical engagement, and retention of incalculable singularity at the heart of the conceptually impossible radical democratic promise — make of a Derridean governance an agonistic ideal of heterogeneity, in which we will always strive to welcome a humanity to come.[31]

Placed in the paradox whereby cosmo-governance is increasingly morally demanded and yet resented, and against backgrounds of total war, globalized instrumentalism and realist geopolitical resurgence, the meta-ethical vision of Derrida's *Voyous*, and its insistence that total democratic reconciliation is a conceptual impossibility, can therefore be read contextually as presenting a singular transcending of the contextual and goal-directed strictures of realist, Marxist and cosmopolitan interpretations. And by the same token, while deformalized answerability elevates governance theorization above pragmatic limitations, the comparison also highlights reasons why non-normative responses are insistently criticized as insufficiently feasible.[32]

Without supporting the dualistic alternatives that cosmopolitanism often employs in self-legitimation, we can certainly review Derrida's preoccupations by airing this cosmopolitan criticism of inoperability. In this context, Derrida's deconstruction of democratic groundings in *Voyous*, via discussion of 9/11, can be understood as bringing out the violence inherent in all rationalization of alterity and heteronomous emergence, including when it is defined as democracy.

Such a deconstruction, for example, might react sceptically to a report by the then contemporary International Commission on Intervention and State Sovereignty (ICISS) *The Responsibility to Protect*, whose justification of intervention in Kosovo and non-intervention in Rwanda essentially re-frames, in cosmopolitan tenor, the continuing 'responsibility' of sovereign states within a developing international context.[33] To this end, the report develops, in a simultaneously descriptive and performative style, its dual function of establishing law and exemplifying the violent exception to law, through justified interventionism on behalf of institutionalized evocations of justice. Derrida would, one imagines, observe how the document notes the need for 'neutralization of domestic opposition' as part of its sophistication of humanitarian intervention, thereby effecting a double rehearsal of the founding violence contained within the report's supposed moral integrity.[34]

Against this demonstration of hyper-ethical sensitivity, however, a cosmopolitan retort, of the kind articulated by Richard Beardsworth, would probably isolate how Derrida establishes, in a paradoxically programmatic way, non-realist distinctions between the emergence of singularity and the practical determination of 'political' context, which are then agonizingly confused in order to throw legal differentiation into aporetic doubt and empirical hypocrisy. The justice-to-come of Derrida's positive disjuncturing of law and singularity would be thus viewed as the endless rehearsal of a hyperbolic ethical conscience that refuses to expound itself as already contained within the modern concept of freedom.[35]

Such objections, delivered often in the name of a cosmopolitan metaprinciple of impartialist reasoning, are as obvious as they are ultimately unsatisfactory, and not just for reasons of subsequent embarrassment.[36] Firstly, they rest on a Kantian juridification of antagonisms and a Habermasian discursive idealism, whose normativisms have been exploded by the deep analyses of hospitality, non-determination, and undecidability in Derrida. Secondly, it is clear that however much David Held's 'metaprinciple' is here dressed up as a heuristic, theoretical, or argumentative 'device', devoted to accountability and inclusion, its ultimate validity and function is to reduce paradox and dissonance in the name of a Habermasian constitutionalization, and so to facilitate the regulatory extension of socio-economic globalization.[37] Viewed in this way, we can argue that, with cosmopolitanism, 'nation-state coercive capability' has been *merely* shifted to the level of 'global institutions' and surpassed only formally, since cosmopolitanism remains ultimately within the cognitive paradigm of capitalist management.[38] Finally, this also underlines that cosmopolitanism's postulated efficacy and greater 'responsibility' rest on a rhetorical sublation of difference, a performance that, without irony, justifies its own hegemonic drives as a post-Washington-Consensus task of making the world safe for humanity, and therefore of needing to impose global justice and impartial rules.[39] This recalls the self-perpetuating logic of the 2004 United Nations high-level panel on threats, challenges, and change, which opened with the statement 'in today's world, a threat to one is a threat to all', and concluded with the view that what was therefore needed in face of such a threat was a strengthening of the Office of the Secretary-General.[40]

In sum, cosmopolitanism's evocation and establishment of a universal moral vocabulary, in the light of a Derridean notion of inoperative governance, can be held to obfuscate the imposition of a particular cosmo-political narrative that quickly becomes imperative in moments of economic crisis or opportunity. Against this supposedly covenantal homogenization, the non-legitimizing agonisms of a philosopher such as Derrida can be said to keep open the interrogation of the political by the ethical, thereby sustaining singularity in the face of cosmopolitanism's pre-determining moralisms. In the ongoing contest of nationalist populisms and supra-national *dirigisme*, the non-foundationalist meta-ethics of Derrida, as articulated in *Voyous* at a time of heightened political categorization, can be read as representing a higher goal, that of a conceptually impossible governance that resists demands to take back control, and encourages instead a continuing belief in the inoperative governance that is founded ideally and non-juridically on each singularity's perpetual possibility.

Notes to Chapter 6

1. Jacques Derrida, *Voyous: deux essais sur la raison* (Paris: Galilée, 2003); *Rogues: Two Essays on Reason*, trans. by Pascale-Anne Brault and Michael Naas (Stanford, CA: Stanford University Press, 2005); this work subsequently referred to as *V* in the main text.
2. Michel Rosenfeld, 'Derrida's Ethical Turn and America: Looking Back from the Crossroads of Global Terrorism and the Enlightenment', *Cardozo Law Review*, 27: 2 (2005), 815–45 (p. 817). For a more involved (half-mourning) notion of 'America' in Derrida, see Geoffrey Bennington, *Not Half No End: Militantly Melancholic Essays in Memory of Jacques Derrida* (Edinburgh: Edinburgh University Press, 2010), pp. 144–48.
3. See also Jean-Luc Nancy, *La Création du monde ou la mondialisation* (Paris: Galilée, 2002). For a parallel analysis of this text's response to globalization, see Seán Hand, 'Being-in-common or the Meaning of Globalization', in *Jean-Luc Nancy: Justice, Legality and World*, ed. by Benjamin Hutchens (London: Continuum, 2011), pp. 177–99.
4. Jacques Derrida, *Khōra* (Paris: Galilée, 1993). On the impossible possibility of the 'event', see also Jacques Derrida, 'A Certain Impossible Possibility of Saying the Event', in *The Late Derrida*, ed.

by W. J. T Mitchell and A. I. Davidson (Chicago, IL: Chicago University Press, 2007), pp. 223–43. It goes almost without saying that there is no reference at all in *Voyous* to such reductionist monolithical paradigms as Huntingdon's notion of a clash of civilizations.

5. Jacques Derrida, 'Force of Law: The "Mystical Foundation of Authority" ', in *Acts of Religion: Jacques Derrida*, ed. by Gil Anidjar (London: Routledge, 2002), pp. 228–98. For various relevant 'head of snake' references, see Thomas H. Kean and others, *The 9/11 Commission Report: Final Report of the National Commission on Terrorist Attacks Upon the United States* (New York & London: Norton, 2004), pp. 54, 59. See also the Palestinian Authority's Deputy Foreign Minister Adli Sadeq's reference to George W. Bush, reported in *Al-Hayat Al-Jadida*, 3 June 2003, and the daily briefing press conference concerning the killing of Osama bin Laden, given by White House Homeland Security and Counterterrorism Adviser John Brennan, 2 May 2011.

6. See Rosenfeld, 'Derrida's Ethical Turn and America', pp. 820, 841–45, and Michel Rosenfeld, 'The Rule of Law and the Legitimacy of Constitutional Democracy', *Southern California Law Review*, 74 (2001), 1307–51. See also Richard Ganis, *The Politics of Care in Habermas and Derrida: Between Measurability and Immeasurability* (Lanham, MD: Lexington, 2010), especially Chapter 2.

7. Jacques Derrida, 'Autoimmunity: Real and Symbolic Suicides — A Dialogue with Jacques Derrida', in Giovanna Borradori, *Philosophy in a Time of Terror* (Chicago, IL, & London: University of Chicago Press, 2003), pp. 85–136 (pp. 91, 98, 99).

8. Jean-Luc Nancy, *Être singulier pluriel* (Paris: Galilée, 1996), and *L'Expérience de la liberté* (Paris: Galilée, 1988).

9. In addition to citing La Fontaine's fable of 'Le Loup et l'agneau' [The Wolf and the Lamb] and Rousseau's *Confessions,* Derrida evokes here the seminar on 'La Bête et le souverain' [The Beast and the Sovereign], begun three months after the attacks of 11 September, on 12 December 2001, and continued until 26 March 2003. See the third and fourth sessions, on 16 and 23 January 2002 where, in addition to the above evocations, Derrida had detailed the status and symbolism of the lycanthrope, or bestial man immune to faith or law, in Lacan, and suggested the anthropomorphic limitations which Derrida sees retained in Levinas's meta-ethics. See Jacques Derrida, *Séminaire: La Bête et le souverain. Volume I (2001–2002)* (Paris: Galilée, 2008).

10. For background to the use of the term, see Robert Litwak, *Rogue States and U.S. Foreign Policy: Containment after the Cold War* (Washington, DC: Woodrow Wilson Center Press, 2000).

11. John Mearsheimer and Stephen Walt, 'An Unnecessary War', in *The Iraq War Reader*, ed. by Micah Sifry and Christopher Cerf (New York: Simon & Schuster, 2003), pp. 419–20.

12. Samuel Huntingdon, 'The Lonely Superpower', *Foreign Affairs*, 75, 2 (1999), 35–49 (p. 42).

13. Noam Chomsky, *Rogue States* (London: Pluto, 2000); William Blum, *Rogue State: A Guide to the World's Only Superpower* (London: Zed Books, 2001).

14. Chomsky, *Rogue States*, pp. 17, 199. Blum, *Rogue State*, pp. 125–67, 184–99.

15. Kean and others, *The 9/11 Commission Report*, pp. 361–62.

16. Ibid., p. 362.

17. Borradori, *Philosophy in a Time of Terror*, pp. 189–90, 103, 86–91, 99, 118, 127.

18. Borradori, *Philosophy in a Time of Terror*, p. 113.

19. Michel Rosenfeld presents this phrase in 'Derrida's Ethical Turn and America' as confirmation of 'Derrida's unequivocal condemnation of global terrorism and his preferences for America's globalizing mission' (p. 831). Such a claim, which forms part of a move towards criticism of the shortcomings of Derridean 'radical singularity' (p. 834) and its ultimate replacement by 'comprehensive pluralism' (p. 844), seems to me to be simply undiscerning and unsubstantiated.

20. Ernesto Laclau, *Emancipation(s)* (London: Verso, 1996).

21. Ibid., p. 78.

22. Ibid., pp. 53, 57.

23. For a comparison between Derrida's reading, and the positions and conceptual language of Habermas and Agamben, see Rodolphe Gasché, ' "In the Name of Reason": The Deconstruction of Sovereignty', *Research in Phenomenology*, 34 (2004): 289–303.

24. See Jacques Derrida, 'Perhaps or Maybe', *Responsibilities of Deconstruction, Warwick Journal of Philosophy*, 6 (1997): 1–18.

25. Borradori, *Philosophy in a Time of Terror*, pp. 28, 42–43.

26. Ibid., pp. 35–38.

27. Jacques Derrida, *De la grammatologie*, (Paris: Minuit, 1967), p. 202.

28. See James Brassett, 'Cosmopolitanism vs. Terrorism? Discourses of Ethical Possibility Before and After 7/7', *Millennium: Journal of International Studies*, 36 (2008): 311–38.

29. Borradori, *Philosophy in a Time of Terror*, pp. 114–15.

30. Ibid., p. 130.

31. See Nick Vaughan-Williams, 'Beyond a Cosmopolitan Ideal: The Politics of Singularity', *International Politics*, 44, 1 (2007): 107–24.

32. See Richard Beardsworth, *Cosmopolitanism and International Relations Theory* (Cambridge: Polity Press, 2011), p. 230.

33. International Commission on Intervention and State Sovereignty, *The Responsibility to Protect* (Ottawa: International Development Research Centre, 2001). See, for example, section 8:1, p. 69.

34. Ibid., sections 8.8, 8.9.

35. Beardsworth, *Cosmopolitanism and International Relations Theory*, p. 208.

36. David Held, *Cosmopolitanism: Ideals and Realities* (Cambridge: Polity Press, 2010), p. 86.

37. Ibid., pp. 86–91, 186–87. See Jürgen Habermas, *The Divided West* (Cambridge: Polity Press, 2006), pp. 159–63.

38. David Held, *Democracy and the Global Order: From the Modern State to Cosmopolitan Governance* (Cambridge: Polity Press, 1995), p. 279.

39. Beardsworth, *Cosmopolitanism and International Relations Theory*, pp. 221, 181–83.

40. United Nations, *A More Secure World: Our Shared Responsibility: Report of the UN High-Level Panel on Threats, Challenges and Change* (New York: United Nations Department of Public Information, 2004), p. 5.

PART III

Freedom and the Subject in Contemporary Philosophy and Theory

CHAPTER 7

The Subject, Abandoned: Jean-Luc Nancy's Spacing of Freedom

Ian Maclachlan

In her consideration of subjectivity, embodiment, and mortality in the work of Jacques Derrida and Jean-Luc Nancy in a chapter of *Mortal Subjects* (2011), Christina Howells at one point recalls 'Derrida's comments on Nancy's willingness to put to his own purposes terminology which Derrida himself finds unusable', placing this key point of resistance between the two philosophers in the context of 'Nancy's defiant project of deconstructive recuperation of notions that have been appropriated by metaphysical, humanistic, and Christian philosophies'.[1] The immediate context of Howells's remark is Nancy's provocative reliance on aspects of gendered sexual embodiment in his fragmentary text on the body, *58 indices sur le corps*,[2] but there could scarcely be a more prominent example of Nancy's defiant maintenance of a contested term that is central to more than one philosophical tradition, and of Derrida's demurral about that terminological stubbornness, than Nancy's treatment of the notion of freedom in his important 1988 volume on *L'Expérience de la liberté* [The Experience of Freedom].[3] As we will also briefly observe, Derrida's reservations about Nancy's gesture, as expressed particularly in *Voyous* [Rogues],[4] his 2003 essay on democracy, will afford a significant role to another feature Howells notes, this time with particular reference to Nancy's weaving of quotations from Derrida's *Mémoires d'aveugle* into his tribute published three years after Derrida's death, in 2007, *A plus d'un titre: Jacques Derrida*, in relation to which she draws attention to an 'intratextual exchange between the two philosophers [that] is both self-conscious and reflexive'.[5] Derrida's own self-conscious deployment in *Voyous* of the textual gesture of quoting from his friend's text, interpolating those quotations with his own parenthetical remarks, serves to provide an implicit textual rejoinder to and qualification of Nancy's notion of an ontologically fundamental *être-avec* [being-with] that is essential to the latter's account of freedom, particularly in relation to the status of the subject.

L'Expérience de la liberté is an attempt at a retrieval or, to use the term sometimes associated with Derrida's deconstructive reworking of key terms, a paleonymy of freedom. It is geared towards, as Nancy himself claims, a liberation of freedom, or a deliverance *from* freedom as it has been construed in the philosophical tradition in order to reach a deliverance *as* freedom, in the sense of being given over or *abandoned* to existence, as Nancy summarizes at the outset, with specific reference to Heidegger's thinking of the 'essence' of *Dasein* as nothing other than its existence:

> Car la liberté ne peut plus être ni 'essentielle', ni 'existentielle', mais elle est impliquée dans le chiasme de ces concepts: il faut penser ce qui fait l'existence, en son essence, abandonnée à une liberté, libre pour cet abandon, livrée à lui et en lui disponible. Peut-être le nom et le concept de 'liberté' ne pourront pas, eux-mêmes, être conservés.

> [Freedom can no longer be either 'essential' or 'existential', but is implicated in the chiasmus of these concepts: we have to consider what makes existence, which is in its essence abandoned to a freedom, free for this abandonment, offered to it and available in it. Perhaps it will not be possible to preserve the very name and concept of 'freedom'.] (*EL*, p. 13; 9)

The enterprise proposed by Nancy will involve a reading of part of the European philosophical tradition (notably Kant, Hegel, and, above all, Heidegger) to uncover the resources for thinking freedom, in a context in which, for Nancy, freedom will prove to be the 'unthought' of philosophy, perhaps even its 'unthinkable', although he does signal the dangers of positing freedom as inconceivable or incomprehensible. Since, in the terms conjoined in the essay's title, experience *just is* freedom, its conceptual elusiveness is in virtue of its unqualified self-evidence: 'La liberté n'est pas "inconcevable"' ('Freedom is not "inconceivable"'), Nancy insists, before adding that, 'c'est elle qui ne se conçoit pas, et c'est en quoi elle est la liberté. Son évidence au-delà de toute évidence [...] tient à ce non-savoir de soi' ('freedom doesn't conceive itself, and this is why it is freedom. Its self-evidence beyond all evidence [...] depends on this non-knowledge of itself') (*EL*, p. 115; 87, translation modified). Philosophy may therefore have always, inescapably, reduced or traduced freedom, in Nancy's sense, but freedom is at the same time what keeps philosophy going, what calls for thought even as it resists comprehension or conceptualizing. Thus it is that Nancy will refer, for example, to 'la liberté intraitable d'où procède la pensée elle-même' ('the intractable freedom from which thought itself proceeds') (*EL*, p. 22; 17, translation modified). Thinking freedom will therefore entail a ceaseless reorienting of the thinking of freedom (which, again, is perhaps what is meant precisely by freedom), to avert the risk, for example, that freedom should appear as a faculty, a property, or some established foundation, on the basis of which, and following which, thinking would proceed (as might mistakenly be supposed from one reading of the remark just quoted).

The bewildering challenge that thinking freedom poses is well summarized in a chapter whose title asks the question: 'Sommes-nous libres de parler de la liberté?' [Are We Free to Speak of Freedom?]. In that chapter's final paragraph, Nancy affirms that, even in the paradoxically compelling obligation to philosophical thought that freedom poses, it remains inescapably philosophy's concern as 'l'ouverture d'un libre espace de sens' ('the opening of a free space of meaning') even in 'l'impasse de ses sens' ('the impasse of its meanings'), going on to conclude:

> Nous ne sommes donc pas libres de penser la liberté ou de ne pas la penser, mais la pensée (c'est-à-dire, l'homme) est libre *pour* la liberté: elle est livrée à cela et délivrée pour cela par quoi elle est d'avance excédée, devancée et débordée.

[We are therefore not free to think freedom or not to think it, but thinking
(that is, the human being) is free *for* freedom: it is given over to and delivered for
what from the beginning exceeded it, anticipated it, and overflowed it.] (*EL*, p.
49; 8, translation modified)

The reductions of freedom that are to be avoided, as Nancy invokes them at various
points in the essay, comprise just about any conception of freedom that has been, or
it seems, could be entertained philosophically: freedom as foundation, or a 'natural'
freedom; positive freedoms in the sense of rights; freedom as a necessity; freedom
as first cause, on the one hand, or indeed as derived, on the other; freedom as free
will, and crucially therefore, in relation to how various European philosophical
traditions have framed this conception — whether that might be in terms of
independence, will, a property, or a capacity — freedom as the attribute of a self-
possessed, self-identical, autonomous, voluntaristic subject.[6]

Earlier in that same chapter, Nancy describes the divorce between such determinate freedoms and the fundamental kind of freedom he's trying to evoke, noting
that the former 'ne saisissent pas l'enjeu de "la liberté"' ('do not grasp the stakes
of "freedom"'), and adding the following of those restricted freedoms: 'Elles
dessinent les contours de leur concept commun — "la liberté" — comme les bords
d'un espace vide, vacant, et dont la vacance pourrait bien en définitive être le seul
trait qu'il faille tenir pour pertinent' ('They sketch the contours of their common
concept — "freedom" — as if these were the borders of an empty, vacant space
whose vacancy could definitively be taken to be its only pertinent trait') (*EL*, p. 42;
2). If a distinction like that tends to echo one that Derrida would make between,
for example, conditional and unconditional forms of justice or of hospitality, then
I think that is indeed a helpful way to conceptualize what Nancy is proposing,
but we'll look more closely at Nancy's thinking of freedom in relation to Derrida
shortly.

To begin to offer a philosophical characterization of this fundamental, existential
freedom, which enables yet withdraws from — in fact, liberates itself from —
determinate freedoms, we could summarize Nancy's account of it as: a fact of
existence, obtaining nowhere other than here and now; however, not to be
thought of as pure immanence (which would offer no possibility, no freedom in
fact, for thought), but as the finite transcendence of existence, to use a language
still deployed from time to time in this 1988 essay (e.g. *EL*, pp. 114, 123; 83, 95),
particularly when the discussion is closest to a reorienting exposition of aspects
of Heidegger's thinking. (Subsequently, Nancy will rather have recourse to the
notion of 'transimmanence';[7] in another Derridean echo that would need further
elaboration than I can offer here, it would resemble what Derrida frames as a 'quasi-
transcendental'.)[8] This finite transcendence would mean something like: existence
as it ex-ists, as it differs from itself in order to be, here and now, what it is. That
very ex-istence *is* freedom for Nancy:

L'ex-istence de l'existant le *livre* à la possibilité de *se livrer* à sa loi, à son existence,
précisément parce que celle-ci n'*a* pas d'essence ni de loi, mais *est* sa propre
essence et sa propre loi. [...] *Le fait de la liberté est cette dé-livrance de l'existence de
toute loi et à elle-même en tant que loi.*

[The existent's ex-istence *gives it over* to the possibility of *giving itself over* to its
law, precisely because the law *has* neither essence nor law, but *is* its own essence
and own law. [...] *The fact of freedom is this de-liverance of existence from every law
and from itself as law.*] (*EL*, p. 37; 30)

Such an account of the freedom of existence echoes the Heideggerian inflection
around the notion of the 'essence' of existence being an abandoned existence,
or an abandonment to existence, that we noted in outlining how Nancy's first
chapter sets up his proposed 'liberation' of freedom. In that chapter, Nancy remarks
parenthetically of this freedom that we might think of it 'peut-être comme une
libéralité ou comme une générosité plus originelles que toute liberté' ('perhaps as
a liberality or generosity more original than any freedom') (*EL*, p. 14; 10); here
again is a formulation where the foundational generosity of this freedom of course
carries a further strong, Heideggerian echo, this time of the ontologically originary
movement of the *es gibt* in the latter's thought.[9]

Remaining with that opening chapter for a moment, I'd like now to consider
how Nancy first brings the notion of *espacement* [spacing] into view as essentially
bound up with this conception of freedom. From the outset, Nancy is set on
activating the temporal as well as the obvious spatial resonances of *espacement*, as
indeed these were heralded by Derrida when he used the term in his reading of
Saussure in *De la grammatologie*, where he pointed out that 'ce mot dit l'articulation
de l'espace et du temps, le devenir-espace du temps et le devenir-temps de l'espace'
('this word speaks the articulation of space and time, the becoming-space of time
and the becoming-time of space').[10] The context of Nancy's introduction of the
term is a discussion of historicity, in which he is endeavouring to disclose what
liberates that historicity from any deterministic causality. Nancy proposes freedom
as that which, in its ceaseless arrival, surprises or indeed takes itself by surprise ('ce
qui *se surprend*', *EL*, p. 20; 15). This entails a view of the freedom of existence as
being open to, or perhaps better, opened by a kind of rhythmic spacing or scansion,
in a movement which he describes as follows:

> Ouverture de l'existence à sa propre essentialité comme à cette scansion ou
> à ce rythme singulier selon lequel l'existant se précède et se succède dans un
> temps auquel il n'est pas 'présent', mais où sa liberté le surprend — ou comme
> à cet espacement (rythme lui aussi, et peut-être au cœur du premier) où
> l'existant se singularise, c'est-à-dire existe, selon l'espace libre et commun de
> son inessentialité.

> [The opening of existence to its own essentiality as well as to this scansion, or
> singular rhythm, according to which the existent precedes and succeeds itself in
> a time to which it is not 'present', but in which its freedom surprises it — like
> the spacing (which is also a rhythm, perhaps at the heart of the former rhythm)
> in which the existent is singularized, that is to say, exists, according to the free
> and common space of its inessentiality.] (*EL*, p. 20; 16)

Freedom as something which surprises in its arrival, or that is the very possibility
of the advent of a future (the terms *advenir* and *à venir* recur repeatedly in Nancy's
account), and that does so according to a rhythmic *espacement*, carries echoes of
Derrida's handling of the event as a radically unforeseeable advent that never simply

arrives in the present, and in fact Nancy will invoke the notion of *différance* on numerous occasions in related contexts (e.g. *EL*, pp. 38 n. 2, 115; 186 n. 8, 87). The temporality of this *espacement* is something on which I'll focus in the latter part of this discussion. For the moment, I'd like to suggest that we think of freedom as Nancy is characterizing it here on the basis of *relation*: we might conceive of this fundamental freedom as a kind of unbound relation, or as the rhythmic movement oscillating between a not-yet-bound and a no-longer-bound relation. In the passage quoted above, this freedom as free relationality, so to speak, affords the opening of a space in which 'l'existant se singularise'. In the context of our theme of freedom and the subject, it is time to dwell a little more on the way in which Nancy styles that (self-)singularizing existent, and to do so I'd like to focus on what is the key chapter in that regard: 'Partage de la liberté. Égalité, fraternité, justice' [Sharing Freedom: Equality, Fraternity, Justice].

This seventh chapter of *L'Expérience de la liberté* opens with Nancy's emphatic rejection of the notion of freedom as the autonomy of an independent, self-contained ('sovereign', in an idiom Nancy will echo on occasion elsewhere, e.g. *EL*, p. 30; 24) subject, and he does so precisely in terms of the impossibility of relation for such a subject:

> La liberté ne se laisse pas présenter comme l'autonomie d'une subjectivité maîtresse de soi-même et de ses décisions, évoluant à l'écart de toute entrave, dans une parfaite indépendance. Que signifierait une telle indépendance, sinon l'impossibilité de principe d'entrer dans le moindre rapport — et donc d'exercer la moindre liberté?

> [Freedom cannot be presented as the autonomy of a subjectivity in charge of itself and of its decisions, evolving freely and in perfect independence from every obstacle. What would such an independence mean, if not the impossibility in principle of entering into the slightest relation — and therefore of exercising the slightest freedom?] (*EL*, p. 91; 66)

Instead, freedom as Nancy proposes it is of *singularities* which, even in their emergence or 'birth' as singularities, are always already in relation, and this is a freedom that recurs with each birth, initiality, or opening: that is, as Nancy repeatedly couches it in the opening of this chapter, the freedom that there should be a singular 'une fois' freely recurs 'chaque fois'. This deployment of a relation between 'une fois' and 'chaque fois' signals an ontologically irreducible *être-avec* that is each time new, and newly given as singular freedom:

> L'existence de l'existant n'a lieu que singulièrement, dans ce *partage* de la singularité, et *chaque fois* c'est la liberté qui est en jeu, parce que la liberté est elle-même l'enjeu du 'chaque fois'. Il n'y aurait pas de 'chaque fois' s'il n'y avait pas chaque fois naissance, surgissement imprévisible, et comme tel inassignable, surprise de la liberté d'une existence.

> [The existence of the existent only takes place singularly, in this *sharing out* of singularity, and freedom is *each time* at stake, for freedom is what is at stake in the 'each time'. There would be no 'each time' if there were not birth each time, unpredictably arising and as such unassignable, the surprise of the freedom of an existence.] (*EL*, p. 93; 68, translation modified)

Of course, the appearance here of the key term *partage* (as sharing and dividing, or sharing *out*, as it is often rendered in English) gives an indication of how we are to understand this free relation of singularities, given the pivotal role that *partage* plays in Nancy's thought. The initial coming into relation this one time ('une fois') of singularity is what constitutes relation each time ('chaque fois'). The unprecedented initiality of singularity is therefore what is shared out ('partagé') in relation, according to the irresolvably conjunctive-disjunctive relation that is marked by *partage*.

What the *partage* of singularity implies, then, is that one should think of singular relation neither in terms, say, of a common substance, on the one hand, nor of atomizing division, on the other, but as a differing that just is what is shared. The following passages develop this idea:

> L'être-*en*-commun signifie ceci: que l'être n'est rien que nous aurions comme une propriété commune, alors même que nous *sommes*, ou bien que l'être ne nous est commun que sur le mode d'*être partagé*. Non pas qu'une substance commune et générale nous soit distribuée, mais l'être *n'est que* partagé *entre* les existants et *en* existants [...]. Ainsi, nous est partagé cela qui nous partage: le retrait de l'être, qui est le retrait de la propriété de soi, et l'ouverture de l'existence comme existence.
>
> [Being-*in*-common means that being is nothing that we would have as a common property, even though we *are*, or even though being is not common to us except in the mode of *being shared out*. Not that a common and general substance would be distributed to us, but rather, being is *only* shared out *between* existents and *in* existents [...]. Thus what is shared us is what shares us out or divides us: the withdrawal of being, which is the withdrawal of the properness of self and the opening of existence as existence.] (*EL*, p. 95; 69–70, translation modified)

Glossing this in connection with the initiality of freedom as relation that was outlined a moment ago, we might say that the initial coming-into-relation, insofar as it *is* initial, may be thought of as a relation that precedes the relata;[11] but that observation would immediately need to be qualified, in light of what Nancy says about the inapplicability of any notion of a 'substance commune et générale', by the proviso that it cannot precede them as substance or presence. Indeed, the exclusion of notions such as the latter is essentially bound up with how Nancy is conceiving freedom: relation, so to speak, *freely gives* singularities over to existence. Singularity is, each time, constituted by the *partage* of that free relation; and to use the language of 'ipseity' (self-relation) that Nancy goes on in the same passage to demarcate from the 'aseity' of being as a kind of *causa sui* ground, ipseity is constituted and deconstituted by *partage* as the differing commonality of singularities.

Nancy reformulates this freedom as the *partage* of singularities in a number of ways that may be helpful: for example, as the constitutive 'being-outside-of-itself' of singularity, and therefore as a freedom that does not return to itself in any movement of self-appropriation:

> Hors de soi, c'est la liberté, ce n'est pas la propriété: ni celle de la représentation, ni celle de la volonté, ni celle de la chose possédée. *La liberté en tant que 'soi' de l'être-hors-de-soi ne se revient pas et ne s'appartient pas.*

[Outside of itself, that's freedom, not property: neither the freedom of representation, nor of will, nor of the object possessed. *Freedom as the 'self' of being-outside-itself does not return to or belong to itself.*] (*EL*, p. 96; 70, translation modified)

In respect of freedom and the *subject*, it's particularly worth noting the terms in which Nancy develops the idea of the *espacement* of freedom as it opens subjectivity in the movement of *partage*, beyond, as he has just insisted at this point, any dialectical recognition and confirmation of its autonomous status:

> [La liberté] est, depuis la naissance et jusque dans la mort — dernière naissance de la singularité — , ce qui jette le sujet dans l'espace du partage de l'être. [...] Le partage ontologique, ou la singularité de l'être, ouvre l'espace que seule la liberté peut, non pas 'remplir', mais proprement espacer. 'Espacer l'espace', cela voudrait dire: le garder en tant qu'espace, en tant que partage de l'être, afin de *partager indéfiniment le partage* des singularités.

> [[Freedom] is, from birth until death — the last birth of singularity — what throws the subject into the space of the sharing out of being. [...] Ontological sharing out, or the singularity of being, opens the space that only freedom is able, not to 'fill', but properly to space. 'Spacing space' would mean keeping it as space and as the sharing out of being, in order *indefinitely to share out the sharing of singularities.*] (*EL*, p. 96; 70–71, translation modified)

This and the other passages I've drawn from the chapter 'Partage de la liberté' touch on three areas on which I'd like to focus briefly in the latter part of this essay, and in each instance, I'll be drawing on Derrida's thinking as a point of comparison: the gesture by which freedom is said here to propel or throw the subject ('ce qui jette le sujet'); the free *partage* in which it is said to be *we* who are related ('nous est partagé ce qui nous partage'); and the spatio-temporal *espacement* invoked repeatedly with regard to the movement of that *partage*. Consideration of these will also involve some close scrutiny of aspects of Nancy's mode of expression in *L'Expérience de la liberté*.

The first of these areas I've singled out is simply to mark a recurring formulation with which Nancy gestures towards the opening of freedom which casts (a verb which we might parse in English as an idiomatic conjunction of 'throwing' and 'shaping') those singularities that he otherwise seems habitually reticent about describing as 'subjects'; namely, the dynamic relation signalled by the thrown initiality of a *-jet* ('-ject') that etymologically inhabits but, in Nancy's terms, conceptually throws open and overspills the *sujet* ('subject'). Having drawn out the '-jectile' movement that opens the *partage* of subjectivity in the passage just quoted above, Nancy returns to this formulation in order, once again, to free up and throw open the notion of subjectivity a few pages later:

> Or l'espace libre ne peut être ouvert, par définition, par aucune liberté subjective. L'espace libre est ouvert, il est libéré, par le fait même qu'il est constitué ou institué en tant qu'espace *par* les trajectoires et les allures qui sont celles des singularités jetées à l'existence.

> [Now, by definition, free space cannot be opened by any subjective freedom. Free space is opened, freed, by the very fact that it is constituted or instituted

as space *by* the trajectories and bearing of singularities that are thrown into existence.] (*EL*, p. 100; 74, translation modified)

And shortly thereafter, summarizing a paragraph in which he has been describing the paradoxically incommensurable measure of justice at work in the very opening of a political space of freedom, Nancy concludes: 'Tel est, pourrait-on dire, le premier jet de la liberté' ('Such is, we could say, the first thrust of freedom') (*EL*, p. 101; 75). It's worth noting, with regard to these formulations, Derrida's unpacking of the notion of a 'jetty' in a text first published in the following English translation, where he exploits the resources of this noun:

> By the word 'jetty' I will refer from now on to the *force* of that *movement* which is not yet *subject*, *project*, or *object*, not even rejection, but in which takes place any production and any determination, which finds its possibility in the jetty — whether that production or determination be related to the subject, the object, the project, or the rejection.[12]

A fuller examination of the parallels between Nancy and Derrida around the gesture or motion described via the figure of the 'jetty' in this admittedly isolated instance would, I suggest, involve tracing the clear connections between that originary '-jectile' movement and another key etymological component in Derrida's thinking: the relational movement of carrying or bearing opened by a *-férence* that, Derrida reminds us, is conveyed not only in difference or, differently, in *différance*, but also in reference, preference, and so on.[13]

Secondly, I'd like to offer a very brief comment on an area that has already elicited a good deal of discussion: Nancy's retention of a notion of commonality and of the first-person plural *nous* to designate the singularities held in relation by an uncertain, connective-disjunctive *partage*, and Derrida's demurral from such a move, particularly in *Voyous*, but also elsewhere. To do so, I'd like just to highlight one passage where Nancy affirms the priority of this *nous*, deploying quotation marks as he does so, in a gesture on which Derrida will comment in turn: 'Le "nous" est antérieur au "je", non comme un premier sujet, mais comme le partage ou la partition qui permet d'inscrire "je"' ('The "we" is anterior to the "I", not as a first subject, but as the sharing out or partition that permits the inscription of "I"'), says Nancy, before going on to qualify that affirmation of the possibility of first-person singular inscription within the further typographical suspension of parentheses:

> (Cela n'implique pourtant pas que 'nous', à ce niveau, fonctionne simplement en tant qu''embrayeur' de l'énoncé sur son sujet énonciateur. 'Nous' fait fonctionner un embrayeur bloqué, écarté de lui-même. On ne peut pas dire qui énonce 'nous'. Il faudrait dire: 'on' sait d'évidence qu'on existe [where Nancy inserts the footnote mentioned below], et c'est ainsi que *nous* existons, partageant la possibilité que *je* le dise à chaque fois.)

> [(This does not, however, imply that the 'we', at this level, functions simply as the 'shifter' of the enunciation over its enunciating subject. 'We' is what causes a blocked shifter, one that is distanced from itself, to function. One cannot say who enunciates 'we'. What would have to be said is this: 'one' evidently knows one exists, and it is thus that *we* exist, sharing out the possibility that *I* should say so every time.)] (*EL*, p. 98; 72, translation modified)

Nancy's declaration of a certain, prior commonality, which 'shares out' (*partage*) the possibility that a singular subject should come to enunciate itself, arrives with an armature of typographical qualifications, hesitations, or displacements — quotation marks, italics, parentheses — and offers a further enunciative rerouting at the very moment when a supposedly prior *nous* is uncertainly trumped by an *on* that elicits the following footnote:

> Ce *on* renverrait alors à celui de Blanchot, ou au *ils* qui lui est parallèle, et qui ne désigne pas l'anonymat d'une banalité, mais qui correspond à l'événement de ce qu'on ne peut 'ressaisir qu'en se dessaisissant (du) pouvoir de dire je'.

> [This *one* would refer to that of Blanchot, or to the parallel *they* which does not designate the anonymity of banality, but corresponds to the event of what one cannot 'get hold of except by losing hold of the power to say I'.] (*EL*, p. 98 n. 1; 192 n. 4).[14]

Alongside the typographical features I've noted here, a sustained analysis would have to draw out the stakes of this shuttling between pronouns (*nous, je, il, on*) and texts (Blanchot, Deleuze-Guattari as also footnoted, and indeed Descartes in a significant reference I've elided), but, at the very least, all these textual features seem to hold open what this passage wants to draw together between 'us'.[15] Given all that he says about the freedom of a *partage* that opens between 'us', I don't suppose Nancy would want to demur from any of that; but in order to flag up a particular difficulty I find in Nancy's account of freedom experienced as a *partage* I want to return in conclusion to the notion of *espacement*, taking parts of Derrida's reading of Nancy as a starting-point for those reflections.

If only in a trivial sense, the textual interruptions and deferrals noted above call for a certain time of reading, and a markedly open time at that, if one wants to pursue a version of the trail sketched by Nancy with his references to Blanchot, Deleuze-Guattari, and others. In his discussion of *L'Expérience de la liberté* in two central chapters of *Voyous*, Derrida is also particularly attentive to Nancy's use of quotation marks, and in what is already quite a close-packed texture of quotation, paraphrase, and analysis, Derrida freely interrupts with his own qualifications and hesitations, often interpolated within material quoted from Nancy's text. In one especially dense passage of close reading, Derrida dwells on what he highlights as Nancy's key premise of 'partage comme espacement' ('sharing out as spacing') (*V*, p. 70; 44, translation modified). This notion seems to be what mitigates the concern that, as he declares, Derrida would otherwise have with regard to the role played in Nancy's account by figures of the *soi*, the *autos*, or of ipseity, which would otherwise risk corroborating the self-identity of subjectivity. Focusing, for example, on a section of the chapter 'Partage de la liberté' which we were discussing earlier, Derrida underscores the spacing of a *partage* which opens the possibility of ipseity but maintains it precisely as open, and therefore, in the same gesture, withdraws the possibility of subjectivity's closure. He quotes Nancy's text, his own bracketed interpolation further suspending Nancy's cautious scare quotes:

> '[...] l'ipséité est elle-même constituée par le partage et comme partage. C'est-à-dire que *l'ipséité de la singularité a pour essence le retrait de l'aséité de l'être.* Aussi,

l'être de son "soi" ["soi" entre des guillemets qui disent toute la difficulté à soutenir quelque "soi" que ce soit] est ce qui reste "soi" lorsque rien ne revient à soi.'

['Ipseity is constituted by and as sharing out. This means that *the ipseity of singularity has as its essence the withdrawal of the aseity of being*. So, the being of its "self" [the quotation marks around "self" tell the whole story about the difficulty of sustaining any "self" at all] is what remains "self" when nothing comes back to itself.'] (*V*, p. 71; 45, quoting *EL*, p. 95; 70, translation modified)

Significantly, I think, it's also at this point of his discussion that Derrida's tentative echoing of Nancy's text revolves around certain temporal expressions. Derrida's reflections on the key role of *espacement* had been launched by Nancy's allusion to the inaugural freedom of an 'espace-temps de *l'initialité*' ('space-time of *initiality*') (*V*, p. 70; 44, quoting *EL*, p. 105; 79, my emphasis). Following some of the analysis of ipseity we've just seen, Derrida quotes at length from this passage, where Nancy alludes to what is lacking ('ce qui manque') in the thinking of democracy 'aujourd'hui'. That little temporal marker elicits a lengthy interpolation from Derrida:

[et il faudrait donner toute la force et la chance de son énigme à cet *aujourd'hui*: où et quand est-ce aujourd'hui, le jour d'aujourd'hui pour le manque dont il va être question? Cet aujourd'hui, vous allez le voir et l'entendre, il va se laisser déterminer par un aussi énigmatique 'jusqu'ici' qui, comme l'aujourd'hui, suppose qu'on a déjà commencé à se rendre au-delà du jusqu'ici, si bien que l'aujourd'hui est déjà hier: ce qui manque aujourd'hui.]

[[and we must allow all the force and chance of the enigma of this *today*: where and when is today, the very day, today, of the lack in question? This today, as you will see and hear, will let itself be determined by an equally enigmatic 'up until now', one that, like the today, presupposes that we have already begun to go beyond this 'up until now', so that this today is already yesterday: which is just what is lacking today.]] (*V*, p. 72; 46, translation modified).

Derrida's caution is prompted, therefore, by the punctuality of Nancy's formulations, which risk collapsing any temporal opening into the self-presence of a moment 'today'. Notwithstanding Nancy's repeated invocation of *espacement* as the spatio-temporal opening of freedom, his constantly reiterated gestures towards initiality, the birth of freedom or, as he puts it in a chapter on 'Liberté et destin' [Freedom and Destiny], the 'pro-venance' of time (*EL*, pp. 144–46; 111–12), seem to underplay a time that would remain otherwise, even in its difference and deferral, and in which there might be a moment for the encounter of free singularities, other than in the apparent simultaneity of their *com-parution* [com-pearance].[16]

  That emphasis on time as punctual initiality remains, for example, when Nancy returns to the topic of freedom in a later, short essay 'La Liberté vient du dehors' [Freedom Comes from Outside].[17] The phrase used by Nancy as his title recalls that freedom, in his sense, cannot be reduced to a property 'internal' to a pre-existing subject. A paragraph that delineates that externality of freedom in relation to any supposedly constituted subject seems to me momentarily to open up a potentially non-punctual time of difference and deferral, only to close it down again with a return to ceaseless initiality. Firstly, Nancy stipulates of freedom that: 'Il n'y a précisément pas de propriété "dedans" qui préexiste: mais toute "préexistence" consiste dans le fait que l'existence se précède elle-même, qu'elle est en elle-même une structure de précédence (et de succession)' [There is precisely no pre-existing property 'within' — but any 'pre-existence' consists in the fact that existence precedes itself, that it is in itself a structure of precedence (and succession)] (*LVD*, p. 135). In the immediately ensuing description of existence as a movement of ipseity outside of itself, the adverbial expression Nancy uses already begins to collapse the open temporality of that movement: 'L'existence est *d'abord et pour finir* l'échappée du "soi" dans le "non-soi", et la liberté est le nom de ce mouvement' [Existence is, *from first to last*, the slipping of the 'self' into the 'non-self', and freedom is the name for this movement] (*LVD*, p. 135, my emphasis). Finally, having qualified this freedom as an 'opening *to*' that opens to nothing other than freedom itself, Nancy's final gesture in this paragraph strikes me as restoring the punctual initiality of such an opening in a manner that, temporally, cannot but risk forestalling that very opening in its freedom: 'Ainsi, le rapport-à-soi du soi s'effectue bien: il s'effectue comme ouverture toujours renouvelée, ouverture qui n'ouvre "à" rien ou "sur" rien, sinon sur un "dehors" qu'elle constitue elle-même' [So it is that the self-relation of the self does indeed take place: it takes place as an ever-renewed opening, and opening that doesn't open 'to' or 'onto' anything, except onto an 'outside' that it itself constitutes] (*LVD*, pp. 135–36).

I should acknowledge that the account I'm offering of time as initiality will come as no surprise to readers of Nancy, since he is elsewhere entirely frank about his espousal of a temporality of interruptive, explosive instantaneity that is deliberately at odds with models of temporal linearity or duration. In the short, polemical piece 'Espace contre temps' [Space Against Time], notably, Nancy combatively embraces a certain spatializing or 'spacing' of time: 'Espace de temps: ouverture d'un *topos* au présent. [...] Il n'y a que du présent, ou plutôt, il n'y a que cet écartement du présent, de sa venue extemporanée' [Space of time: the opening to the present of a *topos*. [...] There is nothing but the present, or rather, there is nothing but this opening of a gap in the present, in its extemporaneous coming]. Moreover, this spacing of time is said, precisely, to militate in favour of a liberation of time: 'L'espace n'est donc contre le temps que pour libérer le temps, sa venue, l'allée-et-venue, lui donner lieu, accueil spacieux, refuser la durée, la succession, le règne des causes, des rétentions, des propensions' [Space is therefore against time only in order to liberate time, its coming, its coming and going, to make room for time, a spacious welcome, to refuse duration, succession, the rule of causes, retentions, propensities].[18] But perhaps finding a place for time, offering it a spacious embrace, may be to restrict its freedom just as much as keeping it in the shackles of duration or succession.

In taking my lead from reservations about Nancy's thinking of freedom hinted at by Derrida, especially in relation to moments in Nancy's text that seem to privilege punctual initiality, I'm also conscious of Ian James's comparative discussion of 'difference' in the two thinkers, in his essay 'Differing on Difference', and especially of the powerful conclusion of his argument, where he insists, persuasively, that 'the legacy of Derrida's thought cannot be one in which philosophical discourses, and particularly those inspired by deconstruction itself, are simply policed or controlled for metaphysical contraband'.[19] One sense in which the gesture I'm making here in claiming a damaging elision of time in Nancy's thinking might elude James's stricture is that, instead of policing Nancy's text for metaphysical contraband, I'm arguing for what looks like a prime piece of such contraband to be smuggled back in. After all, it's not only Nancy who takes aim at a metaphysically constraining view of time. Derrida himself famously declared that: 'Le concept de temps appartient de part en part à la métaphysique et il nomme la domination de la présence' ('The concept of time, in all its aspects, belongs to metaphysics, and it names the domination of presence').[20] But what I am suggesting is that the collapsing of one set of temporal categories, for example of relations to versions of past and future that themselves need to be thought in terms other than past-present or future-present — a time of *différance*, in short — risks consolidating the 'space' of freedom's 'spacing' as no less metaphysical a category.

As a result, the very openings of freedom for which Nancy wants to argue are in danger of stalling in their free movement, as spatio-temporally dynamic aporia gives way to static paradox; or as the temporal disjointedness that always accompanies the movement of deconstruction is reduced to what James, in a curiously rigid formulation, calls 'deconstruction itself'.[21] To return to the textual interplay between Derrida and Nancy that initiated these reflections, that disjointed time might be one in which the criss-cross of texts and voices (the *partage des voix*) would stand a better chance of the freedom of untimeliness, divergence, and dissent.[22] In the interplay of an open *partage*, this might be framed as the time of a democratic irony described at one point in *Voyous* by Derrida, giving rise to an undecidability which 'ouvre donc déjà, pour quiconque, une expérience de la liberté, toute ambiguë et inquiétante, menacée et menaçante qu'elle reste en son "peut-être", avec une responsabilité nécessairement excessive dont nul ne saurait s'exonérer' ('already opens, for whomever, an experience of freedom, however ambiguous and disquieting, threatened and threatening, it might remain in its "perhaps", with a necessarily excessive responsibility with which no one may be quits') (*V*, p. 133; 92, translation modified).[23]

Notes to Chapter 7

1. Christina Howells, *Mortal Subjects: Passions of the Soul in Late Twentieth-Century French Thought* (Cambridge: Polity Press, 2011), p. 199.
2. Jean-Luc Nancy, *58 indices sur le corps, et Extension de l'âme*, suivi de Ginette Michaud, *Appendice* (Quebec: Éditions Nota bene, 2004).
3. Jean-Luc Nancy, *L'Expérience de la liberté* (Paris: Galilée, 1988); *The Experience of Freedom*, trans. by Bridget McDonald (Stanford, CA: Stanford University Press, 1993); this work subsequently referred to as *EL* in the main text.
4. Jacques Derrida, *Voyous: deux essais sur la raison* (Paris: Galilée, 2003), pp. 69–70; *Rogues: Two Essays on Reason*, trans. by Pascale-Anne Brault and Michael Naas (Stanford, CA: Stanford University Press, 2005), pp. 44–45; this work subsequently referred to as *V* in the main text.

5. Howells, *Mortal Subjects*, p. 204, referring to: Jacques Derrida, *Mémoires d'aveugle: l'autoportrait et autres ruines* (Paris: Éditions de la Réunion des musées nationaux, 1990) and Jean-Luc Nancy, *À plus d'un titre: Jacques Derrida* (Paris: Galilée, 2007); Howells also notes the self-consciousness of this intratextual relationship as it is manifested in Derrida's long work on Nancy, *Le Toucher: Jean-Luc Nancy* (Paris: Galilée, 2000).

6. Howard Caygill offers an account of Nancy's conception of freedom in relation to post-Heideggerian thought, focusing especially on Hannah Arendt, in 'The Shared World: Philosophy, Violence, Freedom', in *The Sense of Philosophy: On Jean-Luc Nancy*, ed. by Darren Sheppard, Simon Sparks, and Colin Thomas (London & New York: Routledge, 1997), pp. 19–31. Also drawing on Arendt, there is some helpful exposition of Nancean freedom in the chapter 'Politics in-Common', in Mustafa Dikeç, *Space, Politics and Aesthetics* (Edinburgh: Edinburgh University Press, 2015), pp. 61–81. For an account of freedom in Nancy that instead highlights the Anglo-American tradition, especially as it derives from Humean empiricism, see Peter Fenves, 'From Empiricism to the Experience of Freedom', *Paragraph*, 16, 2 (1993), 158–79. Of the various book-length studies of Nancy, a fairly detailed treatment of his thinking of freedom is to be found in the chapter 'Libertarianism', in B. C. Hutchens, *Jean-Luc Nancy and the Future of Philosophy* (Chesham: Acumen, 2005), pp. 63–84.

7. See, for example, Jean-Luc Nancy, *Le Sens du monde* (Paris: Galilée, 1993), p. 91; for a helpful summary, see Mark Lewis Taylor, 'Transimmanence', in *The Nancy Dictionary*, ed. by Peter Gratton and Marie-Eve Morin (Edinburgh: Edinburgh University Press, 2015), pp. 232–34.

8. For an overview of the quasi-transcendental in Derrida, see Geoffrey Bennington, 'La Série: questions (quasi) transcendantales', in Geoffrey Bennington and Jacques Derrida, *Jacques Derrida* (Paris: Seuil, 1991), pp. 248–63. In an important essay on 'Differing on Difference' (in *Nancy Now*, ed. by Verena Andermatt Conley and Irving Goh (Cambridge: Polity Press, 2014), pp. 110–26), Ian James bases a nuanced distinction between Derrida's quasi-transcendental and Nancy's transimmanence on a claim that the trace in Derrida 'is arguably a *dematerialized* instance since, by Derrida's own account, it necessarily precedes all material sensory experience, being its quasi-transcendental condition of possibility and impossibility' (p. 120). But I think this argument rests on a partial view of Derrida's notion of 'originary technicity' that underestimates how far such a notion undermines the very idea of originarity, allowing James to claim that, for Derrida, the 'economy of inscription and iteration is itself thoroughly material' (p. 119), despite going on to cite remarks from *De la grammatologie* that militate precisely against any such thoroughgoing materiality of inscription. The trace as a quasi-transcendental is no more (or less) dematerialized than it is de-idealized. I return to James's essay towards the end of my discussion.

9. The precise relation to the *es gibt* would require more subtle elaboration than I can offer here. In an earlier essay on 'L'Être abandonné', for example, Nancy says that the *il y a* of his 'abandoned being' may *not* exactly be equated with the *es gibt*; see Jean-Luc Nancy, 'L'Être abandonné', in *L'Impératif catégorique* (Paris: Flammarion, 1983), pp. 141–53 (p. 145); 'Abandoned Being', trans. by Brian Holmes, in *The Birth to Presence* (Stanford, CA: Stanford University Press, 1993), pp. 36–47 (p. 40). For an account of Nancy's ontology of *être-avec* that both attends to his treatment of freedom and draws out some detail of the Heideggerian context, see Marie-Eve Morin, '"We Must Become What We Are": Jean-Luc Nancy's Ontology as *Ethos* and *Praxis*', in *Nancy and the Political*, ed. by Sanja Dejanovic (Edinburgh: Edinburgh University Press, 2015), pp. 21–42.

10. Jacques Derrida, *De la grammatologie* (Paris: Minuit, 1967), p. 99; *Of Grammatology*, trans. by Gayatri Chakravorty Spivak (Baltimore, MD: Johns Hopkins University Press, 1974), p. 68.

11. This last phrase echoes helpful formulations used by Timothy Clark in various contexts; see, for example, his *Derrida, Heidegger, Blanchot: Sources of Derrida's Notion and Practice of Literature* (Cambridge: Cambridge University Press, 1992), p. 50.

12. Jacques Derrida, 'Some Statements and Truisms about Neologisms, Newisms, Postisms, Parasitisms, and Other Small Seismisms', trans. by Anne Tomiche, in *The States of 'Theory': History, Art, and Critical Discourse*, ed. by David Carroll (New York & Oxford: Columbia University Press, 1990), pp. 63–94 (p. 65). The French text was later published, under the same title, in *Derrida d'ici, Derrida de là*, ed. by Thomas Dutoit and Philippe Romanski (Paris: Galilée, 2009), pp. 223–52 (p. 225).

13. See, for example, Jacques Derrida, *Sauf le nom* (Paris: Galilée, 1993), pp. 61–62, and *Spectres de Marx* (Paris: Galilée, 1993), p. 245.

14. Nancy's reference is to Maurice Blanchot, 'La Voix narrative (le "il", le neutre)', in *L'Entretien infini* (Paris: Gallimard, 1969), pp. 556–67 (p. 564), although his page reference is different (there is sometimes divergence in pagination of different Gallimard printings). Although the passage in question does refer to the 'ils' of Kafka's characters, Nancy's third-person plural looks more like a slip: Blanchot's essay revolves entirely around the third-person singular *il* of his titular 'voix narrative'. Moreover, Blanchot does not actually use the pronoun *on* at that point. In this respect, Nancy's account seems reliant on another source to which he refers in this footnote: the take-up of Blanchot's treatment of third-person pronouns by Gilles Deleuze and Félix Guattari, *Mille plateaux* (Paris: Minuit, 1980), p. 324.

15. In a different context, I have explored some of the interplay between Derrida and Nancy, around issues of quotation, typographical marks, and pronominal positions, in 'Contingencies: Reading Between Nancy and Derrida', *Oxford Literary Review*, 27 (2005), 139–58.

16. The coinage *comparution*, also used in *L'Expérience de la liberté*, refers to the being-in-common of singularities. It is described, for example, in Jean-Luc Nancy, *Être singulier pluriel* (Paris: Galilée, 1996), pp. 77–87.

17. Jean-Luc Nancy, 'La Liberté vient du dehors', in *La Pensée dérobée* (Paris: Galilée, 2001), pp. 127–38; this work subsequently referred to as *LVD* in the main text.

18. Jean-Luc Nancy, 'Espace contre temps', in *Le Poids d'une pensée, l'approche* (Strasbourg: La Phocide, 2008), pp. 85–88 (pp. 87, 88). For an account of Nancy's treatment of time that includes discussion of this particular piece, see Verena Andermatt Conley and Irving Goh, 'Introduction: Time in Nancy', in *Nancy Now*, pp. 1–19.

19. James, 'Differing on Difference', p. 126.

20. Jacques Derrida, 'Ousia et Grammè: note sur une note de Sein und Zeit', in *Marges — de la philosophie* (Paris: Minuit, 1972), pp. 31–78 (p. 73); 'Ousia and Grammē: Note on a Note from Being and Time', in *Margins of Philosophy*, trans. by Alan Bass (Chicago, IL: University of Chicago Press, 1982), pp. 29–67 (p. 63).

21. Temporal disjointedness is, of course, a recurring concern of Derrida's *Spectres de Marx*, particularly the chapter 'Injonctions de Marx' (pp. 19–85).

22. Cf. Jean-Luc Nancy, *Le Partage des voix* (Paris: Galilée, 1982).

23. For some thought-provoking reflections on the implications of Derrida's work for thinking about freedom, see Nicholas Royle's chapter 'Be Free', in *Jacques Derrida* (London & New York: Routledge, 2003), pp. 31–45.

CHAPTER 8

The Experience of Freedom Revisited

Ian James

Jean-Luc Nancy's *L'Expérience de la liberté* begins with an epigraph taken from the
first section of Kant's *Critique of Pure Reason*: 'Il s'agit de la liberté, qui peut toujours
franchir toute limite' [For the issue depends on freedom; and it is in the power of
freedom to pass beyond any and every specified limit].[1] As the title of his work
suggests, the freedom in question here is not a principle or question to be taken
up as the object of philosophical inquiry but is rather understood in relation to an
experience, and in particular to a very specific experience of limits: the limits of
philosophy, of theory, of subjectivity and, indeed, of thought itself.

Nancy derives this understanding of experience from an exploration of the
relationship between reason and human freedom in Kantian critical philosophy.
Moreover, for Nancy, the central role played by reason in the architectonic of Kant's
system relates not simply to epistemological concerns but more fundamentally
concerns existence per se. Nancy notes that:

> Lorsque la liberté s'est présentée dans la philosophie comme la 'clef de voûte
> de tout l'édifice de la raison pure' [...] il s'agissait en fait, et d'emblée, d'une
> ostension de son existence, ou plus exactement de sa présence au cœur de
> l'existence.
>
> [When freedom was presented in philosophy as 'the keystone of the whole
> architecture of the system of pure reason' [...] what was in question was in
> fact, and at first, an ostension of the existence of freedom, or more exactly an
> ostension of its presence at the heart of existence.] (*EL*, p. 27; 21).

From the 1970s onwards Nancy's reading of Kant unfolds very explicitly in the wake
of Heidegger's *Kantbuch*.[2] In particular Nancy follows Heidegger in understanding
freedom as being located in the world and *as* worldly existence. More generally,
but no less importantly, Nancy's ontological reading of Kantian freedom and
reason follows Heidegger insofar as it seeks to bring the interpretation of beingness
into a certain relation to time. This is borne out most explicitly in *Logodeadalus:
le discours de la syncope* published by Nancy in 1976 in which he further develops
the arguments of the *Kantbuch* to offer an anti-foundationalist reading of the first
Critique which interrogates questions of philosophical presentation in relation to

the temporality of thought, the schematism and the possibility or impossibility of connecting temporal intuitions to concepts.[3] It is worth noting that Nancy's 1973 doctoral dissertation, supervised by Paul Ricœur, was on Kant, as was his 1987 *doctorat d'état*, supervised by Gérard Granel and then published as *L'Expérience de la liberté* in 1988. To this extent it is arguable that Nancy's reading of Kant, and its attendant problems of presentation, freedom, temporality, and existence, are as fundamental to his formation as a philosopher as the early readings of Husserl were for Derrida.[4]

It is in this context then that freedom, for Nancy, comes to be understood as the *freeing* of existence from any determinate cause, principle, or foundation. This is a freeing that is *experienced* when reason, in and through the temporality of thought, encounters its own ungroundedness *as* reason. So, freedom, in Nancy's reading of Kant, is a *fact* of reason just as it is a 'présence au cœur de l'existence'. Freedom here is that which is not founded in any anterior principle, in any antecedent cause, nor in any substantive ground of any kind whatsoever. To this extent Nancy's freedom resembles its Kantian conception when it is understood as a spontaneity operating in and of itself in the absence of any prior determination or cause. It can therefore be related to Kantian transcendental or cosmological freedom. In the *Critique of Pure Reason* Kant describes cosmological freedom in the following terms: 'By freedom in the cosmological sense [...], I understand the faculty of beginning a state from itself, the causality of which does not in turn stand under another cause determining it in time in accordance with the law of nature'.[5] In Kant, as in Nancy, freedom in this sense is inseparable from a dimension of temporality and of causation or determination. Freedom exists in the possibility of there being or existing something which, within already existing being and its temporal or causal processes, is nevertheless not caused or determined by that which precedes it. A free existence, as a spontaneous emergence, somehow begins anew or again despite the causal or deterministic process from within which it emerges. As a spontaneous 'beginning a state from itself' free existence is therefore an emergence that has no substantive ground or foundation but *as a beginning* is no less part of, and indeed gives in the first instance, an ongoing *temporal* existence.

However, in its mediation via Heidegger and the ontological thinking of existence, Nancean freedom diverges significantly from Kant's more central conception of freedom insofar as it is at no point based upon the autonomy of a willing subject. Indeed, as that which 's'annule à être fondé' ('cannot be founded') (*EL*, p. 16; 12, translation modified) freedom, in Nancy, in fact comes to mark the outer limit point of the philosophy of the subject and thereby also, Nancy argues, marks a certain limit point of philosophy per se.

This is because freedom is not something that thought encounters as a phenomenon in the world, but rather, *as* ungrounded existence, freedom is both that which precedes thought and the thinking subject *and* that *from which* thought proceeds: '[L]a pensée' [...] vient de "l'abîme de la liberté". C'est la liberté [...], qui dispense, sans fond, la pensée' ('Thinking [...] comes from the "abyss of freedom" [...]. It is freedom [...] that groundlessly dispenses thought') (*EL*, pp. 74–75; 52–53). This is why, when Kantian philosophy seeks to secure a foundation or ground for fundamental ontological knowledge in the temporal movement of reason which encounters its own freedom as such, it in fact encounters that which it cannot grasp or secure — it encounters the freedom which makes thought possible and which precedes thought but which therefore also *exceeds* it and thereby marks its outer limit of possibility. In this way, Nancy argues:

> Toute pensée est donc pensée de la liberté en même temps qu'elle pense *par* la liberté, et qu'elle pense *en* liberté. [...] ce qui se passe ici, dans le libre surgissement de la pensée, se passe précisément sur cette limite [...]. Penser est toujours penser sur la limite.
>
> [Every thinking is therefore a thinking about freedom at the same time that it thinks *by* freedom and thinks *in* freedom. [...] what happens here, in the free arising of thought, happens precisely on this limit, as the play or very occasion of this limit. Thinking is always thinking on the limit.] (*EL*, pp. 75–76; 54)

At the very same time this experience of thought and of philosophy at their limit entails a necessary affirmation of existence itself as the free dissemination of an ungrounded and un-circumscribable plurality of singularities. For in the moment that thought in general, and philosophical thinking in particular, fail to secure a ground or foundation for its own existence *as thought*, they fail also to secure a unity or unified horizon to which all the multiplicity of existence per se can be returned.[6] In the absence of such a unity or unified horizon the multiplicity or plural givenness of ungrounded existence can only be thought of in the singular plural. So, for Nancy, the experience of freedom within the temporality of thought necessarily opens onto the fact of: 'l'existence en tant qu'essence d'elle-même' ('the fact of existence as its own essence') and so, 'la liberté ne désigne peut-être rien de plus, mais rien de moins que l'existence elle-même' ('freedom perhaps designates nothing more and nothing less than existence itself') (*EL*, pp. 15, 18; 11, 14). And existence as its own essence necessarily presents or gives itself in the plural, each time singularly.

This experience of thinking, insofar as it is one in which freedom, existence, and thought are co-articulated, gives rise to an affirmation of an existence not simply as both singular and plural, but also, in this very singular plurality, as necessarily *relational*. Insofar as freed existence surges as existence each time singularly in the absence of any ground or foundation it does so only in relation to other singular instances: 'L'être *singulier*,' Nancy writes, 'est dans le rapport ou selon le rapport' ('Singular being is in relation, or according to relation') (*EL*, p. 91; 66). So if freedom is a surging of existence that is *freed* from any ground, cause etc. then it is always each time a singular instance of such surging, but the force of the phrase *each time* here implies that each of these times will always be in relation, or more precisely, will be or exist *as* a relation to other singular instances of surging. Here the alignment of Nancean freedom with Kantian cosmological freedom might be recalled. Cosmological freedom was understood by Kant to be the 'faculty of beginning a state from itself', a state not standing 'under another cause determining it in time'. Such a state would however necessarily be *in some kind of relation* with the temporal, causal, or deterministic processes of nature from which it is 'freed', since it is 'each time' a new beginning or re-initialization of existence that is nevertheless still in relation to other singular existences. As such, despite being a beginning, free existence here nevertheless remains relational through and through (although not in a relation of causation or determination).

It is here that the motif of the 'sharing' of singular plural existence takes on a decisive role: 'L'existence n'a lieu que singulièrement, dans ce partage de la singularité, et *chaque fois* c'est la liberté qui est en jeu, parce que la liberté est elle-même l'enjeu du "chaque fois"' ('The existence of the existent takes place only singularly in this *sharing* of singularity, and freedom is *each time* at stake, for freedom is what is at stake in the "each time"') (*EL*, p. 93; 68). It is in this moment of existence as singularity which 'each time' surges in and by freedom that the structure of temporality as thought by Nancy is most clearly articulated: 'le "chaque fois",' Nancy writes, 'est une structure d'intervalle, il définit un espacement d'espace et de temps [...] L'être [...] n'a d'être que dans la discrétion des singularités' ('The "each time" is an interval structure and defines a spacing of space and time [...]. Being [...] has no being except in the discreteness of singularities') (*EL*, p. 92; 67). The invocation here of a 'structure d'intervalle' is worth noting. The *Petit Robert* defines the French word *intervalle* as a distance between two points or entities or a separation of two different events, dates, or epochs. An interval is therefore intrinsically relational, separating or distancing one point from another but only insofar as they remain in relation. It also implies both spatial and temporal relationality. The temporal/spatial structure of the interval is not one of continuous, linear, causal, or unitary evolution but rather one in which something like a continuous or unitary evolution would be possible in the first instance but which would then also constantly be subjected to the hiatus brought about by the 'each time' of freedom, by the possibility of 'beginning a state from itself'. There is a strong sense here that the structure of the interval itself gives something like a presence of existence insofar as it is both a temporalization and a spatialization. In so doing, it, at the very same time, makes possible or gives time or temporal becoming as such. For if there were only continuous linear, determined, and causal development, then there would be no room for any kind of event. Everything that occurs would be determined by what went before, the future would already be fully coded into the past, everything would in a sense already have happened, and time as such would be abolished. Conversely, if there were only a plural surging into being of singular instances without any relationality of any kind (and for Nancy the 'each time' is always relational) then there would be nothing but an eternal or a-temporal chaos of becoming. Again, time as such would be abolished. The structure of the interval in Nancy separates but also relates and thereby gives ungrounded, singular, and plural existence within *or rather as* a relational, temporal becoming.

So, relation is always in some way primordial and, insofar as freedom gives existence each time singularly, and thereby both spaces and temporalizes singular plural existence, it does so in a sharing of this 'each time' with each and every other time of the 'giving' of existence, such that freedom, as it gives existence, also and at the very same time, gives relation. Freedom is relation, Nancy writes, or at least: '[la liberté] est dans le rapport ou comme le rapport' ('freedom is in relation or as relation') (*EL*, p. 94; 69) and in such a way that the emergence or appearance of any singular existence or entity is always and already a co-emergence or co-appearance. Relation, then, is the spatializing and temporalizing of that which arrives as existence without which there would be no time or space as such. Ultimately what Nancy's experience of freedom gives is the thought of an ungrounded, irreducibly, excessive relational existence: 'l'expérience,' Nancy notes echoing Derrida, 'est donc aussi sa propre *différance*' ('Experience is thus also its own diff*érance*') (*EL*, p. 115; 87). Yet the spatializing and temporalizing at stake here is not a function of phenomenological or intentional consciousness but rather articulates the *real* positioning of singularities in relation to each other in the coming to presence of a world or worlds. As Nancy puts it: 'Le monde n'est pas [...] le corrélat d'une intentionnalité [...]. Le monde n'est d'aucune façon "pour moi": *il est la co-appartenance essentielle de l'existence avec l'exister de toute chose*' ('The world is not [...] the correlate of an intentionality [...]. The world is in no way "for me": it is the essential co-belonging of existence with the existing of all things') (*EL*, p. 202; 159, translation modified).

This point is important to retain and its implications need to be teased out further. For not only does such a formulation imply very strongly that existences are constituted in and by relation and have no status as entities prior to relation. Nancy is also signalling quite clearly that his ontological thinking here is pushing well beyond the phenomenological orbit of intentional consciousness and of the 'givenness' of existence to a strictly human consciousness. If there is a givenness or donation of existence 'for me', or for us as humans more generally, this is because singular plurality, *as relational existence*, is always composed of a sharing between singularities, a giving of singular existence 'each time' to another singular existence. This includes, of course, those singular instances that come into relation with us as some kind of perceptual donation for our experience or consciousness of a world. Yet it would also include all other kinds of relation of singular and plural shared existence that occur independently of human consciousness and of human existence in general. This is what Nancy means by '*la co-appartenance essentielle de l'existence avec l'exister de toute chose*' and it places him, in 1988, squarely within the field of concern that has developed more recently in the context of speculative realism and the overcoming of Kantian 'correlationism'. Yet Nancy's thinking, unlike that of the speculative realists, is able to account for the givenness of existence to human consciousness while at the same time framing that, if you like, 'anthropic' givenness or relation within a wider non-correlational ontology which would account for existence as such and its relationality beyond the orbit or scope of the human.[7]

What this interpretation of *L'Expérience de la liberté* shows is that Nancy's reading of Kant has as its outcome a strictly ontological understanding of freedom, one that implicates human consciousness, but which at the same time yields an ontology that is not restricted to any simple correlation with human consciousness. By extension, then, the thinking of existence as ungrounded and relational singular plurality necessarily yields a *realist* ontology. Singularities, in all their irreducible plurality and multiplicity, are really 'out there' as such and come into *real* relations equally with us and with each other in the sharing of existence. Yet this realist ontology is not foundationalist, it poses no metaphysical ground for being since it emerges as an ontology of singular plurality only in and from the very failure of thought to secure any kind of ground whatsoever in the experience of freedom.

It may seem surprising, if not implausible, that something like a realist ontology could emerge from a reading of Kantian idealist-transcendentalist philosophy mediated by the legacy of phenomenology and existential phenomenology. Yet, as I have argued elsewhere, Nancy's ontology is in a certain sense speculative, experimental, and distinctly minimalist.[8] As realist, however, one might expect that such an ontology might plausibly be brought into a comparative relation with realist ontologies that emerge, not from the tradition of transcendental idealism and its phenomenological and post-phenomenological legacy, but from contemporary scientific theories. Comparing Nancy's ontological thinking of freedom with scientific ontologies would not and should not be understood as an attempt to confer some retroactive authority on his thinking insofar as it might be shown to have a compatibility with science. Experience, as Blanchot once said to Bataille, is the sole authority, and, for Nancy, the experience of freedom will always be an experience *of thought* and will derive its necessity from that experience of thought alone (expiating itself in an absence of metaphysical foundation or ground, no doubt). Nor should it imply an exact identity between Nancean philosophical and scientific-theoretical ontologies. In what follows I will argue that what can be discerned in bringing Nancy's ontology of freedom into a comparative relation with some contemporary scientific theorizing is something like a 'speculative resonance' between philosophy and science. Such a speculative resonance, it will be argued, allows for a *freeing* of the relation between the two domains and for a renewal of the possibilities and scope of speculative thinking that may occur *at the limits* of both philosophical and scientific knowledge.

★ ★ ★ ★ ★

To this end I want to call upon two examples of speculative thought developed by scientists themselves working within the realms of cosmology and theoretical physics. The thinking of physicist Lee Smolin as developed in books such as *The Life of the Cosmos*, *Time Reborn*, and *The Singular Universe and the Reality of Time* (with Roberto Mangabeira Unger) will provide the first example for discussion.[9] The recent recasting of quantum theory by Roger Penrose in *Fashion, Faith, and Fantasy in the New Physics of the Universe* will provide the second.[10] It should be stressed that both Smolin and Penrose are generally considered to be rather controversial or contrarian figures within the wider field of scientific debate, despite having greatly distinguished themselves during their earlier careers as scientists. Smolin in particular is considered to be something of a maverick, particularly in the context of his polemic against string theory.[11] Within this context the speculative resonance between Nancean ontology and contemporary scientific theorizing are Smolin's challenge to the widespread Pythagoreanism or mathematical Platonism within modern theoretical physics and Penrose's reinsertion of probabilistic randomness into a renewed ontological understanding of quantum formalism.

Smolin, like Nancy, argues for a fully relationist picture of the universe. In *The Life of the Cosmos* he points out that most physical theories today are 'based on the point of view that the properties of things arise from relationships' (*LC*, p. 51). On this point he directly cites the phenomenon of quantum entanglement arguing that the 'entangled nature of the quantum state reflects something essential in the world' (*LC*, p. 252). Quantum entanglement tells us that the properties of matter at a fundamental level are deeply interdependent. For Smolin the empirical verification of quantum entanglement is 'one of those rare cases in which an experiment can be interpreted as a test of a philosophical principle' (*LC*, p. 252). So the quanta of quantum theory are in a strong sense always relational, that is, they have no existence prior to relation (as is born out most obviously in theories such as that developed by Smolin's sometime collaborator Carlo Rovelli).[12]

Smolin continues this defence of relationism in his more recent work, arguing in *Time Reborn* that 'every entity in the universe evolves dynamically in interaction with everything else' (*TR*, p. 116; this strongly recalls Nancy's '*co-appartenance essentielle de l'existence avec l'exister de toute chose*'). What is fundamental to the positions adopted by Smolin in *The Life of the Cosmos*, *Time Reborn*, and *The Singular Universe* is the argument that the universe as a whole needs to be understood temporally in its historical evolution and relational becoming and according to the paradigms which inform the *biological* understanding of phenomena. If the whole of the universe can be understood as a singular system or structure evolving in time, Smolin argues, then the 'laws of nature themselves, like the biological species, may not be eternal categories, but rather the creations of natural processes occurring in time' (*LC*, p. 18). The consequence of this insight into the temporal evolution of the cosmos understood as a relational structure is a radical calling into question of the pre-eminent role played by mathematics within modern physical and cosmological theory.

Smolin argues that scientific theory and practice has been underpinned or grounded by perspectives which are essentially theological in nature. He explicitly identifies this tendency with the privileging of mathematics and traces a trajectory that runs from Antiquity to the present day: 'From Pythagoras to string theory,' he suggests, 'the desire to comprehend nature has been framed by the Platonic ideal that the world is a reflection of some perfect mathematical form' (*LC*, p. 177). In *Time Reborn* he launches his full polemic against the metaphysical privileging of mathematics within physics. In the preface to this work he writes: 'If we believe that the task of physics is the discovery of a timeless mathematical equation that captures every aspect of the universe, then we believe that the truth of the universe lies outside the universe' (*TR*, p. xvi). Yet if, as Smolin argues, the universe is nothing other than a singular relational structure evolving dynamically in time, then there can be no such timeless perspective on or grounding of cosmological reality in some eternal mathematical structure.

Smolin's relational cosmos is one which is always evolving fundamentally and singularly *in time*. As Smolin puts it in *Time Reborn*:

> Logic and mathematics capture aspects of nature, but never the whole of nature. There are aspects of the real universe that will never be representable in mathematics. One of them is that in the real world it is always some particular moment. (*TR*, p. 246)

Mathematics, if you like, eviscerates reality of spatial and temporal particularity, and because relational reality is always and necessarily temporal, each time singularly so, the Platonic image of the universe as corresponding to a timeless mathematical object can never be correct.

As a working scientist Smolin recognizes, of course, that mathematics can and must remain an absolutely necessary and extremely powerful descriptive tool, a tool deployed within theoretical constructs or models which should be both predictive and verifiable. This view of mathematics is broadly in line with an intuitionist or constructivist understanding within the philosophy of mathematics and with the idea that mathematics itself maps or models physical reality (but in a never complete or totalizing manner). What this means, though, is that mathematics should never be held up as a royal road or exclusive gateway to a timeless truth that would somehow be situated outside the universe as its metaphysical foundation or its ultimate and eternal reality. In other words, mathematics can never offer an ontological or metaphysical ground and must therefore be stripped of the privilege conferred upon it in the Pythagorean vision in such a way that 'a deep chasm opens up between nature and mathematics' (*SU*, p. 141).

Smolin's (and Unger's) vision of a singular universe resonates strongly with Nancy's ontology of freedom and of being in the singular plural in a threefold manner. First and foremost, it is relational at the most fundamental level. Secondly, it poses the universe as a relationality which evolves dynamically in and as a simultaneous spatialization and temporalization which constitutes singular entities as such.[13] Lastly, this singular universe is entirely without substantive or metaphysical ground. Stripping the abstraction of mathematics of its 'hard' ontological status means that the temporal becoming of this singular universe is not underpinned by any timeless reality or foundation in ideal form. Its existence is its own essence, as Nancy would say. And just as Nancy's experience of freedom represents the impossibility of thought securing a ground or foundation within being, so, for Unger at least, the temporal becoming of the singular universe bears witness to 'our groundlessness — our inability to grasp the ground of being or existence' (*SU*, p. 102).

Roger Penrose, conversely, does not share Smolin's scepticism about the deep connection between mathematical forms and nature or the cosmos (he is a mathematical physicist). However, he does question the extent to which some contemporary physical theories put an inordinately high degree of faith in certain specific aspects of mathematical formalism. The 'objective reduction' theory (**OR**) he elaborates in *Fashion, Faith, and Fantasy* represents an original alternative to the 'many-worlds' interpretations of quantum formalism on the one hand, and to the Copenhagen interpretation on the other. It should be noted that Penrose's theory, although developed within a broader speculative gesture or ambition, also stands as a physical theory as such, that is to say, one which can be subject to empirical testing or be liable to falsification by experiment (and far more so, arguably, than Everett-inspired 'many worlds' theories). In this context Penrose's 'objective reduction' theory can also be read in such a way as to develop and deepen the resonance of Nancy's ontology of freedom with contemporary scientific speculative thinking and does so in relation to the fundamental temporality of physical reality.

In essence Penrose's **OR** theory is a questioning of the status accorded to the wave function (ψ) in quantum mechanics (**QM**) as described by the Schrödinger equation. To recapitulate the basics, what is at stake here is time, causality, and determinism. The quantum world, Penrose notes, differs from its macroscopic classical counterpart insofar as the equations of classical time evolution (referred to as **C**) no longer hold. The quantum world 'has a time evolution — which I denote by the letter **U**, standing for unitary evolution — described by a different equation, called the Schrödinger equation' (*FFF*, p. 142). According to the Schrödinger equation the evolution of the wave function, ψ, is unitary and linear such that **U** is 'a deterministic and local time evolution of the quantum state' (p. 142). Most importantly, ψ involves a superposition of quantum states. The constituent particles of ψ exist in different states simultaneously and are therefore said to be *superposed*. Superposition and deterministic, linear time evolution go hand in hand here, as Penrose puts it: 'this principle of quantum superposition of states is fundamental to the linearity of quantum evolution, which is itself central to the **U** time evolution of the quantum state' (p. 162). In his characterization of the quantum world according to the Schrödinger equation Penrose takes pains to highlight its scope and fundamental status. So, for instance he notes that 'the linearity of Schrödinger's evolution applies to quantum systems completely generally, no matter how many particles might be simultaneously involved' (p. 159). He also underlines what he calls 'the staggering universal scope of quantum linearity. A major feature of the formalism of quantum mechanics is, indeed, the linearity of **U**' p. 158).

Given this 'staggering universal scope of quantum linearity' it is not surprising that it is the exact status of ψ, and of quantum superposition in particular, that lies at the heart of the differing interpretations of **QM**. As anyone familiar with the basics of the 'quantum measurement problem' will know, the key question here is what occurs, or is occurring, when ψ collapses or 'decoheres' and the superposition of particles decays or resolves itself into one or other measurable alternative in the classical macroscopic world. This process is known as the reduction of the wave packet and Penrose refers to this as **R**: 'the effect of **R** is to replace the continuous evolution that **U** has provided us with, by a sudden jump to one of several possible **C** descriptions' (*FFF*, p. 142). So the quantum measurement problem refers to the fact that the state of a quantum system prior to measurement is a superposition of possible results, whereas, after the measurement, it has collapsed into a single result. This is the issue that lies at the heart of Schrödinger's famous cat-related thought experiment where the said feline is *both* alive and dead in a box (the two states being superposed) until the box is opened and it only then appears definitively as *either* alive or dead.

This strange and seemingly impossible situation can be interpreted in different ways. Many-worlds interpretations of **QM**, inspired by Hugh Everett, assume that the quantum superposition and the unitary and linear evolution of ψ, as described by the Schrödinger equation, are all ontologically real. In this context the superposition is a property of the real and not simply a balance of probabilities awaiting to be resolved by observation. When measurement occurs the observer simply views one branch of physical reality and the other state of the superposition constitutes (and continues its linear evolution in) another branch, another alternative possible universe, and one that is no less real, albeit entirely unobservable from our own universe. In essence the quantum measurement problem does not really exist in a many-worlds interpretation of **QM**.[14] Conversely the Copenhagen interpretation (associated with Niels Bohr) assumes that what ψ gives us is not a representation of reality but a 'calculational tool for working out probabilities' (*FFF*, p. 198). So that cat was always *either* alive or dead *in reality* and it is just that we did not know its state until the act of observation occurred. ψ does not, in itself, describe anything ontologically real but just gives a balance of probabilities for what will have turned out to have been real upon measurement or observation.

Penrose's **OR** theory provides a very interesting alternative to many-worlds and Copenhagen-style interpretations of **QM** and can be related to 'environmental decoherence' perspectives which hold that the quantum state of a system can never be isolated from its environment (*FFF*, p. 205). Penrose's key insight is that, at the core of the differing interpretations and strange overall status of **QM**, 'the essential problem is the linearity of **U**' (p. 206). The unitary and deterministic time evolution of the wave function has superposition as a fundamental trait which leads to all the paradoxes and problems of the quantum world. These problems hinge on the fundamental inconsistency between the unitary evolution of **U** and the break, hiatus, or interval enacted in the state reduction **R**. His solution to this problem is to assume that quantum states, being entangled with their environments, are always subjected to gravitational effects of the kind described by Einstein's theories, and, as he points out, in opposition to **U**-style quantum evolution, in Einsteinian gravitation 'the gravitational field itself is fundamentally *non*linear' (p. 208).

What Penrose does here is to hypothesize that gravitational effects have an impact on the collapse of quantum superpositions and do so *all the time* as the quantum state interacts with its environment such that, irrespective of whether measurement occurs or not, 'we find that quantum superpositions do not last forever' (*FFF*, p. 214). Superpositions, and the linear evolution of ψ, are subject to an intermittent spontaneous decay leading Penrose to propose that:

> *All* quantum state reductions arise as gravitation effects of the aforementioned type [i.e. spontaneous decay]. In many standard situations of quantum measurement, the main mass displacements would occur in the *environment*, entangled with the measuring device, and in this way the conventional 'environmental decoherence' viewpoint may acquire a consistent ontology. (*FFF*, p. 215)

According to this theory there would be a more or less constant, albeit intermittent, 'rapid spontaneous reduction of the state to one or another of the alternatives involved in the superposition' (*FFF*, p. 367). This would be occurring irrespective of whether a quantum system was observed or not, experimental observations being simply one specific type of interaction of the quantum state with its environment amongst many other mass displacement effects caused by the effects of gravitational fields. This leads Penrose to conclude that '*all* quantum state reductions (R) arise in the "OR" (objective reduction) way' (p. 354). In effect Penrose takes ψ, U, and R, *all* to be ontologically real and strikes a distinct path between the solutions offered by Everettian interpretations of QM (where U is real and R non-existent) and Copenhagen interpretations (where ψ and U express probabilities and only the results of R are *really* real).

It might be worth stepping back from all this to ask what the philosophical significance of Penrose's 'objective reduction' interpretation of quantum formalism is and, more specifically, what the exact form and status of its resonance with Nancy's ontology of freedom might be. In this context it can be noted that both Everettian and Copenhagan interpretations can broadly be aligned with very familiar philosophical positions. Many-worlds interpretations rely on a strongly realist interpretation of the Schrödinger equation, the unitary and linear evolution of ψ, and of the quantum superposition. As such they align with a realist or Platonist understanding of the status of mathematics (and with the Pythagoreanism that Smolin identifies as widespread in modern theoretical physics). So, despite the fact that the existence of other universes does not appear to be empirically testable their existence is necessarily inferred from the ontological faith placed in the Schrödinger equation itself. Thus many-worlds interpretations are metaphysically grounded in mathematical realism (i.e. in mathematical Platonism and a familiar hinterland of philosophical and metaphysical Platonism). Conversely, Copenhagen interpretations tend towards subjectivism. If ψ contains simply the observer's knowledge of the superposed particle as a balance of probabilities which is only resolved into a real or definite state upon measurement, then the 'reality', such as it is, becomes largely centred on the observer (suggesting a groundedness in subjective experience which is perhaps the most familiar hallmark of so much modern philosophy after Descartes and Kant). This has led some to go well beyond the Copenhagen interpretation to hypothesize that consciousness in and of itself causes the collapse of the wave function (the Von Neumann-Wigner interpretation of QM). So, on the one hand we have a metaphysical Platonism that posits a proliferation of empirically unverifiable universes and on the other a subject-centred philosophical perspective which, when taken to its extreme, appears to move in the direction of subjective idealism.

Penrose's OR theory, whilst it clearly accepts that the mathematical formalism of QM describes some kind of ontological reality, nevertheless and quite strongly places 'a limitation (as yet untested) to current quantum faith' (*FFF*, p. 215). The Schrödinger equation describes, or maps onto, one part of reality (ψ and U) but does not give the complete picture in the manner that the 'faith-like' mathematical Platonism of Everett interpretations assume. At the same time his theory rejects the subjectivism of the Copenhagen interpretation: 'R takes place out there in the world, and it is not something imposed upon the world, in some way, by virtue of a quantum system actually being observed by some conscious entity' (*FFF*, p. 370). The consistent realist ontology that **OR** theory gives to environmental decoherence perspectives on **QM** succeeds, like Nancy's relational ontology of 'freed' singular plurality, in giving a realist picture of what is 'out there' independent of human observation. Yet at the same time it can describe the ontological relationality which is the condition of human observation (in this case quantum measurement as just one possible instance of **R** which is always going on in the environment as the result of gravitational effects).

Moreover, **R** itself introduces a structure of hiatus, interval, or 'beginning anew' into the unitary and linear time-evolution of **U** and therefore introduces nonlinearity, initiality, and a degree of randomness into ontological reality and into what would otherwise be a purely causal and deterministic temporality. If, as Penrose notes, 'the gravitational field itself is *non*linear', and 'the U-violation that necessarily takes place in an objective **R**-process must be gravitationally based', then it becomes possible to talk of 'the random "choice" made by **OR**' (*FFF*, pp. 208, 384–85, 370). It may also be possible, as it were experimentally and by way of their resonance, to talk about the **R**-process in distinctly Nancean terms as a 'structure d'intervalle' which gives time as such and does so specifically as a 'structure d'intervalle [qui] définit un espacement d'espace et de temps' ('an interval structure that defines the spacing of space and time') (*EL*, p. 92; 67). Quantum superposition and the linear evolution of **U** do not, as Penrose hypothesizes, 'last forever' and are subjected to a constant non-deterministic 'rapid spontaneous reduction' due to gravitation effects within an entangled environment.

Can one really take the **R**-process here to be strongly resonant with the relationality and temporality described by Nancy's ontology of freedom in its alignment with Kant's cosmological freedom ('the faculty of beginning a state from itself')? With the ontological faith in the Schrödinger equation as a complete description of fundamental reality overturned or otherwise suspended, Penrose's **OR** theory describes a reality in which, at the most primordial level, linear and deterministic, causal processes are subjected to constant hiatus by nonlinear and random reductions of ψ and of quantum superpositions: unitary time-evolution ceaselessly and spontaneously collapses and starts again because of the 'random "choice" made by **OR**'. Temporal evolution does not find a metaphysical ground in, as Smolin says, 'the discovery of a timeless mathematical equation that captures every aspect of the universe' (*TR*, p. xvi) but rather is continuously ungrounded in a becoming which is composed by the intimate conjunction of the multiple, local, and unitary time evolutions of **U** *and* the rapid, spontaneous, and random outcomes of **R**. This arguably describes an at least very similar structure to that of Nancean ontological freedom as it was elaborated earlier (albeit in very different, scientific-theoretical terms). In this way Nancy's ontology of freedom not only strongly resonates with the physical theory of **OR**, but may appear as a doubling (without necessarily any exact identity) of physical theory within speculative philosophical discourse. In this doubling the realism of Nancy's ontology takes on a sharper profile just as the ontology of Penrose's **OR** theory takes on a more consistently philosophical form.

* * * * *

In *The Life of the Cosmos* Smolin argues that, when it comes to contemporary physics and the limits of our knowledge, 'it is possible, indeed, I would argue necessary, to speculate. Because we cannot invent when we cannot conceive, the construction of a new theory must involve, or perhaps be preceded by, attempts to imagine the outcome' (*LC*, p. 5). Similarly Penrose argues that:

> There are some key aspects to the nature of our actual universe that are so exceptionally odd [...] that if we do not indulge in what may appear to be outrageous flights of fantasy, we shall have no chance at all of coming to terms with what may well be an extraordinary fantastical-seeming underlying truth. (*FFF*, p. xii)

Both are acutely aware that science operates constantly at the limits of what it knows, and that speculation, imagination, or fantasy are both necessary, and perhaps even inevitable, when it comes to thinking or theorizing at that limit. In this context the resonance of Nancy's 'thinking at the limit' with the scientific theories of Smolin and Penrose needs to be understood, not as a mutual or reciprocal conferring of authority or identity between scientific and philosophical discourse. Rather the relation between philosophy and science here is one of a specific set of open, speculative, and non(-self)-identical resonances which might allow us to guide the imaginings and fantasies that may necessarily take place at the limits of thought and knowledge.

On the one hand, the metaphysical and philosophical ideas embedded in scientific theory can be uncovered, clarified, and perhaps even deconstructed from the perspectives of philosophy. On the other, the ontological thinking about reality 'out there' produced by philosophy can be formally clarified, examined, *and recast* from perspectives drawn from scientific theory. Each has their own source of authority such as it is: the authority of an *experience* of thought on the one hand, and, on the other, of a scientifically informed theorizing that sets agendas for empirical verification and experimentation. The resonance between science and philosophy, *such as it is*, should be understood as a conceptually rigorous operator within the necessary and inevitable, speculative, imaginative, and fantastical dimensions of both as they unfold at their limits. Speculation, imagination, and fantasy, if they *are* necessary at these limits, should not be arbitrary or untethered from the experiences of thought embedded in both philosophical and scientific traditions. Indeed, they can perhaps take place most rigorously within the perspectives opened up by the resonances that can be struck between these traditions. Revisiting Nancy's *L'Expérience de la liberté* today, therefore, is less about posing limits as a mode of limitation for philosophical thought and scientific knowledge and far more about the opening of both onto an existence freed from the legacy and prejudices of metaphysical grounding or foundation.

Notes to Chapter 8

1. Jean-Luc Nancy, *L'Expérience de la liberté* (Paris: Galilée, 1988); *The Experience of Freedom*, trans. by B. Macdonald (Stanford, CA: Stanford University Press, 1993); this work subsequently referred to as *EL* in the main text; Immanuel Kant, *The Critique of Pure Reason*, trans. by Paul Guyer and Alan W. Wood (Cambridge: Cambridge University Press, 1998), p. 397 (A317/B374).

2. Martin Heidegger, *Kant and the Problem of Metaphysics*, trans. by Richard Taft (Bloomington: Indiana University Press, 1990).

3. See Jean-Luc Nancy, *Logodeadalus: le discours de la syncope* (Paris: Aubier-Flammarion, 1976). For a critical discussion of questions of subjectivity and temporality related to Descartes, Kant, and Heidegger see Ian James, *The Fragmentary Demand: An Introduction to the Philosophy of Jean-Luc Nancy* (Stanford, CA: Stanford University Press, 2006), pp. 26–63.

4. See also Jean-Luc Nancy, *L'Impératif catégorique* (Paris: Flammarion, 1983).

5. Kant, *The Critique of Pure Reason*, p. 533.

6. Nancy argues very clearly that formal ontology has a choice between two alternatives. Either Being is unique and absorbs all the common substance of the beingness of beings to a unified principle or, there is no being apart from each singular, and therefore unboundedly plural, existence. See *EL*, pp. 91–92; 66–67.

7. For a further development of this argument see Ian James, *The Technique of Thought: Nancy, Laruelle, Malabou and Stiegler After Naturalism* (Minneapolis: Minnesota University Press, 2019), pp. 55–119.

8. Ibid.

9. Lee Smolin, *The Life of the Cosmos* (Oxford: Oxford University Press, 1997); *Time Reborn* (London: Allen Lane, 2013); Lee Smolin and Roberto Mangabeira Unger, *The Singular Universe and the Reality of Time: A Proposal in Natural Philosophy* (Cambridge: Cambridge University Press, 2015); these works subsequently referred to as *LC*, *TR*, and *SU* respectively in the main text.

10. Roger Penrose, *Fashion, Faith, and Fantasy in the New Physics of the Universe* (Princeton, NJ: Princeton University Press, 2016); this work subsequently referred to as *FFF* in the main text.

11. I discuss Smolin's place and reputation in the wider field of science debate and also assess his positions in relation to wider debates within the philosophies of science and mathematics in *The Technique of Thought*, pp. 100-06.

12. Carlo Rovelli, 'Relational Quantum Mechanics', *International Journal of Theoretical Physics*, 35.8 (1996), 1637–78.

13. Smolin and Unger differ somewhat on their exact understanding of the structure of time, with Unger endorsing a notion of becoming that is perhaps closer to Nancy; see *SU*, pp. 518–21.

14. David Wallace, *The Emergent Multiverse* (Oxford: Oxford University Press, 2012), p. 1. Wallace's work is a trenchant defence of the Everettian many-worlds interpretation of **QM**.

CHAPTER 9

Stiegler:
The Freedom of Necessity

Martin Crowley

For a philosopher primarily associated with the constitutive technicity of the form of life called human, and whose work derives initially from the phenomenological and post-phenomenological tradition, Bernard Stiegler makes surprisingly frequent use of a lexicon more associated with existentialism and Kantian moral philosophy: the language of autonomy, of agential sovereignty, responsibility, and freedom. The reason for this is straightforwardly contextual: in Stiegler's analysis, we currently face a critical moment in the history of our relation to technology, in which our tendency to reduce this relation to one of automation and delegation threatens the definitive atrophy of the alternative tendency to adopt technology in more sustaining ways, sacrificed to the short-termist, addictive pleasures of financial speculation. Against this, for Stiegler we need to secure forms of agency through which we might fight for the possibility of constructive, nurturing relations to technical forms: and so his processual understanding of the co-constitution of the human and the technical is enhanced by an at times explicitly Enlightenment language of autonomy and responsibility. The constitutive relation between the two dimensions means that this language is more than a veneer, however: to be properly consistent, Stiegler has to provide an account of how such agency is formed within the flux of individuation that forms his overall framework. The purpose of the current essay is to explore this account, and to set out how its different aspects configure the respective shares of autonomy and heteronomy, or freedom and necessity, in their part of the process.

As Christina Howells shows in her definitive study, Sartre's progressive thickening of the contraints of situation into the weight of the practico-inert nevertheless preserves the *necessity of freedom*, as what Howells calls 'the little gap', or *décalage*, between the internalization and re-externalization of conditioning factors.[1] Stiegler is similarly concerned with something like this *décalage*; and this is of course no coincidence. From the 1940s of Sartre's *L'Être et le néant* [Being and Nothingness], in fact, via the 1960s bookended by his *Critique de la raison dialectique* [Critique of Dialectical Reason] and (for our immediate purposes, as will be seen below) Deleuze's *Logique du sens* [Logic of Sense], to the early twenty-first century which forms the context of Stiegler's interventions, French philosophy has repeatedly found itself wrestling with the relation between situation and event, necessity and freedom; or, to put it another way, with the question of how change is possible. Sartre's shift towards a more strongly dialectical account of contextual determination took place against the backdrop of the structuralist refusal of voluntarism; if the insurrections of the late 1960s gave a new lease of life to spontaneist fantasies, their failure left those still eager for radical change seeking its possibility in the internal mutations of process and flux (Deleuze-Guattari, Lyotard), more or less messianic theorizations of the irruptive event (Badiou), post hoc descriptions of revolutionary subjectivation (Rancière), or neo-Lucretian elaborations of the *clinamen* and its accidental possibilities (Althusser). In this context, Stiegler can be understood as aiming in similar fashion to keep open the possibility of transformative agency within a generally processual account of psycho-social-technical individuation. For Stiegler, as we will see, interiority and exteriority are mutually constituted in a recursive loop, the agent is constituted in its performative assumption of the possibilities opened by the technical forms with which it has been co-individuated, and freedom is generated in this dynamic. This would be the form into which Stiegler morphs Sartre's 'little gap', now articulated *within* a larger process of psycho-social-technical individuation. From the *necessity of freedom*, perhaps, to the *freedom of necessity*: the margin of autonomy opened and maintained by and within the constitutively processual.

Our guiding questions, accordingly, will be the following. What is the structure, or perhaps better, the *rhythm* of responsibility at work here? What, for Stiegler, is the relation between emergence and agency, or constitutive technicity and the will? How does Stiegler insist both that we are produced through processes which logically and chronologically precede us, and that we are charged with responsibility for taking care of ourselves and others, in part by acting into these very processes? How, exactly, are we — heads full of garbage, outsourced beyond our control — to care for the conditions of our own possibility?

Autonomy and Technics; or Freedom, of Necessity

The broad context of this problematic is accordingly Stiegler's understanding of the co-constitution of the form of life we call human, on the one hand, and the technical forms along with which this form of life is individuated, on the other: partly because this is where we see the constitutive role of the relation to technical forms in its fundamental aspect, and partly because already here, Stiegler sets up a relation of mutual implication — or in his terms, *composition* — between what we might be tempted to think of as heteronomy and autonomy.

In Stiegler's account, as established in his reading of Heidegger and Leroi-Gourhan across the first volume of *La Technique et le temps* [Technics and Time], what we call human existence is constituted by the intergenerational transmission of technical forms, which Stiegler describes as the locus of external inorganic memory. This process, which he terms 'epiphylogenesis', allows subsequent generations to inherit the memory of a past they have not lived: encoded in the forms of the objects in question, this memory no longer dies with particular biological individuals, and thereby opens a relation to the deep, immemorial past and the impersonal future.[2] There is here perhaps a paleoanthropological version of what Sartre describes in the *Critique de la raison dialectique* as the 'practico-inert', namely the sedimentation of lived human praxes into impersonal forms and institutions, which in turn come to form the context and conditions of live activity.[3] Where Sartre typically (and somewhat Romantically) sees a struggle between the quicksand of the practico-inert and the vitality of current activity, however, for Stiegler this relation is fundamentally enabling. It is thanks to epiphylogenesis that a relation to time opens as recollection and anticipation: we might even say that without this dimension, the structure of projection which underpins an understanding of human action such as Sartre's would be simply unthinkable. Where Sartre thinks in terms of a dynamic and constitutive opposition between external forms and agential capacity, for Stiegler the constitutive force of these forms is deeper and more intimate: rather than a limit to be negotiated in the play of internalization and externalization that is human agency, they already give the very possibility of something like this play in the first place.

More like Sartre's dynamic of freedom and external constraint is the rhythm of heteronomy and decision found in Stiegler's account of the process through which a particular technical regime is adopted by a collectivity. If the general context of epiphylogenesis forms agency in time, that agency is called to exercise itself in the properly political mechanisms required by the fact of periodic technical change; and here, we accordingly see something more akin to a Sartrean assumption of the constraints and possibilities of situation. According to Stiegler, the arrival of a new technical form produces effects of shock and suspension: of what Stiegler calls *épokhè*. Stiegler's use of this term draws more on the sceptical sense of a 'suspension of judgement' than on the 'phenomenological reduction' it names for Husserl; but Stiegler is also alluding to the everyday sense of an epoch as the opening of an era. For the collective which comes into existence with this new form — with which it is, in Stiegler's Simondonian lexicon, co-individuated — now has a choice: just how is it going to adopt this form? How will the two turn out to have been co-individuated? If the possible agency of this collective is far from unlimited here, constituted as it is in its relation to the form in question, it remains significantly operative: in Stiegler's account, the initial shock and suspension of prevailing conditions produced by the form's arrival can themselves to an extent be suspended by the collective's decision to adopt this new technical regime as beneficially formative. In this process, which Stiegler calls 'epokhal redoubling', we thus see a recursive moment of decision, in which the agency formed through a wholly external process of co-individuation grasps the new technical regime with which it has emerged, assuming its constraints and possibilities and defining itself through this act.[4]

Here, then, we can see the necessity of situation negotiated by agential freedom; and politically, for Stiegler, we might say that freedom just is the possibility of such negotiation — of the pharmacological decisions we take as to the mode in which we will adopt the technical regime with which we have been co-individuated as a collective. In the current context to which Stiegler addresses his writings, this plays out as the struggle between automation and agential autonomy. Not quite as starkly as this: as we will see, in Stiegler's account the tendencies to which we might give these shorthand labels are less opposed than interdependent. Nonetheless, autonomy, duly qualified, is a value for Stiegler here, and automation, as currently practised, a disaster. The algorithmic interpretation of my mind's wandering through time (most obviously in the processing of my online history) sees my secondary retentions (what I might remember, i.e. select, as significant) replaced by pseudo-individualized tertiary retentions (i.e. external memory) amenable to integration into the calculations of finance and governance.[5] The horizon of this, for Stiegler, is the 'annihilation' of the time of reflection, as the social formation of the capacity to pay attention (to do the work of selection and reflection, precisely) is delegated to external programmes, the 'subject' needing to maintain only a low-level, physiological vigilance entirely reliant on the successful operation of these programmes for its relation to what we used to call the world (PS, pp. 183–89; 100–03). In the absence of any meaningful reinternalization of all this externalization, we are ensnared in technological networks beyond our understanding; at which point, further delegation looks like our only option (PS, p. 240; 134), and we find ourselves inhabiting a reductively cybernetic milieu of marketing-led stimulus and response (PS, pp. 188, 230–31; 103, 128).

Against this background, Stiegler wants us explicitly to assume our Kantian inheritance: to understand this tendency to unidirectional delegation as a kind of learned helplessness, a lazy, cowardly abandonment of that aspiration to rational maturity Kant celebrates in 'A Reply to the Question: "What is Enlightenment?"' (PS, pp. 43, 98; 20–21, 51). Through inventing a new industrial model, this mature reason can sustain the responsibility needed to combat the financially-driven short-circuiting of our formative processes: in what would be precisely an example of beneficial 'epokhal redoubling', we can decide to adopt the digital algorithmic technologies whose advent has opened our world in such a way as to nurture both the generations to come (whom it is our responsibility to liberate from these short circuits into long circuits of intergenerational transmission) and the conditions of possibility of this very responsibility (PS, pp. 46–47, 77; 22, 39). Stiegler sees such a decision at work in those groups — notably, online communities — already practising an alternative relation to these technologies: as new figures of the amateur, relaunching the impulse of the learned societies of Kant's Enlightenment, these groupings are inventing new ways to take and share responsibility, new understandings of rational maturity.[6] And if this is possible, in the face of the wholesale delegation of these capacities to financially-integrated forms of automation, it is because mature reason always has potential access to the will and the possibility of acting autonomously. This access is far from guaranteed, given our lazy, cowardly tendency to outsource these capacities (not to mention their constitutive dependence on the exteriority of technicity); and it is true that for Stiegler, they can always be renounced, damaged, or even stifled at source. But they are always available, if only potentially, to 'non-inhuman' existence, inasmuch as this form of existence is characterized by the relation to time opened by epiphylogenesis: as the inheritance of external inorganic memory situates us between recollection and anticipation, the relation to the future remains irreducible: and the future — the future as such, indeterminate and irreducible to all calculability — can only be *willed* (that is to say: it cannot be programmed). The deep structure of the form of life called human gives us access, if only potentially, to the will we need to take care of this future's possibility.

In Stiegler's ecology, there is no formation of the mind other than epiphylogenetic, that is to say, via the inherited technical forms which not only expose this mind to its constitutive exteriority, but are also themselves exposed to the high degree of heteronomy entailed in the social, historical, economic, and political accidents to which they are subject (*EC*, p. 315; 195). In place of the metaphysical definition of subjectivity in terms of an opposition between internal and external, Stiegler thus offers the emergence of noesis in the spiralling movement between internalization and externalization (*PS*, p. 280; 156; *EC*, p. 183, n. 1; 249, n. 11), in which autonomy is no longer opposed to heteronomy, but rather constituted by its adoption of heteronomy as its condition of possibility.[7] For Stiegler, accordingly, we need an understanding of our intellectual and ethical agency (in his terms: of responsibility, autonomy, and reason; of desire, and of the will) in which this agency is inseparable from its technical heteronomy (*EC*, pp. 161, 168–69, 173; 96, 100, 103). Only on this basis will it be possible to articulate a constructive relation between responsibility and technological forms (a relation which otherwise remains the static opposition which favours mere delegation and so exploitation), to practise 'epokhal redoubling' in the mode of positive pharmacology, to inhabit the process of psycho-social formation through technics in such a way as to sustain the possibility of a non-inhuman future.

Emergent Responsibility

So far, then, we have seen that Stiegler views the form of life called human as constituted through its relation to the external inorganic memory encoded in technical forms, that he grants human collectives the ability to make decisions about how to adopt these forms, and that he argues strongly for contemporary practices in which digital algorithmic technologies would be adopted in ways more beneficial than toxic. In terms of our guiding question as to the relation between freedom and necessity, we now need to look further at just how Stiegler conceptualizes the agency on which this ecology depends; we will do this by exploring in more detail the discussions of responsibility that, as we have already seen, come to the fore in his work between 2008 and 2012, namely in *Prendre soin* and *États de choc*.

Many of Stiegler's formulations of agency in these works, notably with reference to the question of responsibility, can easily be read as strongly affirmative of the capacity to act and the moral charge this implies: this is usually what his invocations of Kant, and the Enlightenment more broadly, serve to articulate. Discussing his 'critique of stupidity' in an interview, for example, he describes this as 'an ethics and a praxis against laziness, an ethics and a praxis of courage'.[8] This explicitly Kantian rejection of laziness and promotion of courage is unthinkable without an accompanying belief in an agential capacity to make meaningful decisions in relation to these forms of behaviour. As *États de choc* makes clear, responsibility of any kind is thinkable only on the basis of such capacity: the possibility of responsibility depends on the possibility of formulating alternative forms of action (*EC*, p. 172; 102). It is accordingly in these highly Kantian terms that we should understand a call such as that in *Prendre soin* to assume our responsibility for intergenerational transmission (*PS*, p. 23; 8): if we can be called to such responsibility, it is because we are agents capable of such action. The forces threatening this transmission are those seeking to cultivate a generalized lack of responsibility via the delegation of agential capacities to forms of automation: the goal being to produce a consumer without consciousness or conscience ('la conscience'), which Stiegler defines as the locus of free will, and the capacity for moral and cognitive autonomy (*PS*, p. 327; 184). Ironically, of course, those manipulating such forces demonstrate in these very actions precisely the agential capacity they are seeking to undo, thereby indicating despite themselves its irreducibility: this is of course why their actions are ultimately self-destructive, and the war they are waging a form of blindness (*EC*, p. 237; 146), for all their current lack of punishment (*EC*, p. 287; 177).

Even in the context of the composite and processual formation of the site of any such agency (i.e. the capacity for mature reason of the non-inhuman being, or what Stiegler, in Aristotelian vein, habitually calls the 'noetic soul'), Stiegler emphasizes the importance of a decision in favour of its responsible exercise. Again in Kantian vein, on the constant temptation to immaturity, to the neglect of one's responsibility (the 'intermittence' of the noetic soul, its lived reality as emergent within a process of individuation-disindividuation), he stresses that it is necessary to know this temptation, if one is to be able to fight against it (*PS*, p. 298, n. 2; 228, n. 17).[9] From the force of his repeated injunctions, it is hard to resist the impression that Stiegler considers us capable of bearing full responsibility for our actions, however heteronomous their conditions of possibility. For example: intermittent noesis imposes an *obligation* to activate its potential (*PS*, p. 300; 168); we are charged with the *responsibility* of elevating our drives to the level of desires (*PS*, p. 304; 170); taking care means believing that something better can *and must* be brought into existence (*PS*, p. 318; 179). If these imperatives appear to dramatize a leap from fact to value, from 'is' to 'ought', Stiegler's understanding of retention would oblige us to revisit the terms of this distinction, inasmuch as the selection (retention) of any 'fact' would already be entangled in the skein of those existing retentions (primary, secondary, and tertiary) by — or indeed against — whose criteria it comes to stand out as significant. But more important, for our purposes, are the reflections they invite on Stiegler's configuration of the relation between heteronomy and autonomy.

For as we have seen, Stiegler is more aware than most of the constitutive heteronomy of the agents he is interpellating in this way. The strongest instance of this comes, I think, in a passage considering neural plasticity: here, Stiegler argues that 'social organization' is written into an individual's brain, and so, via this individual, directs his or her physiological organs (*PS*, p. 123; 66). If this crucial 'via' stops this short of the determinism it might seem to imply, it clearly nonetheless poses significant challenges to any thought of strong autonomy. As do references to the historical action of such factors as biopower (which has reduced 'non-inhumankind' to a set of demographic features managed according to criteria of financial viability (*PS*, p. 320; 180)), the world (which has unleashed 'impersonal forces' against itself (*EC*, p. 23; 9)), speculative capital (as fighting a war against investment (*EC*, p. 200; 121)), or the consumerist hyper-industrial model (as imposing 'generalized proletarianization', i.e. exclusion from participation in the circuits of knowledge-production that make life fulfilling (*EC*, pp. 211–12; 129)). In these, as in many other instances, Stiegler follows the standard rhetorical practice of granting agency to anonymous processes. In his case, however, this is more than rhetoric: such statements are part of what emerges as a complex negotiation of the question of agency, between the systemic-processual and the individual-agential. And part of that negotiation entails insisting on the former at the expense of the latter, even to the point, it would seem, of ruling out just the sort of agential sovereignty an emphasis on strong responsibility might be thought to require. How can Stiegler reconcile these dimensions?

In Stiegler's account, explicitly derived from Simondon, the individual 'I' is not thought as a starting-point: the starting-point is the process of individuation from which such an 'I' may emerge (*PS*, p. 114; 60–61), possibly only for a while, given that the disindividuation to which this 'I' may at any moment be subject is not an object of the will, but an irreducible product of the pharmacological facticity of this process (*EC*, p. 105; 61). If disindividuation is not the object of my will, it might seem reasonable — and wholly consistent with Stiegler's emphasis on the primacy of process — to conclude that individuation is similarly something from which I may emerge, but which is quite radically not of my doing. At which point, the (perhaps briefly) individuated 'I', struggling to articulate a constructive process of individuation (say, to impose a relation to tertiary retentions which would shift the process of epiphylogenesis towards long intergenerational circuits), or indeed the noetic soul fighting the temptation of disindividuation, might be thought to be up against impossible odds, indeed making a category mistake: attempting to intervene in a process of which she is not the agent but rather the occasional effect. There is no 'sovereign' agent for Stiegler: this is both a general principle (thanks to the heteronomy introduced by constitutive technicity) and a local, contingent truth (thanks to the financial exploitation of this irreducible heteronomy). So how, exactly, are we to act? Is this a leap of faith? An act of will against a background of radical, constitutive exteriority? *Who*, exactly, are we, if we can be called upon to act *in and through* this heteronomy?

As we have seen, there is in Stiegler's thinking a delicate, even fragile dance between the poles of autonomy and heteronomy which make up the composite that is non-inhuman being. On the question of individuation, for example, he starts from the primacy of process, but nonetheless introduces points of *individual* agency into the flow. The consequences of this are particularly clear in Stiegler's frequent use of the image of the 'quantum leap' in relation to the process of individuation. The quantum leap is, he says (crediting Simondon with this insight) 'the full [*plénière*] modality of individuation' (*T*, p. 47): that is, individuation entails an apparently discontinuous change of state akin to that exhibited by electrons during atomic electron transition. It would be odd, shall we say, to credit the electron in its later quantum state with having brought about its transition to that state: accordingly, this would seem to present individuation as a process independent of the agency of the individuated being, group, or technical form. This is supported by Stiegler's purely processual descriptions of individuation, such as emphasis on constitutive technicity as 'that which constitutes the very process of the phase-shift' (*T*, p. 53), or on invention as a form of infra- and extra-rational quantum leap within individuation (*EC*, p. 134; 79). Against these, however, we can find uses of the image to express the role of individual agency within individuation. In *États de choc*, he describes the individual — against a background of processual disindividuation as the suspension of a previous individuation — as *accomplishing* a quantum leap by crossing a threshold in his or her psychic trans-formation (*EC*, p. 104; 61); elsewhere, he describes those of us 'who still attempt to do philosophy' as belonging to a process 'that would open us up to the possibility of effecting a *leap* in individuation and thus to realize a transindividuation' (*T*, p. 47). Here, against the purely processual versions of the quantum jump, the leap does seem to be akin to a leap of faith: against a background that is beyond my control, I *decide* to jump — or at least, I have the ability to make such a decision.

Against both of these tendencies in Stiegler's descriptions stand instances where the agency behind any such decision remains indeterminate; and it is to these that we should look as we begin to approach some degree of resolution to this issue. One possibility might be to decide that Stiegler shares out heteronomy and autonomy between a constitutive exteriority, on the one hand, and a voluntaristic capacity for action, on the other. But this can hardly be satisfactory, given the dangers of such a separation (namely: lazy delegation to automata) to which he draws our attention. Which means that we have to go further than simply acknowledging autonomy's adoption of heteronomy as its condition of possibility, as mentioned above: the heteronomy-autonomy composite must, in fact, extend beyond the *formation* of the site of agency, and into its *exercise*.[10] But how, in this case, can Stiegler maintain his insistence on conscious free will, on moral and cognitive autonomy? For the beginnings of an answer, we might look to the notion advanced particularly in *États de choc* of the act of will as *performative* (*EC*, pp. 248–49; 153). Emerging from the composite of heteronomy and autonomy that is the process of individuation, the responsible agent *improvises her own capacitation*, that is: *arrives in and as* a site of action and, in acting, finds the capacity to act. The future-perfect temporality of the performative allows Stiegler to affirm agency as what emerges with an agent through a process of individuation, as what her actions *on the basis of* this process *will have disclosed*, and which she may retroactively assume. If this puts considerable pressure on any standard conception of agency in terms of free will, autonomy, and so on, it is wholly necessary if we are to sustain agency as an operative notion in the context of its constitutive exteriority, without separating the two out into discrete moments (formation on the one hand, exercise on the other). Stiegler's endeavours can thus be devoted to developing what he calls an 'individuating performativity' (*EC*, p. 160; 95), without this compromising either the processual nature of individuation, or the agency required for determinate intervention, and without the two having to be naïvely separated. As Stiegler puts it, the noetic soul 'expand[s] its sense in exclaiming it symbolically', and so becomes the noetic soul it has to be to perform this expansion. Stiegler continues: 'This noetic expansion of sense is what Simondon calls psychic and collective individuation. It is this process' (*T*, p. 50). Agent and process are transductively and performatively produced: at which point, the will is no longer the faculty of a self-positing, self-grounding subject, but rather what is secreted by a process of psycho-social individuation, emerging along with this newly crystallized, quite possibly evanescent agent.

While its future-perfect formulation suggests obvious similarities to the forward-flung Sartrean project, the looping, recursive shape of this performative dynamic is particularly identified by Stiegler with the model of transformative agency Deleuze derives from his reading of the Stoics in *Logique du sens*: namely with what Deleuze calls the 'quasi-cause'. Since the world is not of my making, the question for moral philosophy can only be: what relation am I to assume to its radically prior facticity? Against the course of *ressentiment* (which consumes its energies in railing against the way things happen to be, and holds itself prisoner in the vortex of pleasure this affords), Deleuze finds in Stoicism the following imperative: 'Ou bien la morale n'a aucun sens, ou bien c'est cela qu'elle veut nous dire, elle n'a rien d'autre à dire: ne pas être indigne de ce qui nous arrive' ('Either ethics makes no sense at all, or this is what it means, and this alone: not to be unworthy of what happens to us').[11] Not being unworthy of what happens turns out to mean finding in what happens (the mere 'accident', in Deleuze's terminology) the sense of its pure event, willing the event not resignedly but extractively: 'vouloir l'événement, c'est d'abord en dégager l'éternelle vérité, comme le feu auquel il s'alimente' ('willing the event is, primarily, to release its eternal truth, like the fire on which it is fed'); and so the imperative becomes, 'Arriver à cette volonté que nous fait l'événement' ('attaining this will that the event creates in us'), such that 'ce vouloir atteint au point où la guerre est menée contre la guerre' ('this will reaches the point at which war is waged against war') (*LS*, pp. 174–75; 148–49, translation modified). In the quasi-cause, then, we have a model of combative assumption in which agents are constituted by their relation to the situation and the action within which they happen to emerge: constituted, that is, in and by their performance of this relation — or what Deleuze calls 'une sorte de saut sur place de tout le corps' ('a sort of standing jump by the whole body') (*LS*, p. 175; 149, translation modified). Leaping without going anywhere, I emerge as capable of displacing the sense of my context inasmuch as 'I' am simply the site of this displacement, which may or may not come about: if it will have taken place, 'I' will have emerged as the quasi-cause of my situation. Deleuze's delightfully childish image of jumping on the spot gives this possibility a lightness that allows it to float free of all dour heroics, reconfiguring the accident through the performative magic of a game: in a hop and a skip, I may turn out to have performed a quantum leap.

In Stiegler's hands, as we might expect, this model is translated into the terms of epokhal redoubling, and so becomes the name of an active relation to the possible modes of existence opened by technical forms: the transformation of contingent situation into necessity, the assumption of this necessity, and the endeavour to reconfigure the possibilities this offers. Stiegler thus writes: 'Nous ne *faisons* cette forme de vie *effectivement* nôtre qu'en y inscrivant de nouveaux circuits de transindividuation par des *bifurcations* — par où nous devenons les quasi-causes de cette nécessité' ('We *make* this form of life *effectively* our own only by inscribing into it new circuits of transindividuation, via *bifurcations* — through which we become the quasi-causes of this necessity').[12] For Stiegler, then, the pharmacological challenge of epokhal redoubling entails inventing the necessity of the accident (*SA*, p. 209; 115), seeking to become its quasi-cause (*SA*, p. 138; 73): the 'blind necessity' of the accident can be *overturned* quasi-causally (*SA*, p. 133; 70), and our current ordeal consists in 'la dés-intégration totale et le renversement quasi-causal que tout cela requiert' ('total dis-integration, and [...] the quasi-causal inversion that all this requires') (*SA*, p. 121; 64). In this we might even conceivably find our quasi-causal freedom: for Stiegler, as for Sartre, freedom is a question of the adoption and elaboration of an always-prior constraint.

If we now connect this use of the quasi-cause back to Stiegler's model of epokhal redoubling, what we can see is that Stiegler develops an historical temporality composed of breaks — the accident, or the suspension produced by the shock of a new technical form — and their active assumption as opening a new time. And so a possible historical agent crystallizes out of technical change.[13] As individuation is an ongoing, indeed never-ending, process, the emergent agent is moreover in a position to perform her agency by acting *into* this historical process, relaunching it anew, improvising in complete ignorance of its next phase, which is in part to say: of where, how, and indeed whether she will subsequently re-emerge. This, then, is indeed how the heteronomy-autonomy composite extends beyond the formation of the site of agency, and into its exercise: our world-historical responsibility, in Stiegler's terms, is to participate in the invention of new processes of individuation with which to oppose our deathly, unilateral outsourcing, all the while understanding that doing so means exposing ourselves to the radically unpredictable discontinuity of the quantum leap. As Stiegler puts it, 'I put forth my capacity for individuation [...] insofar as it is inscribed at the heart of a *process* that invents itself and in which I attempt to *participate* as an inventor' (*T*, p. 48). This is what Stiegler means by describing the philosophical conception of metastability as Simondon's central contribution to the philosophy of freedom (of autonomy and responsibility) (*EC*, p. 127; 75): first, that from out of a situation of long-term irresolution, there can emerge both a possible agent and a critical moment of decision which opens the incalculable future and so retroactively transforms the situation as a whole, the story of what it will have been; and second, that the long-term stability of the metastable situation allows the meaningful performance of agency, while its underlying instability orientates this performance towards the risk and possibility of the empty future.[14] In sum: we emerge into and as the site of a capacity to act as the result of a process of individuation in which part of the potential of the technics supporting a historical, pre-individual milieu has been actualized; improvising, jumping on the spot, emerge as agents by performing this capacity, acting into this milieu, seeking to participate in the invention of a new moment of individuation; in the event of such an invention, we might re-emerge, transformed, across the space of a quantum leap.

In the Little Gap, a Little Leap

Stiegler's understanding of agency thus encompasses quite a spectrum, across which we have seen different weightings at work in the composition of autonomy and heteronomy, freedom and necessity. If his commitment to constitutive technicity clearly rules out metaphysical fantasies of uncompromised sovereign interiority, Stiegler nonetheless allows for collective decision-making as to the adoption of technical forms, and calls strongly for these decisions to be taken responsibly through the courageous use of mature reason. Given that commitment, however, he also understands that such responsibility must be conceptualized as emergent within purely processual dynamics of individuation; his solution to this is to think its agential site through the twin logics of performativity and the quasi-cause. Consistent with this purely processual understanding, finally, he models the possibility of decisive change as ultimately not within the gift of his emergent agents, whose action consists not in determining the future, but in acting into the flux of tendencies, hoping to promote the beneficial shift they seek. At which point, the spectrum forms not so much a line as a loop: the point of the rational, deliberative, conscious decision-making processes of epokhal redoubling is precisely to enable modes of technological adoption likely to maintain the ongoing possibility of new forms of individuation, keeping open the possibility of the incalculable as the possibility of the future as such. What Stiegler offers us in these terms would accordingly be something like politics as a rational commitment to the incalculable emergence of agency in the *décalage* between necessity and freedom, between the accident and its quasi-cause — in the tiny leap of a hopeful performance.

Notes to Chapter 9

1. Christina Howells, *Sartre: The Necessity of Freedom* (Cambridge: Cambridge University Press, 1988), p. 181.
2. Bernard Stiegler, *La Technique et le temps, 1: La Faute d'Épiméthée* (Paris: Galilée, 1994); *Technics and Time, 1: The Fault of Epimetheus*, trans. by Richard Beardsworth and George Collins (Stanford, CA: Stanford University Press, 1998).
3. Jean-Paul Sartre, *Critique de la raison dialectique, précédé de Questions de méthode, 1: Théorie des ensembles pratiques* (Paris: Gallimard, 1960); *Critique of Dialectical Reason*, vol. 1, trans. by Alan Sheridan-Smith (London: Verso, 2004).
4. Bernard Stiegler, *La Technique et le temps, 2: La Désorientation* (Paris: Galilée, 1996); *Technics and Time, 2: Disorientation*, trans. by Stephen Barker (Stanford, CA: Stanford University Press, 2009).

5. Bernard Stiegler, *Prendre soin: de la jeunesse et des générations* (Paris: Flammarion, 2008), pp. 180–81; *Taking Care of Youth and the Generations*, trans. by Stephen Barker (Stanford, CA: Stanford University Press, 2010), p. 99; this work subsequently referred to as *PS* in the main text.

6. Bernard Stiegler, *États de choc: bêtise et savoir au XXIè siècle* (Paris: Mille et une nuits, 2012), p. 72; *States of Shock: Stupidity and Knowledge in the Twenty-First Century*, trans. by Daniel Ross (Cambridge: Polity Press, 2015), p. 40; this work subsequently referred to as *EC* in the main text.

7. Bernard Stiegler, *Ce qui fait que la vie vaut la peine d'être vécue: de la pharmacologie* (Paris: Flammarion, 2010), p. 42; *What Makes Life Worth Living: On Pharmacology*, trans. by Daniel Ross (Cambridge: Polity Press, 2013), p. 21.

8. Bernard Stiegler, 'The Theater of Individuation: Phase-shift and Resolution in Simondon and Heidegger', trans. by Kristina Lebedeva, *Parrhesia*, 7 (2009), 46–57 (p. 50); this work subsequently referred to as *T* in the main text.

9. On the noetic soul and its intermittence, see also Bernard Stiegler, *De la misère symbolique, 2: La 'catastrophè' du sensible* (Paris: Galilée, 2005), pp. 50–53; *Symbolic Misery, vol. 2: The 'katastrophè' of the Sensible*, trans. by Barnaby Norman (Cambridge: Polity Press, 2015), pp. 23–25. On Stiegler's use of this Aristotelian terminology, see Daniel Ross, 'Politics and Aesthetics, or, Transformations of Aristotle in Bernard Stiegler', *Transformations*, 17 (2009), <http://www.transformationsjournal.org/issues/17/article_04.shtml> [accessed 10 January 2018].

10. Stiegler, *Ce qui fait que la vie vaut la peine d'être vécue*, p. 42.

11. Gilles Deleuze, *Logique du sens* (Paris: Minuit, 1969), p. 174; *The Logic of Sense*, trans. by Mark Lester with Charles Stivale (London: Athlone Press, 1990), p. 149, translation modified; this work subsequently referred to as *LS* in the main text.

12. Bernard Stiegler, *La Société automatique, 1: L'Avenir du travail* (Paris: Fayard, 2015), p. 327; *Automatic Society, vol. 1: The Future of Work*, trans. by Daniel Ross (Cambridge: Polity Press, 2016), p. 183; this work subsequently referred to as *SA* in the main text.

13. Although he would certainly reject any belief in a pre-existing 'historical law', 'realized through the natural selection of accidents', Stiegler would accordingly doubtless agree with Trotsky's subsequent assertion in *My Life* that 'conscious human activity [...] subjects accidents to a process of artificial selection' (Leon Trotsky, *My Life* (1930), Chapter 40, <https://www.marxists.org/archive/trotsky/1930/mylife/ch40.htm> [accessed 10 January 2018]).

14. We should note in passing that Sartre had in fact already used the concept of metastability in *L'Être et le néant*, in relation to questions of consciousness and good faith: see Robert D. Cumming, 'Role-playing: Sartre's Transformation of Husserl's Phenomenology', in *The Cambridge Companion to Sartre*, ed. by Christina Howells (Cambridge: Cambridge University Press, 2006), pp. 39–66.

CHAPTER 10

From the Deconstruction of the Subject to the Clarification of the Clearing: Heidegger, Sloterdijk, and the Genesis of the Clearing of Being

Henry Dicks

One of the key themes of late twentieth-century thought was the deconstruction of the subject. In her 1992 essay 'Sartre and the Deconstruction of the Subject', Howells suggested that the deconstruction of the subject did not ultimately have the 'radical finality' it appeared to have in the 1960s and 1970s:

> Having deposed the subject so firmly and with such apparent haste and delight in the 1960s and 1970s, French philosophers are now seeming to repent at leisure. The 'death of man' (Foucault) and the 'ends of man' (Derrida) are now seen to have lacked the radical finality with which their celebration endowed them twenty years earlier.[1]

Given subsequent developments in Western thinking, it would not be unreasonable to suggest that this moment of repenting was short-lived. Since the early 1990s, one of the major trends in Western thought has been the development of post-humanism, which, while in some respects a rather vague and heteroclite movement, may in its broad outlines be seen as a continuation of the deconstruction of the subject and of man carried out in the 60s and 70s by French philosophers like Foucault and Derrida. Nevertheless, it is also clearly the case that, like postmodernism, post-humanism defines itself relative to what came before, so that humanism remains both the standard and the reference point for thinking. This in turn raises the possibility that whether or not one continues to embrace humanism or, conversely, deconstructs humanism's basic concepts and identifies oneself as a post-humanist in some respects makes little difference, for in both cases no alternative worthy of the name — no new standard or reference point for thinking — has been put forward. In a similar vein, one could also argue that whether one returns to the subject or pursues its deconstruction matters relatively little until some genuine alternative to subjectivity emerges. Even the recent trend towards object-oriented ontology does little to change the overall picture: the modern theoretical framework, with its characteristic subject-object division, is maintained, the only difference being the *orientation* of thinking, which is henceforth turned towards the object rather than the subject.

One thinker whom Howells discusses in her essay who did try to develop a genuine alternative to modern thought and its characteristic concepts of subjectivity, consciousness, reason, man, and so on, is Heidegger. Howells situates Heidegger with respect to two thinkers, Husserl and Nietzsche, who, she notes, take radically opposed approaches to subjectivity. Husserl tries to overcome the division between subject and object, as well as between transcendental subject and empirical self, and may thus be said to aim primarily at healing the rifts and divisions of modern thought, rather than undermining it or posing a radical alternative (*SDS*, p. 324). Nietzsche, by contrast, goes to the other extreme of seeing the very notion of the subject as illusory. In a comparable manner to Hume, for whom the self is merely a 'bundle of perceptions', Nietzsche argues that the subject, the 'I', is but an illusion born of the 'grammatical custom that adds a do-er to every deed'.[2]

According to Howells, Heidegger attempted to go beyond both Husserl and Nietzsche. Following in the wake of Nietzsche's deconstruction of the subject, Heidegger theorized 'non-singular *Dasein* as prior to the individuated self or subject' (*SDS*, p. 325). Likewise, although Heidegger retained Husserl's transcendental method of explaining the a priori conditions necessary for 'the things themselves' to become manifest, he also believed that Husserl problematically retained many of the conceptual and theoretical prejudices of the Western tradition, in particular the transcendental subject. Heidegger's basic aim, on this reading, was thus to propose an alternative transcendental framework to the traditional one espoused by Kant and Husserl: where the tradition talks of the subject, Heidegger talks of *Dasein*; where the tradition talks of consciousness, Heidegger talks of the clearing; and where the tradition studies man via (philosophical) anthropology, Heidegger studies being-in-the-world via phenomenological ontology. Howells does, however, express uncertainty as to whether Heidegger succeeded in his attempt to go beyond Husserl and Nietzsche: 'Heidegger attempts (unsuccessfully?) to go beyond both' (*SDS*, p. 323).

The starting-point of the present essay is precisely this parenthetic question, '(unsuccessfully?)', which I will, as it were, take out of the brackets Howells placed around it. Did Heidegger succeed in going beyond Husserl and Nietzsche? A first important point to note here is that one obvious measure of success is the achievement of one's own aims. For Heidegger, Nietzsche was the final great thinker of the West and, as such, represented the 'end' of Western thought, in the sense of the completion and exhaustion of its essential possibilities.[3] Writing at the time of what he believed to be this ongoing 'end', Heidegger's own thought was oriented towards the emergence of 'another beginning', which, he thought, would repeat — albeit in a radically different way — the first beginning of Western philosophy in the work of what he called the 'early Greeks' (and not the 'pre-Socratics', for that amounts to seeing the Socratic tradition as the standard and reference point for thinking, an ingrained habit that the new beginning would need to circumvent). But this is not to say that Heidegger believed that he himself had initiated this new beginning. On the contrary, he clearly felt that the time was not yet right and that all that he himself could do was to *prepare* the ground for its eventual emergence. It may, therefore, simply be too early to judge whether Heidegger has been successful in his philosophical endeavours. Nevertheless, eighty years after Heidegger first formulated the idea of another beginning, there can be little doubt that it has not yet occurred; the end of Western thinking rumbles on with its continuing accumulation of 'post-isms'.

A second, closely related point is that, although Heidegger's key concepts are not infrequently discussed by subsequent thinkers, they have not for the most part been appropriated and incorporated into a shared philosophical framework. The result is that, whereas 'subjectivity', 'consciousness', and 'man' continue to form significant parts of the basic conceptual vocabulary shared by all or almost all contemporary philosophers regardless of their specific tradition (analytic philosophy, critical theory, post-structuralism, etc.), only a relatively small number of faithful Heideggerians have appropriated such concepts as the clearing or *Dasein*. Further, these faithful Heideggerians have for the most part limited themselves to trying to work out what Heidegger 'really meant', rather than trying to accomplish the task that he saw himself as preparing: the initiation of a new beginning.[4]

One partial exception to the general failure of contemporary Heideggerians to follow through with the task Heidegger set himself may be found in the work of Peter Sloterdijk. Not only does Sloterdijk take up much of Heidegger's basic conceptual and theoretical framework, but he also goes far beyond mere exegesis. This is particularly the case in 'Domestikation des Seins: Die Verdeutlichung der Lichtung' [The Domestication of Being: The Clarification of the Clearing], the central essay of Sloterdijk's most directly Heidegger-inspired work, *Nicht gerettet: Versuche nach Heidegger* [Not Saved: Essays after Heidegger]. As the subtitle of this essay indicates, its initial aim is to shed light on or 'clarify' (*verdeutlichen*) the 'clearing' (*die Lichtung*). To do this, however, Sloterdijk does not simply undertake a reading of Heidegger, as if the clearing could only be clarified exegetically, but instead undertakes a 'fantastic reconstruction' of its genesis — a highly unorthodox project that makes it necessary 'to bracket his [Heidegger's] hostile attitude with respect to all forms of empirical and philosophical anthropology and to put a new configuration between "ontology" and anthropology to the test'.[5]

In what follows, I present a positive appraisal of Sloterdijk's unorthodox project and method, while also arguing that the content of the story he tells is problematic, for it fails to accomplish its stated objective; rather than telling the story of the *clarification* of Being, Sloterdijk ends up telling the rather different story of the *domestication* of Being. This critical reading of Sloterdijk in turn enables me to offer what I believe is a much more lucid account of both the clearing and its genesis, one which I hope will contribute towards Heidegger's goal of developing a genuine alternative to the current framework of Western thought, centred on the subject and on man (or rather humans), and therewith also the emergence of a new beginning.

Sloterdijk on Paleo-anthropology and Paleo-ontology: The Method of Fantastic Reconstruction

The clearing is Heidegger's name for the space or opening wherein Being appears, that is to say, where things are understood *as* things. He further thought that this space was unique to humans. Animals, Heidegger thought, do not dwell in or belong to the clearing; they do not understand things *as* things. This state of affairs, Sloterdijk realizes, raises an intriguing question: how did the clearing originate? Since Darwin, we know that humans were not created by God, but evolved from animals; but how, then, did the clearing come to be?

This question raises significant methodological difficulties. The first and most obvious of these is that, for Heidegger, to be is to appear in the clearing. To study how the clearing came to be would thus appear to *presuppose* the clearing, an apparent case of *petitio principii*. Sloterdijk's answer to this problem is simply to note that the genesis of the clearing is indeed studied from within the clearing, for it is from out of the clearing as it exists today that the story of its genesis is told (*NS*, p. 97).

A second difficulty concerns the method of phenomenological ontology. Phenomenological ontology attempts to describe without prejudice the a priori structures or 'existentialia' of being-in-the-world.[6] But this is clearly impossible with respect to our long-dead 'pre-human' ancestors. If, as Sloterdijk believes, animals inhabit an environment (*Umwelt*), and contemporary humans a world (*Welt*), then, he reasons, the attempt to trace the genesis of the world requires us also to consider the transition from one to the other and therewith also what he calls the 'pre-world' of our 'pre-human' ancestors. But we do not have a direct access to this pre-world, in which case it is clearly out of the question to study it phenomenologically. To drop the phenomenological part of Heidegger's method does not, however, imply the complete abandonment of the transcendental part, though it does call for significant modifications. Indeed, rather than *working back* from phenomenological analysis of the understanding of Being to the a priori structures necessary for that understanding to take place, the aim here is to *work forward*, using a semi-naturalistic approach to trace the genesis not of homo sapiens, but rather of the a priori structures necessary for Being to appear. These structures, being a result of evolutionary processes, are of course contingent; but they are nevertheless necessary *if* Being is to appear, and, in that sense, the method retains a transcendental dimension.

To drop the phenomenological part of Heidegger's method also does not require the ontological part to be jettisoned. To see why, it is helpful to consider Heidegger's analysis of animality in *Die Grundbegriffe der Metaphysik* [The Fundamental Concepts of Metaphysics].[7] Now, phenomenology is again of little direct help here, for, not being animals, we cannot inquire directly into the a priori structures of *their* lived experience. But this is not to say that an ontological approach is also impossible, for, following Heidegger, we may draw on data, theories, experiments, and so on, carried out in the sciences in order to make speculative inferences regarding how — or rather whether — animals relate to Being. This, in a nutshell, is also the method proposed by Sloterdijk for analyzing the pre-world of our pre-human ancestors. Drawing on the empirically-informed theories of various paleo-anthropologists,

Sloterdijk aims to develop not so much a theory of anthropogenesis as a theory of the genesis of the clearing. If, in doing so, he draws on paleo-anthropology, it is thus only as a means to an end: the study of what he playfully calls 'paleo-ontology', understood not in its usual sense as the study of ancient organisms, but rather, differentiated by a hyphen, as the study of the ancient disclosure of Being.

This is not to say, however, that there are not also significant methodological differences between Sloterdijk's paleo-ontology and Heidegger's analysis of animality. For a start, Sloterdijk's aim is not simply to disclose the pre-world of our pre-human ancestors, as if that world were something static and unchanging, but rather to disclose the dynamic processes involved in the transition from the complete hiddenness of Being to its disclosure in the clearing. Further, it is also obviously the case that, unlike the animal species analyzed by Heidegger, the various pre-human species no longer exist. This in turn means that we can only infer what relation, if any, they may have had to Being from the *traces* they left behind, whether in the form of bones, DNA, tools, and dwelling sites, or in traits that persist in the deepest levels of our own being, a state of affairs that adds significantly to the 'fantastic' nature of the task.

A Home in the Clearing: Critique of Sloterdijk's Paleo-anthropology

The stated aim of Sloterdijk's inquiry is to clarify the clearing, and it is with this end in view that he sets about his fantastic reconstruction of its genesis. Knowing how anything came to be may shed light on what it is, and the clearing, Sloterdijk suggests, is no exception to this. But how is this aim to be realized in practice? After all, paleo-anthropologists have revealed a plethora of seemingly important phenomena involved in anthropogenesis — upright posture, advanced tool-use, changes in sexuality, bigger brains, spoken language, and so on — and it is far from immediately apparent which of these, if any, are relevant to the project of clarifying the clearing via the study of its genesis. Some sort of guiding thread is clearly required.

The guiding thread Sloterdijk settles upon derives from Heidegger's famous remark, made in 'The Letter on Humanism', that 'language is the house of Being' (NS, p. 107). Reflecting on this remark, Sloterdijk argues that it is not only in language that Being is 'housed'. Indeed, he thinks that the key evolutionary developments that taken together distinguish humans from animals are all ultimately directed towards the creation of a 'house' wherein Being discloses itself, hence both the main title of his text, 'The Domestication of Being', and his explicit proposal to 'imagine the genesis of the human being itself as an actual house affair, a drama of domestication, in the radical sense of the word' (NS, p. 108). This radical sense implies something more fundamental than the construction of houses and the domestication of plants and animals; it is the process of creating a frontier between an inside and an outside, and thus also a protective 'sphere' for dwelling.[8]

The process of domestication, Sloterdijk further argues, may be broken down into four key mechanisms, the synergistic interaction of which is responsible for

Being's disclosure. The first of these is 'insulation from selective pressure', a notion proposed by the nineteenth-century geologist Hugh Miller. It involves living in large groups such that the most vulnerable members at the centre of the group — particularly the infants — are protected from environmental threats and may thus evolve new traits that do not directly reflect the selective pressures exerted by the surrounding ecology. The second mechanism is what the early twentieth-century anthropologist Paul Alsberg calls the 'deactivation of the body'. This expression reflects the fact that tool-use, which even our distant ancestors already took much further than other species, involves the interposition of a protective, intermediary entity between the body and the physical environment. Drawing on the pioneering work of the early twentieth-century biologist and anatomist, Louis Bolk, the third mechanism Sloterdijk proposes is neoteny: the slowing down of ontogeny and the preservation of juvenile traits into adulthood, a phenomenon whose viability depends directly on the previous two mechanisms, for without the protection afforded by large groups and tools (weapons included), the preservation of juvenile characteristics would render the slow-developing infant too vulnerable to survive. And the fourth and final mechanism is 'transference', by which Sloterdijk means the ability to remember and thus to some extent recreate previous spheres of domesticity following a catastrophe (NS, pp. 111–33).

Sloterdijk's account of domestication as the driving process behind anthropogenesis is in many respects highly convincing; and yet it depends on a fundamentally problematic assumption. To see why, it suffices to note an important change of focus that takes place at the very outset of his project. Having set himself the task of drawing on paleo-anthropology to clarify the clearing, Sloterdijk immediately proposes the house (understood in his radical sense) as the guiding thread required to carry out this project. The clearing of Being, Sloterdijk thus assumes, is the same thing as the house of Being. This assumed identity between the house and the clearing in turn enables Sloterdijk to turn his attention exclusively to the house, thus overlooking the possibility of examining the clearing as a separate phenomenon requiring investigation in its own right. The consequential result is that, whereas the house is discussed and elaborated to the point that it grounds and pervades the entirety of Sloterdijk's fantastic reconstruction, the same cannot be said for the clearing, which assumes instead the status of what Ricœur calls a 'dead metaphor', that is, a metaphor that is no longer recognized as such and which instead assumes the role of an abstract concept.[9] And yet, as I shall presently show, just as it is theoretically possible to take a radical understanding of the house as the guiding thread of anthropogenesis, so it is also possible for the clearing, understood in a comparably radical sense, to play much the same role, albeit at a more primordial level. To see how this is possible, however, it is first necessary to take a journey back in evolutionary time.

It is well known that the common ancestor we share with our closest living relative, the chimpanzee, inhabited the dense tropical forests of Africa. Further, it is also generally accepted that the ecological shift that underpinned the evolution of the genus Homo was the thinning out of these forests, most likely as a result of climate change.[10] Thus it was that the fundamental driver of the first five or so million years of anthropogenesis was the transition from a heavily forested environment to one that was increasingly punctuated by clearings. Further, according to the French paleo-anthropologist, Pascal Picq, the defining trait of the first true species of the genus Homo, which he thinks appeared around 1.5 million years ago in the form of *homo ergaster* or *homo erectus* (so not the 'misnamed' *homo habilis* or *homo rudolfensis*), lay in the fact that they had *completed* the transition to open environments.[11] So, whereas paleo-anthropologists often posit some physiological or psychological change or set of changes as the distinguishing feature of the genus Homo, especially bipedalism, increased brain size, tool-use, or language, for Picq the overarching shift that explains the emergence of the genus Homo is the specifically *ecological* one of transitioning from a forested habitat to the clearings left behind as the forest thinned out. We are, as Jean-Jacques Hublin puts it, 'le cousin [du chimpanzé] qui a quitté la forêt pour vivre dans les paysages ouverts' [the cousin [of the chimpanzee] who left the forest to live in open landscapes].[12]

It is also not hard to see that it was the ecological shift to open environments that made necessary the various mechanisms of domestication discussed by Sloterdijk. No longer assured of the protection of the trees and the fruits of the forest, our ancestors had increasingly to fend for themselves. Living in large groups afforded greater protection from environmental threats, and increased recourse to tools served the twin aims of both warding off predators or rivals and helping procure otherwise inaccessible food supplies, notably by digging for roots and tubers, breaking open carcasses, and, later on, hunting. It was, in short, precisely because the protective sphere of the forest dwindled away, and our ancestors were increasingly left vulnerable in the midst of a hostile clearing, that a new 'home' had to be created. So, while Sloterdijk is no doubt right to talk of the 'exodus from uncleared nature into the danger that is called the clearing' (*NS*, p. 96), he does not ever think to interpret 'uncleared nature' in terms of forests and the clearing in terms of the open, non-forested environments in which our distant ancestors set about creating a home.

From the Domestication to the Clarification of Being: Critique of Sloterdijk's Paleo-ontology

The narrative presented in the previous section already adopts an oblique perspective with regard to paleo-anthropology, for its primary focus is not anthropogenesis, understood in terms of purely physiological or psychological changes to the human being, but rather the paleo-ecological transition out of forested habitats and the consequent need to create a home in the clearing. Just as Sloterdijk thinks that anthropogenesis is not the primary phenomenon to be investigated but rather a 'side effect' of the process of creating one's own habitat (*NS*, p. 124), my alternative account holds that anthropogenesis is ultimately just a 'side effect' of: a) coming to dwell in clearings; and b) creating one's own habitat therein. But this theory of the *ecological* foundations of anthropogenesis is still a long way from an *ontological* account of the genesis of the clearing; the paleo-ecological narrative of the transition to open environments must be connected with the paleo-ontological one of Being's disclosure.

At the outset of Sloterdijk's narrative, there occurs a problematic shift of inquiry from the clearing to the house. A similar shift also occurs with respect to Being. Despite Sloterdijk's initial aim of clarifying the clearing of Being, he does not ever engage in a direct discussion of Being, at least if Being is understood, as it is in *Being and Time*, as the 'as' or the 'is'. There may be extensive discussions of such key Heideggerian notions as truth, world, openness, ex-stasis, space, and so on, but Being — the understanding of things *as* things — is not directly discussed. So, whereas Levinas, for example, describes anthropogenesis in terms of the transition from experiencing mere qualities (e.g. blueness) to also experiencing the things or substances that underlie these qualities (e.g. the sky that *is* blue), no comparable transition is described by Sloterdijk: the emergence of the 'as' and the 'is' remains shrouded in darkness.[13]

How, then, are we to understand the 'as' and its emergence? Although Sloterdijk's narrative focuses on the paleo-ecological, or perhaps rather paleo-economic, issue of domestication, his principal paleo-anthropological references relate mainly to physiological or behavioural changes (living in large groups, deactivating the body, neoteny), the ontological implications of which he then seeks to tease out. In proceeding in this manner, he largely overlooks paleo-anthropological theories regarding the origin and nature of specifically human psychological traits. Drawing on recent work in this area carried out by Michael Tomasello, I will in what follows propose a fantastic reconstruction of the clearing, which, in an analogous manner to the previous section, not only undermines the traditional focus on the genesis of the human being, but also demonstrates the priority of the clearing of Being with respect to the house of Being.

In Tomasello's early work, he argues that what differentiates humans from animals is joint intentionality (or joint attention). In joint intentionality, a 'triadic' relation between self, other, and thing occurs in which one party attends to the thing while at the same time being aware that another party is also attending to the same thing. Whereas animals either attend to others or to things, humans alone, Tomasello initially argues, can attend to a thing while simultaneously being aware that another party is also attending to the thing.[14] As Tomasello later acknowledged, however, experimental research with great apes has revealed a problem in this account: great apes can in some cases become aware that another is also attending to a thing (*OHC*, pp. 31–33). Further, it has also proved possible to teach great apes to point at things, and thus to draw the attention of another to the thing in question (*OHC*, pp. 34–37).

There is, however, a key difference between the way great apes and humans point: the pointing of great apes is only ever imperative; they point because they want another party, only ever a human, to retrieve something for them (*OHC*, pp. 37–38). Human pointing may of course also take this form, but, as Tomasello points out, human pointing is also frequently 'declarative'. Humans point simply to show that there is something worthy of interest (*OHC*, p. 38). For Tomasello, the importance of this distinction between imperative and declarative pointing is the following: whereas pointing in apes only occurs in an egoistic context, humans also point at things in a cooperative context. Declarative pointing brings things to joint attention in such a way that it becomes possible to cooperate with respect to them.

From the perspective of anthropology and psychology, there is certainly much truth in Tomasello's account, but, viewed from an ontological perspective, it misses what is truly essential in human pointing: in human pointing *the being of the thing may become open*. This may occur in declarative pointing if, for example, something is pointed out by one party, but another party then disagrees with respect to it: one party may think that some specks on the horizon are a group of humans, another that they are a group of animals; one party may think some approaching humans are dangerous, another that they are harmless. Further, much human pointing is also inquisitive, a phenomenon particularly visible in young children, who often point at things in order to obtain some sort of clarification about them, a state of affairs that is in keeping with Tomasello's observation that 'there is no evidence that other animals ever ask one another for clarification' (*OHC*, p. 83). In declarative and inquisitive pointing, it may thus become an open question as to what, or what exactly, a thing is: whether it is for this or for that, whether it is indicative of some other thing or not, whether it was caused by this or that thing, whether it is mine or yours, and so on and so forth.[15] There is, to focus on a single example, a world of difference between the joint intentionality involved in competing for possession of a thing, as occurs in apes, and the joint intentionality involved in disagreeing as to whether the thing 'is' mine or yours, as occurs in humans.

Further, it is only because of this prior openness of Being — and therewith also the possibility of clarifying and agreeing with respect to the being of things — that specifically human forms of cooperation are possible. If we do not agree and, if necessary, obtain clarification about what something is, whether it is dangerous or harmless, whether it is to be done in this or that order, and so on, then cooperative behaviour with respect to the thing in question will not be able to get off the ground. This is not to deny that other species may cooperate with respect to things attended to jointly, such as wolves when hunting, but in these instances the thing is always intended in basically the same instinctual manner, such that there is no need for its being to become open. In the case of humans, by contrast, any entity — a seashell, a lightning strike, a footprint — may not only become the focus of joint intentionality, but may also become open as to its being, and thus intended in all sorts of different ways (i.e. 'as' a, b, c...).

In the light of this argument, let us now briefly reconsider tool-use, which Sloterdijk thinks makes a key contribution to Being's disclosure. Now, it could be objected here that great apes also make extensive use of tools. This may be true, but their tool-use is always egoistic. In humans, by contrast, the need to create a shared 'home' in the clearing means that tool-use is essentially cooperative. So, while great apes may use tools, these tools do not, to employ Heidegger's vocabulary, form part of an 'equipmental totality' that refers back to non-singular *Dasein*. Moreover, in order for this equipmental totality to exist, there must first be some sort of shared agreement as to what the various different items of equipment are for; and in order for that to be possible they must first have become open with respect to their being.

A similar principle also applies to language, which, unlike tool-use, arises because of the need to make present something that would otherwise be absent (*OHC*, pp. 66–71). Without any form whatsoever of language, even such simple tasks as agreeing on whether there is a water source over the other side of a hill would be extremely difficult to achieve. Agreements as to the being of absent things may thus have been limited at first to only the most basic set of cases, such that it was only over time that both genetic and cultural changes — in particular those linked to the development of fine-tuned spoken language — made possible agreement and clarification regarding ever more complex cases of otherwise absent things, including, in particular, abstract concepts. But if language differs from human tool-use in that it is concerned with otherwise absent things, it resembles tool-use in that it is only after the being of things becomes open that it may arise. Language arises precisely because of the need to agree, to share common assumptions, about the being of otherwise absent things, and, on that basis, coordinate behaviour. There could never be, as Wittgenstein rightly notes, a private language.[16] In this respect, however, language obviously differs from non-human tool-use, which, we have already seen, may be carried out egoistically.

To Wittgenstein's private language argument, it is also necessary to add that there can be no private understanding of the being of things prior to the openness of Being. Prior to this openness of things, it is not the case that our ancestors had their own private understanding of the being of things, but that, lacking language, they were incapable of expressing any disagreements they may have had, for, as long as they lacked the shared project of constructing a 'house', there was simply no need for the being of things to be understood at all. Understanding the being of things only arises — and only can arise — on the basis of their becoming open not to an individual, but rather to a plurality of individuals, who, on the basis of this openness, may arrive at mutual agreements with respect to their being. Once the being of things has been mutually agreed upon, individuals may then go on to experience 'anxiety', a state of mind in which the commonly accepted understanding of the being of things falls away and individualized *Dasein* is left cut off from its usual involvement in the world of the 'they' (*das Man*) — a state of mind that Heidegger revealingly describes as 'not-being-at-home' (*nicht-zuhause-sein*). But any 'authentic' and initially private understanding of things that may arise subsequent to the experience of anxiety will only ever be *secondary* with respect to the shared understanding of the being of things characteristic of the 'they' (*das Man*).

To see the experience of anxiety as 'not-being-at-home' indirectly confirms the idea that the mutually agreed understanding of the being of things is none other than the 'house' of Being. But the very need to house Being, to provide protection and shelter for precious and hard-fought clarifications and agreements regarding the being of things, as occurs in both cooperative tool-use and language, only arose at all because of the prior openness of Being. Things must first enter the clearing, and, in so doing, become open as to their being, in order thereafter to be 'housed'. So, just as Sloterdijk overlooks the fact that the need to construct houses arose in clearings in the forest, he also overlooks the fact that the very need to create a house for Being, thus providing durable protection and shelter for hard-fought clarifications and agreements as to what things are, only arose because of Being's prior emergence into the clearing.

By way of conclusion, I would like to provide a brief indication of how I think the present essay may contribute to Heidegger's objective of grounding a new beginning. The key methodological insight underlying this essay is that it is possible to pursue a form of transcendental philosophy, not, as was the case in early Heidegger, by means of phenomenological inquiry into the clearing, understood as the basic a priori structure necessary for the understanding of Being, but rather through a semi-naturalistic inquiry that seeks to shed light on the clearing through a 'fantastic reconstruction' of its genesis.

Applying this method in the context of a critical reading of Sloterdijk's 'The Domestication of Being' led to the idea that the clearing is not to be understood *anthropologically*, as the distinctive trait of human beings, in the way that Kant sees transcendental subjectivity as the distinctive trait of human beings, but *ecologically*, as an open, non-forested space in which there unfolded the 'drama of domestication' that Sloterdijk convincingly argues is the guiding thread of anthropogenesis.[17]

This *ecological* conception of the clearing had in turn to be articulated with an *ontological* conception of the clearing. This, I argued, may be achieved via the following semi-naturalistic argument: the hostile nature of clear, open environments called for the cooperative construction of a shared 'house'; but, in order for this cooperative construction to take place, the being of things had first to become open such that these things could, thenceforth, be allotted an appropriate and commonly accepted place within that 'house'.

But in what way does this ecological and ontological conception of the clearing contribute to the possible emergence of a new beginning? The answer, I suggest, is the following: by returning to the clearing, to the bare and open ground that precedes the construction of a shared house for Being, we raise the possibility not simply of deconstructing Being's current house, but also of building another quite different one.

Notes to Chapter 10

1. Christina Howells, 'Sartre and the Deconstruction of the Subject', in *The Cambridge Companion to Sartre*, ed. by Christina Howells (Cambridge: Cambridge University Press, 1992), pp. 318–52 (p. 331); this work is subsequently referred to as SDS in the main text.
2. Nietzsche, cited in SDS, p. 325.
3. Martin Heidegger, *Basic Questions of Philosophy: Selected 'Problems' of 'Logic'*, trans. by Richard Rojcewicz and André Schuwer (Indianapolis: Indiana University Press, 1994), pp. 115–16.
4. See, for example, Thomas Sheehan, *Making Sense of Heidegger: A Paradigm Shift* (London: Rowman & Littlefield, 2015).
5. Peter Sloterdijk, *Not Saved: Essays After Heidegger*, trans. by Ian Alexander Moore and Christopher

Turner (Cambridge: Polity Press, 2017), p. 96; this work is subsequently referred to as *NS* in the main text.

6. Martin Heidegger, *Being and Time*, trans. by John Macquarrie and Edward Robinson (Oxford: Blackwell, 1995).

7. Martin Heidegger, *The Fundamental Concepts of Metaphysics: World, Finitude, Solitude*, trans. by William McNeill and Nicholas Walker (Indianapolis: Indiana University Press, 1995).

8. This radical sense of domestication is clearly linked to Sloterdijk's overall philosophical project of 'spherology'.

9. Paul Ricœur, *La Métaphore vive* (Paris: Seuil, 1975).

10. See, for example, Jean-Jacques Hublin and Bernard Seytre, *Quand d'autres hommes peuplaient la terre: nouveaux regards sur nos origines* (Paris: Flammarion, 2008); Yves Coppens, *Histoire de l'homme et changements climatiques* (Paris: Fayard, 2006).

11. Pascal Picq, *Au commencement était l'homme* (Paris: Odile Jacob, 2009), p. 100.

12. Hublin, *Quand d'autres hommes peuplaient la terre*, p. 18.

13. Emmanuel Levinas, *Totalité et infini: essai sur l'extériorité* (The Hague: Martinus Nijhoff, 1961), p. 115.

14. Michael Tomasello, *The Origins of Human Cognition* (Boston, MA: Harvard University Press, 2000); this work is subsequently referred to as *OHC* in the main text.

15. The being of things, it follows, should not be understood in this context solely as their 'essence', as opposed to what they are only 'accidentally', for, depending on context, it may be relevant to consider things under all sorts of different aspects.

16. Ludwig Wittgenstein, *Philosophical Investigations* (Oxford: Basil Blackwell and Mott, 1958).

17. Immanuel Kant, *Anthropology from a Pragmatic Point of View* (Cambridge: Cambridge University Press, 2012).

CHAPTER 11

The Subject of Recognition in International Relations: Axel Honneth

Jeremy Ahearne

Formal legal notions of 'recognition' have long been a staple component of theories of international law.[1] Debates have revolved around the performative or constative potency of the recognitive act — does it 'constitute' states as such or simply 'declare' that they do indeed exist? It is only quite recently, however, that more extensive theories of recognition have been mobilized to explore the immanent dynamics of international relations.[2] Up until then, the most sustained treatments in political philosophy had tended to focus on subnational levels. The most influential among these treatments were those of Charles Taylor and Axel Honneth, which both derive in different ways from Hegelian *Urtexts*. While Taylor is best known in this respect for his work on identities and multiculturalism, Honneth's work is characterized by an emphasis on the central importance of recognition both in the formation of the individual subject and in more general struggles around social emancipation.[3]

Although he is a recurrent reference in the nascent International Relations recognition literature, Honneth himself has not been a prime mover in this turn. Its enabling conditions have been certain 'constructivist' challenges within International Relations to the 'realist' or 'neo-realist' traditions, which posited the polarities of material capacity as the dominant determinants of inter-state relations.[4] Honneth himself, who has not worked extensively in the area of International Relations, has expressed some doubts as regards the relevance of his fully articulated recognition theory for understanding state-to-state relations.

I would like in this paper to explore Honneth's expression of these doubts, or more precisely the way in which he works in and through them upon a terrain with which he is not familiar. I will focus in particular on a text taken from his 2010 collection *Das Ich im Wir* [The I in We], which extends into various fields the recognition theory which he first expounded systematically in the classic 1992 work *Der Kampf um Anerkennung* [The Struggle for Recognition]. The text is entitled 'Anerkennung zwischen Staaten. Zum moralischen Untergrund zwischenstaatlicher Beziehungen' [Recognition between States: On the Moral Substrate of International Relations]

(*IW*, pp. 181–201; 137–52). It is clear in several comments that Honneth does not feel altogether at ease in the domain of international relations, and his position shifts somewhat within the text about the extent to which this domain might be suited to an application of his own brand of recognition theory. But these very hesitations, and the sticking points they lead him to articulate, are what make the text an interesting piece for thinking with. The text as a whole is certainly dense with suggestions for empirical analysis (my own engagement with the text arises from a wider project exploring aspects of French foreign policy as forms of recognition-seeking behaviour within mutating international orders of recognition).

As Christina Howells and Oliver Davis rather invited us to do in preparing our contributions to the colloquium from which the present volume arose, I will intertwine two readings of the text as I go. On the one hand, I will intermittently consider Honneth himself, at least in this purely textual figuration, as the subject of Theory (with a capital T). It seems to me that his very lack of familiarity ('Vertrautheit', *IW*, p. 184; 139) with the subject-matter interrupts that self-confidence ('Selbstvertrauen') which Honneth sees in his general philosophy as necessary for an 'unbroken' relation of the subject to himself. This 'break' problematizes and foregrounds the place of the theorizing subject in ways that are not so apparent in pieces where Honneth is more routinely at home. On the other hand, at the level of content, I will consider how his somewhat ambivalent introduction of subjectivity (or affect) into inter-state relations opens up for analysis a bounded freedom for manoeuvre for political agents that is actualized by interpretative political acts. I will finish by considering some potential limits of his approach.

The Subject Muted by Theory

The text first seems to give us a somewhat flattening encounter between the subject as a neophyte with an assortment of presumptive notions about recognition and international relations, and the stern rejoinders of established Theory. At a 'pretheoretical' level, Honneth writes, as evidenced in the 'Meinungsaustausch' [everyday exchange of opinions] in which we are immersed, questions of recognition seem to saturate international relations (*IW*, p. 181; 137). Just to cite recent examples equivalent to those given by Honneth: Turkey complains that the Dutch government is not recognizing its citizens' rights; China complains that, by recognizing the Taiwanese government, the USA is derecognizing China's own territorial and symbolic identity; the Kurds, the Catalans, and the Palestinians, in very different circumstances, claim that their rights to form a state are not recognized. These and other such instances appear to offer ample territory for the 'carrying across' of the category of recognition from interpersonal relations and social movements to inter-state relations.

What Honneth calls 'die offizielle Theorie' (*IW*, p. 182; 138), however, tells the neophyte not to be so naive. Firstly, states are not people, they are not 'subjects' in that way, and they do not have the consciousness required to carry recognitive exchanges. Secondly, exchanges between states follow functional, quasi-technical channels determined by the 'Aufgabe [...], nach außen hin die territorialen Grenzen, den ökonomischen Wohlstand und die politische Sicherheit des eigenen Landes zu wahren' [the task of preserving their own country's borders, economic well-being and political security] (*IW*, p. 185; 140). Such functions are 'eigengesetzlich' (they follow their own 'laws'). Thirdly, even when states do appear to talk the language of recognition, they are lying, this is simply a cover for pursuing their more fundamental economic and security agendas (*IW*, p. 182; 138).

We may wonder about the precise configuration of the 'official Theory' projected by Honneth here, which is certainly not the German strand of 'critical theory' with which he has been intellectually and institutionally associated. It appears instead to be a particularly hard version of what is called the classic 'realist' or 'neo-realist' school of International Relations.[5] One might already raise questions, as do more 'constructivist' approaches to International Relations, about the culturally mediated quality of entities like frontiers or feelings of security, or even how the prospect of a lying state may complicate matters. However, the initial reaction of the would-be neophyte as it figures in Honneth's text is one of discouragement. The subject's 'pretheoretical opinions' do not 'stand up' to the demystifying force of the established 'scientific models', which posit as the determining factor in international relations materially backed acts or potential acts of self-assertion immune to the back and forth of recognitive relations: 'Die Vorstellung, staatliche Akteure und Regierungen verfolgten ausschließlich Interessen der kollektiven Selbstbehauptung, besitzt eine solche suggestive Kraft, daß wir nach erneuter Überprüfung unsere Alltagsintuitionen schnell wieder fallenlassen und uns dem Standardschema der bloßen Nutzenorientierung verschreiben' [The idea that state actors and governments pursue exclusively the interests of collective self-assertion has such suggestive power that, after reconsidering, we quickly abandon everyday intuitions and turn to the standard scheme of purely utilitarian motives] (*IW*, p. 182; 138). Fortunately for the interest of the piece, however, the thinking subject here is cowed but not quite silenced in its train of thought. It knows that it is not quite thinking straight, but it seems unable, when thinking about the action of states, to do without recourse to this apparently unclarified metaphor: 'Etwas hilflos und verlegen sprechen wir dann vom Anerkennungsstreben oder vom Respektbedürfnis einzelstaatlicher Akteure, obwohl wir doch wissen, daß solche psychologischen Begriffe die genannten Sachverhälte nicht angemessen beschreiben' [We speak, rather helplessly and awkwardly, of the striving for recognition or the need for respect on the part of individual state actors, even though we know that such psychological concepts do not adequately describe these matters] (*IW*, p. 184; 139). We might also translate 'verlegen' here as 'embarrassedly' — the departure from Theory is a cause of shame for the writing subject. Unable to divest himself of the perceptions gathered under the rubric of 'everyday intuitions', he experiences in the first instance a kind of malaise in Theory, and is initially tempted to relinquish, as it were, the voice of his own thinking.

States as Subjects

Honneth might have produced quite a different text had his point of entry into International Relations been not the realist and neo-realist traditions, but the work of a theorist like Alexander Wendt. For Wendt, who is obviously 'at home' in his speciality of International Relations, the discipline's analysts have for long been sleepwalking in a pretheoretical mist of their own when they quasi-instinctively refer to state actions as though they are the actions of subjects ('Algeria was humiliated by France's dismissive attitude', etc.). In Wendt's view, however, this is not because they are wrong to do so, but because they do not develop the full consequences of the fact that international relations cannot be adequately described by reducing states to their constituent elements. On the contrary, he argues that, as a 'real' emergent entity, the state is best understood as a subject in its own right, and indeed as a 'person' (not just in a thin sense as a moral and legal 'person', but in a much thicker sense on grounds of collective intentionality, persistence as a superorganism, and, more arguably, consciousness). Few would go as far as Wendt along these lines, but his contributions have undoubtedly made it easier to conceive inter-state relations as 'inter-subjective' relations of a peculiar kind.[6] On the basis of Honneth's own recent Hegel-inspired definition of freedom as feeling 'at home in the other' (a 'Bei-sich-selbst-Sein im Anderen') (*IW*, pp. 37–38; 21–22), we could imagine he would have found such constructivist ground, had he been aware of it, hospitable for a less inhibited theoretical inquiry.[7] At the same time, it is precisely the unauthorized cognitive dissonance set out above — a kind of localized *Unbehagen* or thwartedness in theory — that sets Honneth to work down tracks of his own.

Honneth has no qualms elsewhere in his work transposing the language of recognition-striving from the realm of interpersonal relations to that of certain kinds of social movements (workers' rights, gay rights, minority rights, etc.). Indeed, such applications were part of the social rationale of his recognition work in the first place (*IW*, p. 105; 76). I think this is due partly to the commonality of purpose inherent in such movements, creating shared structures of feeling and intentionality, but also to the 'progressiveness' of their purposes, which allows them to figure as evidence for his general thesis about the dynamics of recognition struggles as a progressive motor of history. The matter of nation states poses more of a problem to him. The reason he himself puts forward for his reluctance to attribute collective recognition-seeking aspirations to states as such is their high level of agglomeration as social entities: they are, as a rule, so large and so internally heterogeneous that we baulk at the idea of describing them as if they were a single subject (*IW*, p. 185; 140). A second reason one might add is that, much more than liberal social movements do, relations between states display less frequently a 'progressive' historic vector, and indeed confront us more regularly with what some analysts call the 'dark side of recognition'.[8]

Honneth nonetheless continues to write, after the moment of textual malaise discussed above, in such a way as to ascribe subjecthood to states, as if to see where this transitional fiction will get him. The first way he does this is by invoking Hans Kelsen's classic distinction from 1941 between the 'cognitions' and 'recognitions' carried out by states.[9] For Kelsen, when a state acknowledges that another state does indeed possess the established attributes of statehood, this is simply a cognition that registers a fact (Honneth translates the act as a 'schlichte Zurkenntnisnahme eines Faktums' rather than an 'Anerkennung' (*IW*, p. 187; 141)). Kelsen distinguishes this from a decision to pursue a fuller 'political' recognition of another state, which signals a voluntary move to an actively maintained relation with that state. For Honneth, this distinction opens up an 'Entscheidungsspielraum' (a space or a play of decisional freedom) within the iron cage of realist perspectives on international relations. A space is opened up between greater or lesser degrees of recognition — other analysts might speak of a continuum between thin and thick, or perhaps cold and warm, forms of recognition.[10]

This move in itself does not, however, get us beyond the initial problems of assigning subjecthood, and free subjecthood, to states. It simply shows that the actions of states can indeed, perhaps uncannily, be described as though they were the actions of free subjects, without giving us an indication of why that description might so often ring true.

Honneth's next move is more far-reaching. Those in charge of states, even authoritarian states, can seldom simply do as they like in their public dealings with other states. They are bound by the requirement to maintain their legitimacy, notably among their own population. They must frame their actions and words such that a sufficient proportion of that population feel represented. And members of that population maintain certain normative expectations about how the state with which they identify should be recognized by other states. This necessity (for legitimacy) opens up in Honneth's account a bounded space for political freedom which we may describe as interpretative.

For such collective horizons of expectation are notoriously difficult to pin down. Not only are there a plurality of viewpoints among such highly agglomerated common entities as nation states. These viewpoints are not cold cognitions. They are unstable and saturated with high levels of affect. The vocabulary Honneth uses to describe the mode of existence of these expectations is interesting in its own right. He evokes 'die in der Bevölkerung schwelenden, uneinheitlichen und kaum organisatorischen Empfindungen' [the smouldering, diverse and scarcely organized sentiments in the population] (*IW*, p. 192; 144); 'diffuse Wünsche nach Anerkennung' [diffuse wishes for recognition] (*IW*, p. 191; 144); 'grassierende Empfindungen' [rampant sensitivities]; a 'lähmendes Unbehagen' [paralyzing unease] (*IW*, p. 193; 145). Indeed, all this brings out an undercurrent of affective repulsion in the critical theorist Honneth himself: he describes the collective enthusiasm displayed by sports crowds as 'irritating', and the 'pride' that people take in collective historical achievements in which they had no part as 'naïve' (*IW*, p. 189; 142). It may be that this irritation prevents Honneth from integrating more fully such nationally refracted affect into his own theoretical framework. Nation states may not be, *pace* Wendt, psychological entities that can seek recognition. But to use Honneth's habitual Hegel-inspired parlance, nation-state affiliations are potent mediatory references in the practical relation of subjects to themselves.

The solidity or 'unbrokenness' of this relation-to-self is dependent on the external recognition of this mediating reference.

These expectations for recognition that are 'gehegt' [harboured or nursed] by many individual subjects are portrayed as swirling, smouldering, raging, or dispersing among 'fragile' and 'porous' collective bodies (*IW*, p. 191; 144). It was their indeterminacy that discouraged Honneth from seeing in the state a single subject of recognition along the lines of individuals or issue-based social movements. Yet this same indeterminacy sets up a space of political action (Honneth speaks of a 'Spielraum' for competing interpretations (*IW*, p. 192; 144)). It allows political actors to project competing 'narrative syntheses' bringing together some pockets of expectation, marginalizing others. Again, the vocabulary Honneth uses to describe such acts is interesting in its own right: political actors can 'hervorkehren' [parade] either the 'reconciliatory' or the 'hostile' components of their population's attitudes (*IW*, p. 192; 144–45); they can 'zuspitzen' [sharpen] the edges of such attitudes, in a kind of weaponization (*IW*, p. 193; 145); 'anerkennungswürdige Züge' [recognition-worthy traits] of the country can be 'zur Darstellung gebracht' [channelled into a quasi-theatrical representation], in which implicit signalling is as important as explicit statement (*IW*, p. 189; 143); they can 'wachrufen' [awaken] prejudices and resentments when they lie dormant (*IW*, p. 199; 149). Political actors are thus free to interpret the political mood of their populations, both in the sense of laying out its purportedly true meaning, and in the musical performative sense of playing upon and thus accentuating this or that cluster of expectations. The examples Honneth adduces are those of Hitler 'sharpening' the ressentiment of German populations in the 1930s, or Obama working the attitudes to the outside world of a post-Bush USA. Other perhaps discouraging examples might come to our minds in the current climate. But Honneth underlines, in terms very reminiscent of Gramsci, that political actors are decisively bound in this interpretative play. Their 'narrative syntheses' around national identity must chime with a critical mass of existing structures of perception and feeling, which themselves have, of course, always already been produced by an accumulation of preceding narrative syntheses.

Honneth is reluctant to introduce into inter-state relations the taxonomies of recognitive relations with which he usually works (distinguishing broadly between the realms of close interpersonal affective relations, legal rights, and social esteem). This is because the swirl of greater or lesser recognitive expectations among millions of individuals is likely to be too internally heterogeneous for such clear-cut distinctions. However, one could argue that the 'Beschaffenheit' [composition] (*IW*, p. 195; 147) of these syntheses is clearer than the 'raw materials' with which they work. On that basis, these syntheses can offer a hold for the kinds of conceptual distinctions that Honneth elaborates elsewhere in his work. These could be analyzed in terms of a spectrum moving from demands for parity of legal recognition, to strategies for the securing of esteem, to the kinds of affective dimension that perhaps the famously hard-headed Talleyrand had in mind in his instructions to his ambassadors: 'Faites aimer la France' [Make them love France].[11]

Despite such hesitations about fully deploying the resources of his established recognition theory upon this new territory, one can trace over the course of the argument an amplificatory process through which Honneth writes himself into a space of greater assurance. He begins this process with a striking but tentative metaphor, suggesting that the 'collective striving for recognition' does not represent a separate function for state action, but 'färbt und grundiert vielmehr die Weise, in der von den politischen Akteuren die ihnen verfassungsgemäß zugewiesenen Aufgaben wahrgenommen werden' [colours and undercoats the way in which their constitutionally assigned tasks are perceived by political agents] (*IW*, p. 189; 143). He goes on to say that the 'moral pressure' of recognitive conflicts 'determines' the perception of external interests to such an extent that the two categories cannot be analytically separated out (*IW*, p. 192; 144). This inseparability goes on to receive its confirmation in metaphors of materiality, first in liquid terms (a 'fusion of interests and values' (*IW*, p. 194; 146)) and then as a solidly cast and recalcitrant reality — a specific 'Legierung' [alloy] of interests and values (*IW*, p. 198; 148). By the end of his text, Honneth is even berating (his projection of) established International Relations Theory for its 'prozedurale Phantasielosigkeit' [unimaginative procedural myopia], insofar as it focuses only on the balancing out of interests and legal agreements and fails to consider 'die kollektiven Empfindungen von Anerkennung oder Demütigung durch andere Staaten' [collective sensitivities for recognition and humiliation through other states] which, he now asserts, play an incomparably greater role (*IW*, pp. 198–99; 149). This subject of theory appears free now of his earlier inhibitions, 'at home in the space of the other' — indeed perhaps just a little bit too much so.

Yet the initial doubts expressed continue to surface here and there. Honneth is convinced by the end of his text that he has gone some way to addressing a gap in classic 'realist' Theory of international relations, by introducing questions of 'psychology' and 'mood' into his descriptions. However, he still maintains that these cannot form part of the necessary 'Theoriesprache' [theoretical language] itself, but must be the 'object' of that theory (*IW*, p. 194; 146). One might question, in one's turn, this rather sharp distinction between 'theoretical language' and its vernacular object. For some, the most productive parts of Honneth's piece might be the adjectives he selects without fanfare to describe the mode of existence of quasi-viral sentiments (diffuse, raging, smouldering), and the vernacular verbs he selects to describe the interpretative acts of political leaders (parading, sharpening, staging, reawakening).

Recognition Inflated and Dispersed

I have certainly found Honneth's formulations useful in analyzing the actions of French leaders upon 'certain ideas of France' which they look to feed, satisfy, inflect, or sharpen among their own electorates through their outward-directed policies.[12] More than is perhaps suggested by Honneth's piece, these ideas likewise act upon and model the *habitus* of those leaders and associated elites themselves, who in this respect are subjects like any others.[13] However, a final use of Honneth's articulated framework here is that it brings into relief some aspects of contemporary recognition dynamics that do not quite fit into it, or that square awkwardly with its orientation. I will draw here on some of my own work on contemporary France as a source of illustration.

Firstly, Honneth tends to work within what Cillian McBride has called a 'recognition-deficit' normative model.[14] For Honneth, pathologies, inhibitions, and injustices within interpersonal and inter-group relations are usually to be solved where possible by the granting of greater or thicker recognition. I think, however, that there is an obverse problem to which Honneth has been less attuned, and which one could describe as recognition inflation, that is escalating demands for recognition and recognizability which cannot be peaceably met, and that if anything need to be reined back. It is true that Honneth in his later work on recognition has gone some way to engaging with such issues. He has explored, in an engagement with Althusser's notion of 'interpellation', the idea of 'recognition as ideology'; and he has considered, rather along the lines of Boltanski and Chiapello, the ways in which institutions have captured and channelled for their own purposes individual aspirations for 'emancipatory' recognition.[15] Honneth's approach has tended to be to expose such practices as 'distorted' forms of recognition which betray the underlying meaning of the concept (this is due in part to the intrinsically affirmative sense of the German *Anerkennung* in contrast to the more neutral and polyvalent English 'recognition' or French *reconnaissance*). For Honneth, the 'surplus' of unmet or potential recognition claims over and beyond actual practices of recognition in a given society (a 'Geltungsüberhang') is what drives societies towards more progressive settlements (*IW*, pp. 224–25; 171). However, one can see in this inexhaustible 'surplus', both remedy and poison, the seeds of an altogether more problematic dynamic.

One symptom of this might be seen in the rise of the term 'insécurité culturelle' [cultural insecurity] in French public discourse, which was virtually inexistent as a collocation before about 2010, but has become quite a pervasive reference thereafter.[16] It refers to insecurity about the values and rituals that make up a group's lifeworld, and was originally deployed in France by analysts broadly on the left to capture something of the 'mood' that had led significant tranches of the working and lower middle classes to forsake the left for the far right. It was subsequently seized upon, however, by influential figures on the nationalist and far right as a legitimating term for their own programmes. The term carries with it a double recognition claim — both that a certain traditional native French culture be more assertively 'recognized', and that the terrains of that culture be purged of elements that are foreign, unrecognizable, *méconnaissables*. I have argued elsewhere that one should not demonize the term or the notion as such.[17] If appetites for recognition are so ingrained, and are perhaps accentuated under conditions of modernity, it is doubtless because both world and subject are recurrently *méconnaissables*. At stake is a certain ontological security. However, the hankering after such security, and its interpretative sharpening and parading by political actors, produces a potentially toxic spiral, an inflationary politics of recognition claims.

Secondly, I think there is a new dimension of state recognition-seeking that somewhat falls out of the frame of a Honnethian account. Recognitive exchanges in Honneth tend to be broadly dyadic, taking place between two entities: agent and agent; social pressure group and englobing collective entity; state and state. Certainly, the laying out of mediating third terms is a key part of the analysis, but the core action of granting and withholding recognition seems to happen between two entities. Yet something different appears to be happening in a new type of instituted mechanism through which states now engage in recognition-seeking. That is the international ranking or league table. One might consider in this respect the ways states invest themselves in a number of normatively potent league tables: university rankings; the OECD PISA rankings of fifteen-year olds' performances in literacy and maths; global cities; international media channels; global languages, etc.[18] There is seldom a single state actor that lays out the parameters of these ranking tables. They come to function rather like contingently formed apparatuses of governmentality insofar as they shape, orient, and inflect behaviours. Moreover, states do not simply bring their attributes for evaluation — they have to reshape those attributes to make them recognizable in the first place, so that they figure on the radar of these international rankings. A classic single example would be the case of French higher education, whose most prestigious institutions were simply not picked up as 'universities' by the most prominent of the relevant ranking systems. As a result, they have been engaged in over a decade of awkward institutional reengineering with the key objective of gaining more recognition not by a specified partner, but by these oddly compelling though uncertainly localized apparatuses of hierarchical classification.[19]

Despite moments of possible subjection to a somewhat forbidding 'realist' Theory of international relations, Honneth is of considerable help in embedding recognitive exchange between states in the bounded play between the interpretative acts of political leaders and relatively indeterminate swirls of recognitive expectations on the part of agglomerated subjects. Some important things do seem to fall outside his framework, but at the same time the framework can help us put them into relief. Thus, because recognition as such tends to feature as 'a good thing' in Honneth's work, he is less attuned to the dangers of recognition inflation, or recognition as object of unruly appetite. Also, his emphasis on recognitive exchange between two parties or entities allows us to flag up as something potentially novel the workings of more structural recognition regimes through the establishment of diverse global ranking systems. While Honneth elsewhere defines the condition of 'substantive freedom' for the social subject as the possibility of 'feeling at home in the other', the text in question reminds us that uncomfortable exposure to foreign territories can free a theory's subjects from the ruts in their own thinking.

Notes to Chapter 11

1. Hans Kelsen, 'Recognition in International Law: Theoretical Observations', *American Journal of International Law*, 35 (1941), 605–17.
2. See for example Hans Agné and others, 'Symposium on "The Politics of International

Recognition"', *International Theory*, 5 (2013), 94–176; *Recognition in International Relations: Rethinking a Political Concept in a Global Context*, ed. by Christopher Daase and others (Basingstoke: Palgrave Macmillan, 2015); *The International Politics of Recognition*, ed. by Thomas Lindemann and Erik Ringmar (Abingdon: Routledge, 2016).

3. Charles Taylor, 'The Politics of Recognition', in *Multiculturalism: Examining the Politics of Recognition,* ed. by Amy Gutmann (Princeton, NJ: Princeton University Press, 1994), pp. 25–74; Axel Honneth, *Kampf Um Anerkennung: Zur Moralischen Grammatik Sozialer Konflikte* (Frankfurt am Main: Suhrkamp, 1992); *The Struggle for Recognition: The Moral Grammar of Social Conflicts*, translated by Joel Anderson (Cambridge: Polity Press, 1995); Nancy Fraser and Axel Honneth, *Redistribution or Recognition? A Political-Philosophical Exchange* (London: Verso, 2003); Axel Honneth, *Das Ich Im Wir: Studien Zur Anerkennungstheorie* (Berlin: Suhrkamp Taschenbuch, 2010); *The I in We: Studies in the Theory of Recognition*, translated by Joseph Ganahl (Cambridge: Polity Press, 2014); this work subsequently referred to as *IW* in the main text. Translations are my own, but the second page reference on each occasion refers to the corresponding passage in the published English edition.

4. On the history of these theories, and their relation to international history as such, see Robert Frank, 'Histoire et théories des relations internationales', in *Pour l'histoire des relations internationales,* ed. by Robert Frank (Paris: Presses universitaires de France, 2012), pp. 41–82. The classic work of neo-realist theory is Kenneth N. Waltz, *Theory of International Politics* (Reading, MA: Addison-Wesley, 1979). Prominent examples of constructivist challenges opening a space for questions of recognition are: Alexander Wendt, *Social Theory of International Politics* (Cambridge: Cambridge University Press, 1999); Erik Ringmar, 'The Recognition Game: Soviet Russia against the West', *Cooperation and Conflict: Journal of the Nordic International Studies Association,* 37 (2002), 115–36; Richard Ned Lebow, *A Cultural Theory of International Relations* (Cambridge: Cambridge University Press, 2008).

5. On Honneth and the German 'critical theory' tradition as incarnated in the works of authors such as Horkheimer, Adorno, Habermas, and Honneth himself, and as associated with the Frankfurt Institute for Social Research, and also its relations with other traditions of 'critical theory', see Katia Genel, 'Jacques Rancière and Axel Honneth: Two Critical Approaches to the Political', in Axel Honneth and Jacques Rancière, *Recognition or Disagreement*, ed. by Katia Genel and Jean-Philippe Deranty (New York: Columbia University Press, 2016), Chapter 1. On realism, neorealism, and their history see note 4 above.

6. Wendt, *Social Theory of International Politics*; Alexander Wendt, 'The State as Person in International Theory', *Review of International Studies,* 30 (2004), 289–316. For readers who think that the case for 'self-conscious' states is simply fanciful, a suggestive thought experiment might be to consider the issue *a contrario*. It is not shocking to read analysts who speak of dysfunctional 'phantom states' and 'zombie states' (for the former in relation to the Central African Republic, see Philippe Baumel, *Rapport d'information par la commission des affaires étrangères sur 'La stabilité et le développement de l'Afrique francophone'* (Paris: Assemblée Nationale, 2015), pp. 54, 68; for the latter in relation to the UK itself in its post-referendum limbo, see for example Polly Toynbee, 'Britain has Become a Zombie State', *Guardian*, 21 November 2017). Now a 'phantom' may usually be understood as a mind without an effective body, and a 'zombie' as a body without a conscious mind. One could therefore conclude that our intuitive conception of a properly functioning state involves the integration of a certain kind of institutionally supported 'body' with a certain kind of collectively maintained 'mind'. Of course, this thought experiment is not a proof, but simply an indication that the idea of a self-conscious state is not as removed as we may initially think from our underlying beliefs.

7. The English translator renders 'bei sich' as 'with itself', but I am leaning here and later on Charles Taylor's suggestion that 'bei sich' 'exactly translates into French as "chez soi", and carries also a connotation of presence to self', and that it can be rendered in English as 'at home' (in his *Hegel* (Cambridge: Cambridge University Press, 1975), p. xi).

8. Cf. Mattias Iser, 'Recognition between States? Moving Beyond Identity Politics', in *Recognition in International Relations: Rethinking a Political Concept in a Global Context,* ed. by Christopher Daase and others (Basingstoke: Palgrave Macmillan, 2015), pp. 27–45 (pp. 36, 40).

9. Kelsen, 'Recognition in International Law'.

10. On thin and thick recognition, see Alexander Wendt, 'Why a World State Is Inevitable', *European Journal of International Relations*, 9 (2003), 491–542 (pp. 511–12).

11. Cited in François Chaubet and Laurent Martin, *Histoire des relations culturelles dans le monde contemporain* (Paris: Armand Colin, 2011), p. 117. Mattias Iser also argues, though on different grounds, that the kinds of conceptual distinction used for the analysis of recognition in interpersonal relationships can be applied fairly unproblematically to relations between states, and proposes his own 'sketchy' framework for doing so (basic legal recognition; equal respect; esteem; trust/friendship) (Iser, 'Recognition between States', pp. 36–40).

12. The implicit reference here is to de Gaulle's famous phrase, 'Toute ma vie, je me suis fait une certaine idée de la France' [All my life I have had a certain idea of France] (the first words of *Mémoires de guerre*, vol. 1, *L'Appel: 1940–1942* (Paris: Plon 1954), p. 1).

13. On the sociology and ethnography of foreign policy elites, see Pierre Jardin, 'Groupe, réseau, milieu', in *Pour l'histoire des relations internationales,* ed. by Robert Frank (Paris: Presses universitaires de France, 2012), pp. 511–27; Christian Lequesne, *Ethnographie du Quai d'Orsay* (Paris: CNRS, 2017).

14. Cillian McBride, *Recognition* (Cambridge: Polity Press, 2013), pp. 6–7, 35–38, 40, 102.

15. See *IW*, Chapters 5 and 10.

16. For the term's discursive history in the anglophone world and, more recently, in France, see Jeremy Ahearne, 'Cultural Insecurity and its Discursive Crystallisation in Contemporary France', *Modern and Contemporary France,* 25 (2017), 265–80.

17. Ibid.

18. See respectively, for these domains, Christine Musselin, *La Grande Course des universités* (Paris: Presses de la Fondation Nationale des Sciences Politiques, 2017); *Pisa, Power, and Policy: The Emergence of Global Educational Governance*, ed. by Heinz-Dieter Meyer and Aaron Benavot (Oxford: Symposium Books, 2013); Göran Therborn, *Cities of Power: The Urban, the National, the Popular, the Global* (London: Verso, 2017); Jean Chalaby, *Transnational Television in Europe: Reconfiguring Global Communications Networks* (London: I. B. Tauris, 2009); Louis-Jean Calvet and Alain Calvet, *Les Confettis de Babel: diversité linguistique et politique des langues* (Paris: Éditions Écriture, 2013).

19. Musselin notes that the 'problem' highlighted for France by the Shanghai world university rankings in 2003 'was not — or not only — the weak presence of French universities in this ranking, but the fact that *none* of our institutions (neither *grandes écoles*, nor universities, nor research bodies) possessed the characteristics enabling them to be measured against those establishments figuring in the "top 10" of the Shanghai ranking'. Attempts not only to give higher education institutions more 'autonomy', but also to reshape the perimeters and attributes of 'universities' in line with global templates, had emerged in the 1990s, but gathered pace with the proposal (in 2004) and energetic promotion (after 2008) of 'Pôles de recherche et d'enseignement supérieur' (PRES). These were rebaptized as 'Communautés d'universités et établissements' (COMUE) in the major higher education law of 2013 (see Musselin, *La Grande Course*, Chapter 5).

CHAPTER 12

Franking (and)
the Subject of Theory

Serge Trottein

The three concepts which constitute the object of this volume: freedom, subject, and theory, are profoundly interconnected, to the point of becoming indistinguishable one from another. Can they be dissociated? Is there another way of thinking freedom in its relationship to theory? Could another kind of theory offer new possibilities of overcoming the traditional obstacles encountered along the theoretical track? The object of this essay is to propose a fourth concept for the reader's reflexion, that of 'franking', of *affranchissement*, in order to free the subject of/from theory, and to free freedom itself from its historical links to subjectivity and theory.

There is a certain necessity for freedom to be the subject of theory — or of these essays for that matter. Freedom, the subject, and theory are not just related vaguely on the contingent occasion of a conference, or a work, even one dedicated to a 'philosopher, dramatist, novelist, critic and moralist' whose 'major preoccupation was, throughout his life, always the same — freedom, its implications and its obstacles': those are the first words by which Christina Howells introduces the subject or object of her book, *Sartre*, rightly subtitled *The Necessity of Freedom*.[1] That freedom has, as a matter of fact, been 'a particular preoccupation' not only of Sartre, but of French theory in general, is all the less surprising since these three concepts have acquired a certain degree of equivalence which characterizes the contemporary state of theory, especially when approached from a much wider perspective.

This wider perspective, which would make freedom, subject, and theory appear more than related, indeed almost synonymous, is that of the history of philosophy, and more specifically of the history of metaphysics. It is not absent from Christina's book, which also puts Sartre's work into perspective, especially in its last chapter, offering a 'contemporary perspective' in its effort to understand the 'current disaffection with Sartre in French philosophical circles' (*NF*, p. 194). For this disaffection is 'almost total', she writes, Sartre's views (or theories) having been 'subjected' to a 'cacophony of polemical criticism', as if the subject of theory could not be freedom or its necessity, and certainly not Sartre, at least as far as French theory is concerned — 'French theory' meaning here of course 'the Structuralist and Post-Structuralist movements', not *la théorie française*, a formulation which, in

French and in France, does not exist. Her chapter briefly mentions several authors indebted to Sartre as well as a list of subjects of French theory that 'have been, at least in part, of Sartre's making': the 'decentred subject, the "death of man", the paradoxes of *qui perd gagne* and of "différance", the rejection of Hegelian dialectics and the recognition of the impossibility of ultimate synthesis' (*NF*, p. 194). However, after pointing out several similarities, analogies, or even parallels between their bodies of thought, her analysis soon focuses on 'the reasons underlying Derrida's almost too vehement rejection of Sartre's early philosophy' (*NF*, p. 195), and more precisely on what Christina describes as 'a fundamental mode of recuperative transformation which tempts both thinkers whilst being repudiated by them'. This is, she explains, 'the transformation effected by the principle of *qui perd gagne*, loser wins, and represented in its inauthentic form, in the view of both Sartre and Derrida, by negative theology and Hegelian dialectics' (*NF*, p. 198).

Were we to develop these vivid metaphors, emphasizing some of their French or etymological overtones, we would find ourselves viewing (theorizing) a scene where a woman, a seductress, is tempting two lovers — or perhaps trying to win back two husbands — of different generations, who are trying not only to resist her charms but to repudiate and divorce her. This would seem merely *théâtre de boulevard* if the two mythological heroes were not 'doing battle', as we finally learn, with a 'philosophical hydra'. Now, if the Lernaean hydra had seven heads, this philosophical hydra has at least two: negative theology and Hegelian dialectics, and maybe two more, existentialism and *différance*, in which the text recognizes multiple forms of the *qui perd gagne* strategy: authentic, inauthentic, Hegelian, Sartrean, Derridean — it would take time to sort them all out. These strategies tend to become indistinguishable even to the point of being identical. But do losers win? Does Sartre, or Derrida for that matter, really survive this ongoing battle, or are we not ultimately left to struggle in our turn with the philosophical hydra?

The problem is not that of knowing or deciding who won or lost the battle against the previous generation of philosophers; philosophy is, in this context, rightly described as an unruly monster whose multiple heads unceasingly grow back, a monster literally recapitulated by its ultimate figure, Hegelian dialectics. Understanding the epics of our contemporary heroes, whether they be still modern or already post-modern, requires putting distance between ourselves and the battle-field, for fear of being snatched by one of the serpent's heads. In other terms, it is not only the necessity of freedom in Sartre's work, or that of *différance* in Derrida's attempts to evade dialectical totalization, that need to be questioned or reaffirmed, but in a more general perspective the necessity of theory or philosophy itself as they are confronted with the whole of metaphysical discourse. For the hydra, with its many heads which seem to be multiplying faster than they can be neutralized, is only one of the appearances assumed by a heritage which we have no other choice than to accept, since it has always already inhabited our language and our relationship to everything that is.

This inescapable heritage is that of metaphysics, of which Heidegger tried to make us aware. Even if one does not follow or agree with each detail or aspect of his analyses, it is nevertheless worth referring, if only briefly, to 'European Nihilism', for example, one of the main chapters of his *Nietzsche*, where the metaphysics of modern times is characterized as the metaphysics of subjectivity.[2] Evaluating the 'situation of "theory" today' would amount to a very futile exercise if one did not remember to take into account the whole historical process of which today's theory is only the most recent outcome, an outcome which must necessarily be thought in terms of accomplishment or, on the contrary, of overcoming. Theory, if we take seriously what the title and rationale of this volume call for, is not just this or that theory, not even the complete collection of the more or less subjective views expressed by contemporary authors regarding today's world, problems, or aspirations; theory is the task left or passed on to us by history, the task of thinking in thankful response to the successive metamorphoses and translations incurred by the concepts with which we have been trying to grasp and understand our relation to what surrounds us. And for this task, freedom and subject are not simple themes that we are free to choose or not to choose, to adopt, or to reject, in an arbitrary or capricious manner: they force themselves on us or on theory, by way of a history that we must assume while eventually trying to overcome, to go beyond the determinations limiting our thinking. The subject of theory is not just the subject who theorizes, who freely makes theory, and decides that freedom will be at the centre of his or her theoretical enterprise; it is first and foremost subjected to theory, a theory whose subject is the subject as that which is thrown and lies or stands in plain sight, before the eyes of the one who sees, the theorist, as the very foundation or ground of theory. The subject of theory brings us back to the Greek *hypokeimenon* (substance), which became the Latin *subjectum*, and finally, from Descartes on, the subject of modern philosophy.[3] Whether this derivation needs to be thought in terms of evolution, translation, or mutation, whether it results from a new interpretation of the truth of being within the history of Being, as Heidegger claims to explain, these further questions cannot be dealt with in this framework.

What separates and unites Sartre and Derrida, or French theory, is their two ways of doing battle against the philosophical hydra, that is of overcoming the metaphysical theory of the subject, which Hegel unceasingly recapitulates by theorizing the dialectical process of substance becoming subject. Heidegger himself had to engage in this battle, this gigantomachia. Every philosophy since Hegel and Nietzsche has been an effort to overcome the modern metaphysics of subjectivity, which every attempt at thinking tries to evade, as if thought had been condemned to repeat and confirm endlessly the conceptual framework of Cartesian subjectivity, Kantian representation, or the Hegelian system of absolute knowledge. For there is no theory outside these limits, which function like the walls, moats, gates, and barriers protecting and constituting conceptual thought while at the same time imprisoning it. And it is not a simple question of evading confinement, or escaping from jail, or clearing (*franchir*) an obstacle, for freedom itself is part of the frame.

As truth becomes certitude and *hypokeimenon* becomes subject, the Cartesian *ego cogito* gives way to the spontaneity of the transcendental subject of the *Critique of Pure Reason*. But behind the scenes, in the background of representation, so to speak, where reality is always that of an object (*Gegenstand*) resisting, set against, or lying before (*ob-jectum*) a subject, lurks the thing in itself, which already in the first *Critique* announces a new metamorphosis or mutation of the subject into the will, clearing the way to Schelling, to Schopenhauer (who conceives *The World as Will and Representation*), and to Nietzsche (and his will to will or will to power). This appearance of the will on the scene of theory, which began as *theoria*, that is the simple view, observation, or contemplation, in particular of a spectator attending a celebration or a procession, is also the advent of freedom in theory, even though this advent can also be thought by Heidegger in terms of liberation from medieval doctrines and scholastics. What is new in modern, as opposed to medieval, times, is that man takes the initiative, which results from a 'liberation' from Christian truth, but presupposes also a new determination of the essence of liberty, in terms of necessity, of law, and of obligation. Freedom has therefore two faces: a dark side, license and arbitrariness, or liberation from faith in revelation; and a luminous side, the claim of a necessity, the inauguration of a multiplicity of what man can and wants to set as necessary and obligatory, making his own law, to speak in Kantian terms, whether it be human reason (*Aufklärung*), the real (positivism), classical humanism, or the Nietzschean superhuman.[4] Later, again, Heidegger will think the relationship between Hegel and Nietzsche in terms of liberation. It is however Kant who makes us 'touch' or 'hit upon' what is essential at the beginning of modern times, 'the proper structure of a fundamental metaphysical position', even though freedom already appears as essential, for example in Descartes's fourth Meditation.[5]

The two faces of freedom are to be found in Kant's own philosophy, whose development leads from the real to the Idea, from reception to spontaneity, and from scientific knowledge to political and ethical praxis. The thing in itself, which may first appear to be the real object of theory, is only a thing at the level of transcendental aesthetics, that is at the level of the sensibility of the subject who seeks to apprehend it. As its limits become more apparent, as it becomes more and more obvious that it cannot be perceived or thought in itself, but as conditioned (*bedingt*), it soon appears as a *noumenon* at the level of transcendental analytics, i.e. the level of the categories of understanding, and finally, toward the end of the *Critique of Pure Reason,* as a transcendental Idea, the Idea of a systematic knowledge of all objects of experience. Beyond the first *Critique*, the thing in itself as Idea actually ends up finding an order or domain where it can become unconditional (*unbedingt*), and, as the Idea of freedom, constitutive instead of simply regulative. Kant's *Metaphysik der Sitten* [Metaphysics of Morals] will clearly identify Idea and thing in itself, giving as an example of the thing in itself the Idea of a perfect human juridical constitution. Thus the thing in itself, as the object of theory (of theoretical reason), reveals itself to be freedom, as the subject of praxis (of practical reason). To state it even more briefly: freedom has become in modern times the true subject of theory, it belongs to the very essence of modernity.

The subject, source of all syntheses up to systematicity, is then also to be thought as ultimately liberating itself as practical reason, as autonomy, as will. Later, these two faces of freedom will explicitly become, in Schopenhauer's main opus, the two faces of the world, as will and as representation — a work which constitutes the main and direct source of Nietzsche's philosophy and of theories like that of the will to will, or will to power, one of the primary subjects of Heidegger's *Nietzsche*.

Freedom is thus necessarily the subject of modern theory, inasmuch as freedom defines, in multifarious ways, the subjectivity or 'subjectity' of modernity. What then would it mean to overcome modernity or to become postmodern? To liberate oneself (again, as subject?) from liberty, from that essence of freedom that makes up the frame to be exceeded, the walls to escape or the limits to cross? And how would French theory be able to accomplish such a feat?

First, certainly, by meditating a little longer and more precisely on Heidegger's *Nietzsche*. Then maybe by questioning also the origins not only of theory, but of what makes it French. The theory in question is said to be French from a non-French perspective — or perhaps conversely is it in fact more French than a strictly French perspective on theory would be? Nothing may make it French other than the national origin of the theorists involved. Let us think for a moment about what it could also mean for theory to be French, or the direction to which this notion might lead. What would we inherit? To what would we be obligated if we had the choice of accepting or not such a heritage?

Montesquieu once repeatedly asked: 'Comment peut-on être persan?' [How can anybody be Persian?]. I am not asking now 'how can theory today be (or not be) French?', but it may be useful nevertheless to remember that the word 'French' derives from 'Frank', and if not Montesquieu, Voltaire at least could help us understand what it originally means. Voltaire wrote the article 'François ou français' for Diderot's *Encyclopedia*, a rather long article whose last paragraph, on philosophy, reads thus:

> On ne devoit pas attendre que le françois dût se distinguer dans la Philosophie. Un gouvernement long-tems gothique étouffa toute lumiere pendant près de douze cents ans; & des maitres d'erreurs payés pour abrutir la nature humaine, épaissirent encore les tenebres: cependant aujourd'hui il y a plus de philosophie dans Paris que dans aucune ville de la terre, & peut-être que dans toutes les villes ensemble, excepté Londres. Cet esprit de raison pénetre même dans les provinces. Enfin le génie françois est peut-être egal aujourd'hui à celui des Anglois en philosophie, peut-être supérieur à tous les autres peuples depuis 80 ans, dans la Littérature, & le premier sans doute pour les douceurs de la société, & pour cette politesse si aisée, si naturelle, qu'on appelle improprement urbanité.

> [One would not expect the French to excel in Philosophy. A long-time gothic government snuffed out all light for almost twelve hundred years; and teachers of errors paid to make human nature brutish deepened darkness even further: today however there is more philosophy in Paris than in any city on earth, and maybe more than in all cities together, except London. This spirit of reason has even penetrated into the provinces. In a word, the French genius is probably at present equal to that of England in philosophy; while for the last four-score years France has been maybe superior to all other nations in literature; and has undeniably taken the lead in the courtesies of society, and in that so easy and natural politeness, which is improperly termed urbanity.]

Voltaire is also the author of the article 'Franchise', which is even more pertinent in this regard: *franchise* means freedom, he writes, no matter how it is used (whether designating rights, privileges, immunities, asylums, given to a nation, a city, a corporation or individuals, and finally a discourse). The word, Voltaire adds, comes from the Franks, who used to be free:

FRANCHISE, s. f. (*Hist. & Morale.*) mot qui donne toûjours une idée de liberté dans quelque sens qu'on le prenne; mot venu des Francs, qui étoient libres: il est si ancien, que lorsque le Cid assiégea & prit Tolede dans l'onzieme siecle, on donna des *franchies* ou *franchises* aux François qui étoient venus à cette expédition, & qui s'établirent à Tolede. Toutes les villes murées avoient des *franchises*, des libertés, des priviléges jusque dans la plus grande anarchie du pouvoir féodal. Dans tous les pays d'états, le souverain juroit à son avenement de garder leurs *franchises*.

Ce nom qui a été donné généralement aux droits des peuples, aux immunités, aux asyles, a été plus particulierement affecté aux quartiers des ambassadeurs à Rome; c'étoit un terrain autour de leurs palais; & ce terrain étoit plus ou moins grand, selon la volonté de l'ambassadeur: tout ce terrain étoit un asyle aux criminels; on ne pouvoit les y poursuivre: cette *franchise* fut restreinte sous Innocent XI. à l'enceinte des palais. Les églises & les couvens en Italie ont la même *franchise*, & ne l'ont point dans les autres états. Il y a dans Paris plusieurs lieux de *franchises*, où les débiteurs ne peuvent être saisis pour leurs dettes par la justice ordinaire, & où les ouvriers peuvent exercer leurs métiers sans être passés maîtres. Les ouvriers ont cette *franchise* dans le faubourg S. Antoine; mais ce n'est pas un asyle, comme le temple.

Cette *franchise*, qui exprime originairement la liberté d'une nation, d'une ville, d'un corps, a bientôt après signifié *la liberté* d'un discours d'un conseil qu'on donne, d'un procédé dans une affaire: mais il y a une grande nuance entre *parler avec franchise, & parler avec liberté*. Dans un discours à son supérieur, la liberté est une hardiesse ou mesurée ou trop forte; la *franchise* se tient plus dans les justes bornes, & est accompagnée de candeur. Dire son avis avec liberté, c'est ne pas craindre; le dire avec *franchise*, c'est n'écouter que son cœur. Agir avec liberté, c'est agir avec indépendance; procéder avec *franchise*, c'est se conduire ouvertement & noblement. Parler avec trop de liberté, c'est marquer de l'audace; parler avec trop de *franchise*, c'est trop ouvrir son cœur. *Article de M. de Voltaire.*

[A word which always gives an idea of liberty in whatever sense it is taken; a word derived from the Franks, who were always free. It is so ancient, that when the Cid besieged and took Toledo, in the eleventh century, *franchies* or *franchises* were given to all the French who went on this expedition, and who established themselves at Toledo. All walled cities had franchises, liberties, and privileges, even in the greatest anarchy of feudal power. In all countries possessing assemblies or states, the sovereign swore, on his accession, to guard their liberties.

This name, which has been given generally to the rights of the people, to immunities, and to sanctuaries or asylums, has been more particularly applied to the quarters of the ambassadors of the court of Rome. It was a plot of ground around their palaces, which was larger or smaller according to the will of the ambassador. The ground was an asylum for criminals, who could not be there pursued. This franchise was restricted, under Innocent XI. to the inside of their palaces. Churches and convents have the same privileges in Italy, but not in other states. There are in Paris several places of sanctuary, in which debtors cannot be seized for their debts by common justice, and where workers can pursue their trades without being freemen. Workers have this privilege in the Faubourg St. Antoine, but it is not an asylum like the Temple.

The word 'franchise,' which originally expresses the liberties of a nation, city, or body, has soon afterwards been used to signify liberty of speech, of counsel, or of a law proceeding; but there is a great difference between speaking with frankness and speaking with liberty. In a speech to a superior, liberty is a studied or excessive boldness; frankness keeps more within its just bounds. To speak with liberty is to speak without fear; to speak with frankness is to listen to one's heart. To act with liberty is to act with independence; to proceed with frankness is to conduct oneself openly and nobly. To speak with too much liberty is to display audacity; to speak with too much frankness is to be too open-hearted.][6]

Thus, behind French one can read or hear *franchise* (or exemption), but also *franchir* (to pass, or to go beyond, or above an obstacle, to cross difficult places, large spaces, borders), as well as *affranchissement*, franking. We seem to be progressively slipping from very ancient manifestations of political, economic, and judicial freedom into the much more recent history of postal administrations — from liberating a slave to stamping a letter: what could such different practices have in common, and what could they bring to theory, especially in these postmodern times of digital communication when stamping a letter has already almost become a thing of the past?

Frankly, nothing else seems to be left to philosophy other than to rememorate the traces of its evolution, or to collect the marks of its history, the vestiges of sendings (are they *envois de l'Être*? designing a *Geschichte*?), sendings which may never have reached their destination. Such may be the state of theory today, that there is no possible overcoming of the limits imposed by the metaphysics of subjectivity and the doctrines of liberty implied in each of its achievements or accomplishments, from Kant to Nietzsche, including Heidegger and their post-structuralist readers and analysts. Unless the practice of stamp-collecting, this apparently futile divertissement to which the theorist is condemned toward the end of modernity, conceals new possibilities of thinking: let us try once again, like Heidegger, to go back to the Greek origin of what we seek to understand. Stamp-collecting is the modern translation of *philatelia*, or is it?

In fact, *philatelia* has never been a Greek name, for it is French. The word *philatélie* is a modern creation (by a certain Gustave Herpin, in 1864, just a few years before the appearance of Nietzsche on the philosophical scene), borrowing from *philos/philein* (to like or to love, which we also find in philosophy) and *ateleia*, which means absence of *telos*, exemption of tax and charges, in one word: *affranchissement*. The philatelist is he or she who likes, who is enamoured of, franking. In the present situation of French theory, the philosopher has to be not only a historian of philosophy, or a genealogist, in order to understand fully the underpinnings and stakes of the discourse of which he or she is to remain the prisoner, but also a philatelist. To be a philatelist-philosopher (and only later an artist-philosopher, if that is still possible) means looking for what might be called 'thought frankings', *des affranchissements de pensée* — passages, mostly textual, where thought has been able to escape or to free itself, *s'affranchir*, from dominant, metaphysical discourse — collecting them as used traces, forgotten or obliterated vestiges of a counter- or para-history of theory that needs to be carefully restored or reconstituted. These marks of free thinking, these theoretical franchises can be found even in the most metaphysical or determinant texts when closely read or analyzed, whether those of Hegelian dialectics or Heideggerian history of Being. But no example is more enlightening than that of Kant's aesthetics, where love of *ateleia* metamorphoses into the pleasure of legality without law, purposiveness without purpose, and finality without end: no longer freedom in the modern sense, but free play or simple philatelic reflexion, already postmodern, under the condition of not constantly reintroducing, reinjecting in it and re-subjecting it to regulation, finality, systematicity, and determination in general. Philately being also the pleasure of sharing and exchanging vignettes, rather than the mere speculation it has sometimes threatened to become, I can only hope for many more and longer occasions to express my always renewed admiration of Christina's exemplary collections.

Notes to Chapter 12

1. Christina Howells, *Sartre: The Necessity of Freedom* (Cambridge: Cambridge University Press, 1988); this work subsequently referred to as *NF* in the main text.
2. Martin Heidegger, *Nietzsche, Volumes Three and* Four, ed. by David Farrell Krell (New York: HarperCollins, 1991). See especially volume IV: *Nihilism*, part I: 'European Nihilism', sections 15 ('The Dominance of the Subject in the Modern Age') and 19 ('Nietzsche's Position vis-à-vis Descartes').
3. Heidegger, *Nietzsche, Volumes Three and Four*, p. 130: 'The subject is the human "I." The concept of substance is never, as Nietzsche believes, a consequence of the concept of the subject. But neither is the concept of the subject a consequence of the concept of substance. The subject-concept arises from the new interpretation of the *truth* of the being, which according to the tradition is thought as *ousia*, *hypokeimenon*, and *subiectum*, in the following way: on the basis of the *cogito sum* man becomes what is properly foundational, becomes *quod substat*, substance. The concept of the subject is nothing other than a restriction of the transformed concept of substance to man as the one who represents, in whose representing both what is represented and the one representing are firmly founded in their cohesion'.
4. Heidegger, *Nietzsche, Volumes Three and Four*, pp. 97–98: 'We have gathered from these introductory remarks on the distinction between Protagoras' saying and Descartes' principle that man's claim to a ground of truth found and secured by man himself arises from that "liberation" in which he disengages himself from the constraints of biblical Christian revealed truth and church doctrine. Every authentic liberation, however, is not only a breaking of chains and a casting off of bonds, it is also and above all a new determination of the essence of freedom. To be free now means that, in place of the certitude of salvation, which was the standard for all truth, man posits the kind of certitude by virtue of which and in which he becomes certain of himself as the being that thus founds itself on itself. [...] If we say pointedly that the new freedom consists in the fact that man himself legislates, chooses what is binding, and binds himself to it, then we are speaking Kant's language; and yet we hit upon what is essential for the beginning of the modern age. In its unique historical form, this essence is wrought into a fundamental metaphysical position for which freedom becomes essential in a peculiar way (see Descartes, *Meditationes de prima philosophia*, Med. IV). Mere license and arbitrariness are always only the dark side of freedom. The bright side is the claim of something necessary as what binds and sustains. Of course, these two "sides" do not exhaust the essence of freedom, nor do they touch its core.

For us, it remains important to see that the sort of freedom whose obverse is the liberation from faith in revelation does not simply lay claim to something generally necessary, but rather makes its claim in such a way that man in each case independently posits what is necessary and binding. [...] Viewed metaphysically, the new freedom is the opening up of a manifold of what in the future can and will be consciously posited by man himself as something necessary and binding. The essence of the history of the modern age consists in the full development of these manifold modes of modern freedom. Because such freedom implies man's developing mastery over his own definition of the essence of mankind, and because such being master needs power in an essential and explicit sense, the empowering of the essence of power as fundamental reality can therefore become possible only in and as the history of the modern age'.

5. See the French translation of Heidegger's *Nietzsche: Nietzsche II*, trans. by Pierre Klossowski (Paris: Gallimard, 1971), p. 116: 'Si nous disons de façon plus précise que la nouvelle liberté consiste en ce que l'homme se donne lui-même la loi et choisit l'obligation de s'y lier, nous parlons le langage de Kant et touchons tout de même l'essentiel du début des Temps modernes, qui historialement dégage de haute lutte la structure propre d'une position métaphysique fondamentale, position pour laquelle de manière toute particulière la liberté devient essentielle'.

6. See Voltaire, *The Works of Voltaire: A Contemporary Version. A Critique and Biography by John Morley, notes by Tobias Smollett*, trans. by William F. Fleming, 21 vols (New York: E.R. DuMont, 1901), v (*Philosophical Dictionary*, part 3 [1764]), <https://oll.libertyfund.org/titles/voltaire-the-works-of-voltaire-vol-v-philosophical-dictionary-part-3> [accessed 29 January 2019]. The translation has been modified where necessary.

PART IV

Theorizing Pathologies and Therapeutics of Freedom

CHAPTER 13

Taking the Body Seriously:
A Critical Synthesis of the Work of
Christina Howells and Drew Leder

Marc Lafrance

In her most recent book, *Mortal Subjects*, Christina Howells presents us with a series of close and critical readings of some of France's most influential scholarship on subjectivity.[1] Focusing on phenomenology and existentialism, religious philosophy, psychoanalysis, and deconstruction, Howells argues that thinking about subjectivity in the twenty-first century requires that we carefully consider the relationship between mind and body and how it is invariably informed by embodied experiences of death and dying. As she explains in her opening chapter, considerations of this sort remain relatively rare in the scholarly literature on subjectivity. Instead, what 'is generally explored in the theorisation of subjectivity is its genesis, its constitution, its essence (or lack of essence), its identity, and its relation to otherness, not its disintegration, weakness, and ultimate dissolution in the radical alterity of death' (*MS*, p. 20). Precisely because theories of subjectivity have tended to avoid accounting for the human being's inevitable encounters with disintegration, weakness, and dissolution, they 'rarely allow for conceptions of subjectivity which already manifest the vulnerability and fragility which they claim characterize the subject as it should be understood' (p. 21). By placing the subject's vulnerabilities and fragilities at the centre of her study, Howells provides us with an imaginative approach to how we might think about the subject's fleshly frailties.

Like that of Howells, Drew Leder's book *The Absent Body* reflects on mind-body dualism by exploring themes of pain and suffering.[2] These themes, as Leder shows, prove to be highly useful for making sense of why subjects often experience a kind of lived separation between the mental and the physical. Opening with the claim that '[human] experience is incarnated', Leder's book is characterized by a decidedly non-dualist approach to thinking critically about human subjectivity (*AB*, p. 1). But this does not mean that he sets out to forge a framework that does away with dualism altogether. Instead, Leder attempts to understand what dualism has to teach us about the mind-body relationship, for it is only by understanding this relationship as it is lived that we will be able to appreciate why dualism remains entrenched both epistemologically and ontologically. To do so, Leder sets out to understand why the body is, in periods of relative health and well-being, absent from consciousness. While this emphasis on absence may appear to encourage rather than discourage dualist thinking, Leder posits that the opposite is true. He writes:

> It is often assumed that this dualist paradigm is shaped by ontological commitments at the expense of attending to lived experience. However, I will argue against this view. I will suggest that experience plays a crucial role in [...] supporting Cartesian dualism' (AB, p. 3).

By developing a phenomenological account of why this kind of dualism is so persuasive, Leder hopes to 'break its conceptual hegemony, while simultaneously reclaiming its experiential truths' (p. 3).

Both Howells and Leder are informed by twentieth-century French existential phenomenology. And while, as I mentioned above, the scope of Howells's book spans far beyond her engagement with this particular school of thought, I will focus on her readings of three of its key proponents — Jean-Paul Sartre, Maurice Merleau-Ponty, and Simone de Beauvoir — in order to show how she and Leder work with similar conceptual tools but arrive at different, albeit complementary, conclusions. Insofar as they are both interested in human frailty and how it might be understood in the context of embodied subjectivity, the two books are ripe for analytic synthesis. Ultimately, my goal is to bring these two authors into dialogue with one another so that the contributions of each may enrich those of the other.

Fragility, Vulnerability, and Mortal Subjectivity

Attempts to make sense of the mind-body relationship have been ongoing since the ancient Greeks (MS, pp. 1–15). And while philosophers ranging from Aristotle and Descartes through to Spinoza and Wittgenstein have found various ways of accounting for this relationship, the apparent oppositions and peculiar paradoxes with which it is often associated continue to preoccupy those interested in the complex workings of subjectivity. As Howells puts it, 'the human need to understand what [...] seems to be a dualism between mind and body at the heart of experience never really disappears' (MS, p. 16) even if, as she is careful to point out, the nature of this need changes according to the epistemological concerns and commitments of the day. For many philosophers, reflecting on the mind-body problem has meant trying to 'solve' it. And here solving the mind-body problem has tended to mean trying to find ways of 'explaining away' the many conceptual and experiential contradictions bound up with it. Yet part of what makes Howells's work both interesting and important is that she does not set up the mind-body problem as one to be solved but, rather, as one from which to learn. And in order to learn from this problem, she shows us that we must be willing to dwell in the ambiguities that appear to so deeply define it.

For Howells, thinking critically about the mind-body relationship means resisting the temptation to try to reach a point of absolute certainty and, above all, analytic closure. She does exactly this when she proposes the suggestive notion of *qui perd gagne*. A conceptual shorthand, *qui perd gagne* emphasizes the paradoxes of the human condition and how useful they are for helping us to understand the basic structures of subjectivity. Howells writes: 'Subjectivity and mortality are [...] linked in an aporetic structure in which subjectivity is simultaneously created and abolished by mortality: made possible at the same time as made impossible' (*MS*, p. 221).

As a 'mode of thought', *qui perd gagne* makes itself felt in a number of ways across the theoretical formations Howells considers. For the existentialists, it is, as Howells explains, 'precisely our failure to achieve self-identity that allows us to be free'; for the psychoanalysts, 'the death drive is essential to life' while 'the pleasure principle protects us from an excess of *jouissance*'; and, for the deconstructionists, '*différance* ensures that the (self-) presence we may yearn for is forever impossible' (*MS*, p. 218). *Qui perd gagne* allows us not only to accommodate but also to account for the paradoxical structures of subjectivity and, in doing so, to insist that identity and alterity are mutually productive, that transience is constitutive of experience, and that freedom is always already conditioned by constraint. Simply put, *qui perd gagne* allows us to work with, rather than against, the constellation of contradictions that characterize human subjectivity.

At once a methodological approach and an open-ended conclusion, Howells's notion of *qui perd gagne* is one of her study's key contributions to contemporary debates on subjectivity. But there is another contribution that I wish to discuss here, and that is her emphasis on '[reconciling] experience with philosophical reflection' (*MS*, p. 1). It is precisely this emphasis that makes her thinking in *Mortal Subjects* so conceptually productive. And here I am not referring to the fact that her thinking has been driven by what she herself calls 'an acute personal experience of love and death' (p. 1). What I am referring to, more specifically, is how Howells engages with experience — and particularly embodied experiences of fragility and vulnerability — as a legitimate, and perhaps necessary, mode of enquiry. This is made especially clear in her critical analyses of the work of existentialists such as Sartre, Merleau-Ponty, and Beauvoir. In these analyses, Howells reflects on how embodied experiences of fragility and vulnerability might be taken up as a way of 'testing' the explanatory potential of the philosophical approaches in question. Ultimately, as I will show, the approaches that appear most able to do justice to the suffering that results from these experiences tend to be those which Howells claims are most useful for thinking about the human subject.

For existentialists like Sartre, the body is that which 'enables us to act, to carry out our projects, to express our desires, to communicate with others, to know the world' (*MS*, p. 26). Sartre describes the body as the 'necessary' and 'essential' condition for consciousness to exist' as well as 'the situation from and in which consciousness makes its free choices' (p. 30). Yet despite the fact that Sartre is 'reso-lutely anti-dualist', he is, according to Howells, 'arguably unable to accept all the implications of embodiment' (p. 26). This is especially so where pain and illness are concerned, neither of which Sartre sees as 'overwhelming, or even significantly affecting, consciousness, but rather as experiences towards which consciousness remains free to choose what attitude it will adopt' (p. 33). To support his position, Sartre discusses the examples of stomach ache and eye pain, claiming that in both cases 'I cannot be infirm without choosing myself as infirm'. Howells, however, is unconvinced by these claims for at least two reasons. To start, Sartre's examples are, as Howells herself demonstrates, 'far from exhausting the range of illnesses and are indeed among the least significant'. Put differently, neither stomach ache nor eye pain is severe enough to entirely overpower consciousness and, as a result, neither poses a serious challenge to Sartre's claims. More serious challenges might have included the ravages caused by cancer and its associated treatments, the unrelenting demands of a physical disability, or the maddening agony that often accompanies chronic pain management. But there is another reason why Howells is critical of Sartre's accounts of pain and illness, and it relates to what she refers to as their 'externality'. This externality results in what Howells calls 'a limited attitude' that 'seriously impoverishes' his work — and especially his earlier work — on the human subject (p. 39).

So what does externality really imply in this instance? It appears to imply that Sartre's position as an outsider — as someone who had neither experienced extreme physical debilitation nor accompanied another as they did so — substantively interferes with his ability to truly capture that about which he writes. Of course, this is not to suggest that one must experience something in order to be able to write about it in a phenomenologically evocative manner. But it is to suggest that something seems to be missing from Sartre's accounts. Howells, for her part, argues that 'what Sartre seems to be lacking here is imagination' (*MS*, p. 38). I, however, want to make a slightly different and perhaps bolder claim: what Sartre is missing is in this instance is compassion.

Compassion, in the context of this paper, should not be defined as 'feeling sorry for someone'. Instead, it should be defined according to its Latin roots *cum* and *patior*, 'which together can be literally translated as "to suffer with"'. For Leder, 'the Latin notion of *patior* is not used solely in reference to pain and misfortune; more broadly it means to suffer something [...]; that is, to undergo an experience' (*AB*, p. 161). In other words, compassion is less about giving something to someone and more about experiencing it with him or her. And insofar as it is about experiencing with, or indeed suffering with, compassion is a most useful mode of thought — one that encourages the thinker to be both absorbed by and in communion with the fragilities and vulnerabilities of another and, by extension, to understand these experiences of absorption and communion as legitimate forms of knowledge production. To be sure, adopting a compassionate approach to subjectivity is not just about doing justice to those who suffer. That may well be important, especially for those who wish to put their scholarly work in the service of social justice, but it is not the point I wish to make here. More epistemological than sociopolitical, I argue that a compassionate approach quite literally allows us to see and understand things about subjectivity that we would not otherwise be able to perceive or comprehend.

What, exactly, does it mean to adopt a compassionate approach to thinking about subjectivity? To start, it means considering embodied experience in its most strained forms rather than just its more habitual ones. This requires a willingness to take the human being's extreme encounters with pain and illness seriously and, in doing so, to understand them as important ways of illuminating the intricacies of that which makes subjectivity what it is. This, as Howells points out, is something that Merleau-Ponty does more effectively than Sartre.

While it is certainly true that, like Sartre, Merleau-Ponty sees the body as 'an intrinsic element in the activities of consciousness', the two men differ in no small way on how this body's fragilities and vulnerabilities ought to be taken up in the context of debilitating discomfort and catastrophic disease. As Howells explains, Merleau-Ponty's 'examples of phantom limb pain and of brain damage [...] rather than stomach ache and eye strain are themselves indicative of the seriousness with which he takes the body'. And it is precisely because of the seriousness with which he takes the body — particularly the ill body — that he is able to understand, as Howells puts it, 'the worldview of the sick man as irremediably affected by his physical condition'. So if, for Sartre, we are free to choose how we relate to our illness, then for Merleau-Ponty, 'it is only through that illness that we exist at all'.[3] Given the phenomenological insistence on the idea that 'I am my body', illness 'cannot be viewed as something extraneous that we can simply transcend' but must, instead, be seen as something that constitutes us in the deepest and most meaningful ways (MS, p. 46).

Understanding embodied experiences of pain and illness as fundamentally constitutive of our relationship to, place in, and perspective on the world is a necessary part of adopting a compassionate approach to subjectivity. For it is precisely these experiences that allow our more abstract thinking about embodiment to be tested by its more concrete limitations. And this, according to Howells, is exactly what happens when Beauvoir writes about ageing and dying. Like Sartre, Beauvoir endeavours to 'espouse the radical existential position which insists that we are free to take up our chosen attitude with respect to our own ageing'. Yet this proves difficult, if not impossible, as her own body changes over time and becomes increasingly frail (MS, p. 64). Similarly, in her work on death and dying — the most notorious of which describes in very vivid terms Sartre's mental and physical degeneration at the end of his life — it becomes clear that the radical claims of her existential philosophy tend to 'fall away as useless in the face of the most extreme situations she has to face' (p. 67). Yet Howells does not criticize Beauvoir for her inability to adhere to the positions she outlines in her earlier work. Quite the contrary: it is precisely when Beauvoir fails to do away with the aporias associated with her own thinking that Howells deems her to be at not only her most passionate but also her most intelligent. For Howells, then, Beauvoir's best thinking on subjectivity is that which is characterized by contradictions — contradictions that are themselves the product of intensely embodied experiences of suffering.

As I mentioned above, Howells applauds Beauvoir for her candid discussions of the 'insurmountable contradiction' that results from the 'inevitable alienation' caused by her close encounters with the body's deterioration and decline (MS, p.

64). Not only does Beauvoir find it almost impossible to identify with a body that is, for all intents and purposes, degenerating, but this very degeneration is exactly what interferes with her capacity to '[easily transcend]' the body so that she may, as Howells states, 'best enjoy her embodiment' (p. 65). Howells has identified an important paradox here and, in order to make sense of it in both epistemological and ontological terms, we must think carefully about why exactly the body is at its most 'enjoyable' when it is 'easily transcended'.[4] In order to do this thinking, I will introduce Leder's work as it relates to and resonates with that of Howells.

Presence, Absence, and Mind-Body Dualism

Leder argues that the body is largely absent from consciousness in periods of relative health and well-being. He claims that understanding how and why this is the case is crucial if we hope to reveal the essential structures of subjectivity. Like his most important interlocutors, Sartre and Merleau-Ponty, Leder is resolutely anti-dualist. However, this does not mean that he thinks dualism ought to be completely dismissed while alternative epistemological frameworks are forged. Like Howells, Leder maintains that we must be able to account for why dualism has had, and continues to have, such an enduring appeal; we must, in other words, see dualism as something from which we can learn in order to better understand the complexities of embodied experience.[5] In many cases, this means that we must be willing to risk dualism before we can hope to do away with it. To fully appreciate what it means to risk dualism in this context, we must briefly consider Leder's conceptualization of bodily absence and how it relates to embodied experience.

Leder outlines two types of bodily absence in his now widely-cited book: that which characterizes the body's surface and that which characterizes its viscera.[6] For Leder, the body's surface is substantively different from the viscera insofar as it constitutes the site on and across which perception takes place. And while there are certainly differences between the structures and functions of the perceptual organs, the one thing that they all share is that they open the body onto the world and '[direct it] away from itself' (*AB*, p. 19). To highlight what he calls the 'radical paradox of the present-absent body' (p. 21), Leder makes use of the term *ecstasis*. He explains:

> This word includes within it the root *ek*, meaning "out," and *stasis*, meaning "to stand." The ecstatic is that which stands out. [...] The body always has a determinate stance [...]. But the very nature of the body is to project outward from its place of standing. (*AB*, pp. 21–22)

Put simply, Leder maintains that insofar as we perceive through an organ, 'it necessarily recedes from the perceptual field it discloses' (*AB*, p. 14). He points out that we do not see our eyes seeing, smell our noses smelling, hear our ears hearing, or taste our taste buds tasting but, rather, we 'perceive with and through such organs'. In this way, our being in the world 'depends upon [our] body's self-effacing transitivity' (p. 15).

Having described how the body's surface falls away from conscious awareness in periods of relative health and well-being, Leder turns his attention to the body's depths or, as I put it earlier, its viscera. Leder points out that even thinkers like Merleau-Ponty, thinkers for whom subjectivity is essentially embodied, tend to privilege the body's surface at the expense of its depths. Leder writes:

> Ecstatic functions such as perception will necessarily stand out for the phenomenological observer. [...] The same cannot be said of my spleen. This organ gives rise to no projective field. Moreover, it is largely unavailable to my own awareness or that of others. (*AB*, p. 37)

Over and above the spleen, Leder's visceral body includes the digestive, respiratory, cardiovascular, urogenital, and endocrine systems — all of which are inaccessible both to visual apprehension and physical manipulation. 'Neither subject nor object of direct engagement', the visceral organs disappear into the depths of human embodiment and 'recede from the arc of personal involvement' (*AB*, p. 54).

If, for Leder, healthy bodies are largely absent bodies, then unhealthy bodies are a different story altogether. It is precisely when the body is ill or in pain that its parts and processes concern and, indeed, consume us the most. Fragile and vulnerable bodies are neither ecstatic nor recessive in the ways I outlined above. Instead, these bodies seize our awareness when they are in a state of break-down. In this way, ill bodies and bodies in pain do not *disappear* but rather *dysappear*. Leder writes: 'In contrast to the "disappearances" that characterize ordinary functioning, I will term this the principle of *dysappearance*. That is, the body appears as a thematic focus, but precisely as in a *dys* state' (*AB*, p. 84). *Dys*, as Leder explains, is derived from the Greek prefix signifying bad, hard, or ill, and is found in English words such as dysfunctional. When the body dysappears, it does so in ways that are experienced as 'aversive, involuntary, and disruptive' (p. 75). Moreover, this dysappearance brings with it what Leder calls a two-fold 'telic demand' that incites the subject to both assiduously interpret and obsessively repair what is wrong with his or her body (p. 92). In and through these ongoing attempts to interpret and repair, the dysappearing body becomes increasingly objectified and, ultimately, 'emerges as a foreign thing' (p. 75). And when the ill or painful body is experienced as an object or a foreign thing — something that is 'separate from the essential self' — then identifying against it is likely to yield some relief and re-establish the subject's integrity in the face of a destabilizing irritant or compromising threat (p. 75). It is precisely experiences of this nature that, according to Leder, 'play a part in buttressing Cartesian dualism' (p. 70).

Leder's argument requires us to question the idea that bodily awareness is always already associated with bodily identification. After all, Leder's analysis suggests exactly the opposite; that is, we may well be our bodies, but our bodies do not always feel like us. In fact, the body is often experienced as other in the context of both health *and* illness. With respect to the former, it is experienced in this way because we are for the most part unaware of it. Indeed, insofar as the body serves as the seat of perception, we tend to turn away from it while turning toward that which it perceives. Here, as Leder puts it: 'the body is alien by virtue of its disappearance, as attention is primarily directed toward the world'. With respect to the latter, however, the body is other because it is experienced as that which no longer belongs to us. In other words, the body is no longer 'alien-as-forgotten, but precisely as-remembered, a sharp and searing presence threatening the self'. These two types of bodily alterity are complementary and, indeed, correlative phenomena: in the case of the former, alterity is enacted as 'a mode of silence' while, in the case of the latter, it is expressed as a 'manner of speech' (*AB*, p. 91).

Here we might reasonably ask: is Leder's approach to the experience of embodiment expansive enough to account for the many ways in which we relate to our bodies? And aren't these ways of relating to our bodies defined not only by absence but also by presence? Our everyday experiences of embodiment certainly suggest that this is so. Consider, for example, the extraordinary feelings of physical aliveness associated with athletic performance: we feel the acceleration of our heartbeat, the quickening of our breathing, and the perspiration on our skin. Here the body is, without a doubt, more present to us than it is absent. Similarly, consider the enormous pleasure we gain from our intimate encounters with others: our erogenous zones are excited, our sensory capacities are intensified, and our bodily parts and processes are associated with a kind of gratification that is largely inaccessible to us as we engage in the everyday activities of life. That said, our experiences of bodily presence are not limited to the exhilaration of physical exercise or the satisfaction of sexual intimacy. Our bodies are present to us in a wide range of other situations as well, many of which are downright banal: when we brush our teeth, wash our faces, stretch as we get out of bed, and look in the mirror as we get dressed for the day to come. Indeed, our daily body maintenance practices are necessarily bound up with a kind of physical awareness that Leder's notion of bodily absence does not elucidate or explain. How, then, does Leder account for this awareness?

Leder does not deny that our bodies are often present to us in ways that cannot be reduced to what he calls dysappearance. He acknowledges that both positive and negative experiences of the body are experienced as present, but he is also careful to point out that the former are to be distinguished from the latter because they do not exert the same kind of 'telic demand' on the subject. This demand, as I mentioned earlier, is two-fold in nature in that it induces the subject to both interpret and repair that which causes his or her body to dysappear. Unlike the more pleasurable or what we might call 'neutral' experiences associated with embodiment, the more embattled experiences that Leder emphasizes in his work are not optional; they cannot, as he states, 'be volitionally pursued or neglected according to personal and social preferences'. Instead, bodily dysappearance compels our attention insofar as it heightens sensory awareness of the body's frailties and, in doing so, demands that we sense-make and problem-solve in order to subdue the suffering caused by them. In this way, negative experiences of the body are bound up with an attentional demand that positive experiences are not. But this attentional demand is not the only one at issue here; bodily dysappearance is also associated with an existential demand in ways that set it apart from more positive or neutral experiences of embodiment. Unlike athletic performance, sexual intimacy, or everyday body maintenance practices, pain and illness tend to reorder the subject's existence by reorganizing his or her projects and reorienting his or her relationship to the world. As Leder explains: '[neutral] kinesthetic, visual, and tactile self-experiences may play as crucial a role in the construction of our body image, but they do not place upon one the same demand for an affective and metaphysical wrestling with embodiment' (*AB*, p. 92).

Thus far, my discussion of Leder's work has focused on what he calls organic dysappearance; that is, dysappearance that results from a breakdown in the body's biophysiological or sensorimotor systems. However, the phenomenon of bodily dysappearance is not confined to the organic realm; it is also, quite crucially, to be found in the realm of the social. Drawing on Sartre's now iconic account of the look, Leder argues that the gaze of the other plays a crucial role in constituting our experiences of embodiment. Like organic dysappearance, social dysappearance can give rise to a split between mind and body and, in doing so, can make us feel as though our bodies are objects that do not belong to us. As Leder asserts:

> In social dys-appearance, this split is effected by the incorporated gaze of the Other. But not just any gaze will bring about such a rupture; it is the objectifying gaze that refuses cotranscendence. [...] Internalizing this perspective, I can become conscious of my self as an alien thing. (*AB*, p. 96)

Social dysappearance, then, is not unlike what we might call social marking; that is, it is enabled by and through an oppressive logic of visibility whereby bodily awareness is unevenly distributed across dominant and subordinate groups.[7] Those who make up the dominant groups are unmarked and can, therefore, enjoy the privilege of being able to forget about their bodies. Those who belong to subordinate groups, however, are marked and must wrestle with the burden of being reduced — in sometimes dangerous and often deterministic ways — to their flesh and blood.

Leder too points out that members of marginalized communities bear a disproportional burden where social dysappearance is concerned. And though he himself does not develop this point, other critical cultural theorists do. For example, feminist theorists inspired in large part by the work of Michel Foucault have shown that women are surveilled in ways men are not and that this surveillance has a way of inscribing the power relations of the day into the bodies of those subjected to it;[8] similarly, as critical race theorists influenced by the work of Frantz Fanon have demonstrated, members of racialized groups are often reduced to their skin colour by means of what he calls the *schéma épidermique racial*.[9]

In summary, Leder argues that dualism is appealing to us because it allows us to account for the ways in which the body can and often is experienced as an object in both our organic and social worlds. In situations such as these, the dualist interpretation of the body makes its own kind of sense. But this interpretation is, as Leder makes clear, a misinterpretation. And it is a misinterpretation not only because embodiment is, as the existentialists and the phenomenologists teach us, fundamentally reflexive but also because it is meaningful in ways that only something that is vitally constitutive of me, my situation, my perspective, and my projects can be. Put succinctly, my body's problems matter to me to the extent that they do because I am the matter of my body's problems.

Closing Remarks

When read alongside one another, Christina Howells and Drew Leder allow us to shine a light on what has long been a blind spot in contemporary theorizing on subjectivity: namely, the embodied experience of suffering. And, as I have tried to show, both Howells and Leder do this in four key ways: first, by working with rather than against the paradoxes of the mind-body relationship; second, by exploring exceptional states of embodiment rather than merely its more 'normal' states; third, by being open to the everyday life of the body — that is, the body as it is lived in both its moments of splendour and vitality and its moments of breakdown, decomposition, and degeneration; and fourth, by allowing themselves to wade, with a careful tentativeness and considered uncertainty, back into the waters of the dualism debate to attempt to do justice to the often deeply felt separation between mind and body. Together, Howells and Leder provide us with an epistemologically persuasive and ontologically powerful approach to embodied subjectivity, one that, above all, takes the humanness of the human seriously.

Notes to Chapter 13

1. Christina Howells, *Mortal Subjects: Passions of the Soul in Late Twentieth-Century French Thought* (Cambridge: Polity Press, 2011); this work subsequently referred to as *MS* in the main text.
2. Drew Leder, *The Absent Body* (Chicago, IL: University of Chicago Press, 1990); this work subsequently referred to as *AB* in the main text.
3. Howells is, however, careful to point out that Sartre's understanding of embodiment changes considerably over the course of his lifetime. His later work, she argues, is more attuned to embodied experiences of pain and suffering than his earlier work (*MS*, p. 33). She writes: 'Sartre himself was highly critical of his own position, commenting in an interview in 1970: "It's incredible: I really believed it"' (*MS*, p. 40).
4. For another discussion of precisely this paradox, see Oliver Davis, *Age Rage and Going Gently: Stories of the Senescent Subject in Twentieth-Century French Writing* (Amsterdam: Rodopi, 2006), pp. 33–63.
5. Here, again, it is worth mentioning that Leder's approach is reminiscent of that taken by Oliver Davis when he discusses Beauvoir's suggestion that old age is a time of Cartesian contradiction. Future research on the productive nature of thinking through, rather than against, contradictions of this sort would do well to consider Davis's work alongside that of Howells and Leder.
6. For a relevant example of work informed by Leder's book, see Nick Crossley, *Reflexive Embodiment in Contemporary Society* (Milton Keynes: Open University Press, 2008).
7. For more on how logics of visibility operate in contexts such as these, see Nick Mansfield, *Subjectivity: Theories of the Self from Freud to Haraway* (New York: New York University Press, 2000), pp. 118–36.
8. See, for example, the work of feminist theorists such as Sandra Bartky, *Femininity and Domination: Essays on the Phenomenology of Oppression* (London: Routledge, 1990); Susan Bordo, *Unbearable Weight: Feminism, Western Culture and the Body* (Berkeley: University of California Press, 1993); and Cressida Heyes, *Self-Transformations: Foucault, Ethics and Normalized Bodies* (Oxford: Oxford University Press, 2007).
9. Frantz Fanon, *Peau noire, masques blancs* (Paris: Seuil, 1965). For more on this topic, see the work of critical race theorists such as Lewis Gordon, *What Fanon Said: A Philosophical Introduction to his Life and Thought* (New York: Fordham University Press, 2015); Paul Gilroy, *Against Race* (Cambridge, MA: Harvard University Press, 2000); and Kobena Mercer, 'Reading Racial Fetishism', in *Representation: Cultural Representations and Signifying Practices*, ed. by Stuart Hall, Jessica Evans, and Sean Nixon (London: Sage, 1997), pp. 280–87.

CHAPTER 14

Philosophy and Other Addictions: On Use and Abuse in the History of Life

Gerald Moore

From the levers and pumps that inspired Enlightenment models of the heart and lungs, to twentieth-century accounts of the computational brain, our self-understanding of the dynamics and potentialities of human life is interwoven with the evolution of technology. Configurations of the human around metaphors drawn from technology nonetheless tend to differentiate us from machines, introducing causal gaps that leave mechanical and deterministic explanations of our behaviour under-determined. More recent emphases on our structural openness to the outside ensure that we can never quite be reduced to automata, always retaining, in Kantian terms, a potential for *autonomy* that cannot be automated away by the causal overriding of free will. For both Peter Sloterdijk and Bernard Stiegler, for example, the effect of technology is to reinvent and bring about changes in the function of human organisms that would otherwise risk enslavement to biological drives: 'anthropotechnological' media 'tame' and 'sublimate' the unthinking, instinct-led beasts that dwell within us.[1] But as Stiegler repeatedly observes in reference to the ambivalent therapy-toxicity of the technological object as *pharmakon*, both cure and poison, the very technologies that 'liberate', or 'disautomate', us, can also induce regression to pathological modes of automation, most notably in the form of addiction.[2] His claim is consistent with contemporary neurobiology, which is moving away from the idea of addiction being rooted in a combination of genetic pathology and a 'disease' of brain chemistry triggered by a narrow range of potent addictogens, and towards understanding it as an extreme case of experiential learning. Sometimes criticized for an excessive dilution of the concept, emerging research treats addiction as an increasingly negative feedback loop that takes hold when (neuro)plastic life adaptively reshapes itself around environmental sources of stimulus most associated with potential reward — be they opioids, digital screens, or even books.[3] Building on this, and on other advances in the ecological approach to addiction, let us go further and posit that nowhere is the rewriting of our interiority by our prostheses more pronounced than in technology's capacity for monopolizing attention, pushing the dopamine system to 'automatize behaviour' around *pharmaka* that distract us from the instabilities of the surrounding world.[4] Evidence for the impact of increasingly intense modes of technological stimulation is found in what we might speculatively diagnose as historical waves of addiction, coinciding with periods of 'disadjustment' between the technological reorganization of society and the social and political norms that govern our consumption of technology. This is one way of making sense of Catherine Malabou's recent claim, made though reference to the 'biohistory' of Daniel Lord Smail and the 'psychotropic' bases of capitalism, that 'history is the history of addictions', beginning with the trade in dopamine-arousing spice and sugar and culminating in the chronic, manic, consumption of the Anthropocene.[5]

With its eternal return to weakness of the will and to the transcendence of reason over the appetites, we can read the history of philosophy as a series of responses to the threat of nervous automation posed by becoming locked in to the craving for dopamine. But what if philosophy, too, were susceptible to becoming an addiction — an antisocial bad habit whose pretensions to a higher form of love and meditational retreat were just another technique of anxiolytic withdrawal? The pursuit of disautomation works by attaching ourselves to forces that stand outside the habitual, narrowing, attentions of the addict, but these new attachments can also turn pathological.

Varieties of Automation

The concept of life and, above all, of specifically human life, has evolved alongside the history of technology, the dialogue between biology and our exosomatic organs dating back at least as far as Aristotle. The systematic zoological observations Aristotle undertook on the island of Lesbos are frequently cited as the birth point of the scientific method, but, for Georges Canguilhem, the Stagirite's artifactual environment was also of decisive significance. 'Genuine working artifacts', meaning simple automata, became more common from around the time of Aristotle, and he makes several references to them in his later biological writings.[6] In *De motu animalium*, he observes that 'the movements of animals' are comparable with, but strictly irreducible to, 'those of automatic puppets, which are set going on the occasion of a tiny movement (the strings are released, and the pegs strike against one another)', but lack both the accompanying qualitative change in sensation and the internal origin of motion that would characterize organic life.[7] Without mechanical contraptions to serve as the contrastive model against which he could develop a theory of life, it has been argued, he could not have arrived at the idea of 'soul', or 'vital principle', through which he differentiates the living from that which might only appear to be alive.[8] As Canguilhem puts it:

> L'assimilation de l'organisme à une machine présuppose la construction par l'homme de dispositifs où le mécanisme automatique est lié à une source d'énergie dont les effets moteurs se déroulent dans le temps, bien longtemps après la cessation de l'effort humain ou animal qu'ils restituent.

[The comparison of the organism to a machine presupposes man-made devices in which an automatic mechanism is linked to a source of energy whose motor effects continue well after the cessation of the human or animal effort they reproduce.][9]

And yet in Aristotelian circles, as in those of Plato before him, we also see glimpses that we, too, are intermittently susceptible to an automation that trumps autonomy, via the ingestion of psychoactives whose effect on our behaviour lasts well beyond the immediate moment of consumption. (Pseudo-)Aristotle's 'Problema XXX', on melancholy, muses, for instance, on the effect of *pharmaka* like wine, while indicating that their transformation of subjectivity is differentiated from mere mechanical automation by its accompanying changes at the level of experience.[10]

Canguilhem proposes that automata exerted a similarly decisive influence on the formulation of Cartesian dualism.

Quand Descartes cherche des analogies pour l'explication de l'organisme dans les machines, il invoque des automates à ressort, des automates hydrauliques. Il se rend par conséquent tributaire [...] des formes de la technique à son époque, de l'existence des horloges et des montres, des moulins à eau, des fontaines artificielles, des orgues, etc.

[When Descartes turns to machines to find analogies in his explanation of the organism, he invokes spring-loaded and hydraulic automata. He is thus a tributary [...] of the technical forms of his age: of the existence of clocks and watches, water mills, artificial fountains, pipe organs, etc.][11]

Off the back of this reading, Ian Hacking has proposed that modernity began not so much with Descartes's *cogito* in 1641, but with 'the invention or proliferation of free-standing machines' that made it possible to envisage isolating the soul from a mechanical body.[12] The Cartesian epiphany becomes but one moment in the more protracted emergence of a modern technical system grounded in the mechanization and automation of work, already hinted at in Aristotle, and which lays down a firmer foothold in the Renaissance before intensifying alongside the growth of industrialization. But this history of the machine set apart from the soul still tells only half the story — that of envisaging mind and body as metaphysically distinct. The other half cuts in the very opposite direction, concerning the permeability of the subject's interiority: no longer irreducibly free and a site of resistance to external automation, but itself automatable, lending itself to reorganization by habits that penetrate to the innermost core of the nervous system.

The ensuing modernity bears witness to a series of attempts to salvage something of humanity from subjection to ever more invasive forms of habituation, whose manufacture moreover becomes both a powerful engine of the consumerist economy and the palliative precondition of our adaptation to the traumas of capitalist exploitation. Modern anxiety incorporates not just the uncanniness of mechanicity and the broader social effects of its reordering of society, but also and perhaps moreover a parallel history in which we are vitiated and restructured by *pharmaka* in the fullest sense, encompassing both the tools and machines that organize the economy and society, and the pharmaceuticals that, by one means or another, keep us well enough to cope with their demands. This is the history of capitalism as what we might call 'dopamining'. From the refining equipments and techniques of preparation used to enhance the potency of agricultural crops, to the printing of books and the mass production of televisual screens that, via the hand and the eye, interface with the brain, this history consists, on one hand, in the cultivation of a long line of increasingly accomplished technologies for the delivery and exploitation of dopamine hits. The successive waves of stimulation for sale provided by these dopamining technologies take the edge off the labour of adaptation that, on the other hand, pushes us towards addictive, anxiolytic habits as a way of coping with the economic instability of accelerating rates of technological change and the perpetual reorganization (now 'disruption') of social norms. Pathologies pertaining to these manufactured habits don't really get diagnosed under the modern rubric of addiction until the late eighteenth-early nineteenth centuries. The coalescence of amateur experimentation into the formalized disciplines of the modern medical sciences is profoundly intertwined with the birth of the pharmaceutical industry from the engineering and commercial exploitation of ever more powerful forms of pain medication. The medicalization of pathological consumption as a disease and subsequent addiction-specific modes of therapy like Alcoholics Anonymous (AA) are even slower to take off, emerging only between the nineteenth and late twentieth century — and even then with decidedly mixed success. But we can find proto-addiction therapies at work as early as Plato, in a deployment of reason against weakness of the will that can speculatively be traced to the context of an addiction epidemic at the end of the fifth century BCE.[13] A comparable practice is at work in the critical philosophy of Immanuel Kant, which might similarly be read as a response to the disadjustment of an early industrial society firmly marked by automation, both technological and of the nervous system. Kant identified resistance to such automation with the capacity to anchor oneself to a point of externality standing outside the tightening grip of the addict's dopamine craving, albeit in what would amount to advocacy of a higher form of therapeutic addiction. In so doing, he sets the pattern for what would follow with AA's 'god'.

Spectres of Vaucanson

In the mid-sixteenth century, a foot-high automaton of a praying monk appears to have been thought so 'miraculous' in its construction that it could make for a fine ex-voto, commemorating the miracle return to health of Spain's crown prince, Don Carlos, presumed to be on the brink of death.[14] A century later, vastly more complex automata were common enough for Descartes to posit that all animal life was basically clockwork, though crucially, he could still rely on the immateriality of the soul to immunize humans against the threat of collapse into mechanical behaviour. By the time his *Meditationes* turned one hundred, however, the dualist defence was beginning to look out of kilter with the age, at least philosophically. The years 1737–40 saw Jacques de Vaucanson build and exhibit revolutionarily lifelike mechanical automata, before turning his attentions to industry and the automation of French manufacturing. His clockwork musicians and defecating duck created panic and suspicions of witchcraft, and his attempts to reorganize the silk trade around punch-card-programmed mechanical looms provoked rioting by guildsmen in the city of Lyon.[15]

If the fears of French silkmen turned, in the first instance, towards unemployment and the prospect of skilled artisans reduced to automata, the thinkers of the age dwelled on a more metaphysical terror, namely the realization that, if replaceable by machines, then machinery was perhaps all we had ever really been. Vaucanson's engineering helped lead the empiricist philosopher Julien Offray de La Mettrie to conclude, in *L'Homme-machine* of 1747, that 'le corps humain est une Machine qui monte elle-même ses ressorts' [the human body is a self-winding machine], the complex organization of which is alone enough to account for rational thought. He saw further evidence of the absence of a soul in the ease with which states of consciousness can be transformed by such stimulants as coffee, wine, and opium.[16] Hobbes and Spinoza had, by this stage, already grappled with the philosophical implications of human life being reduced to a chain of material cause and effect, the former going so far as to infer the necessity of creating another tier of automation, namely a Leviathanic and absolutely sovereign 'Artificiall man' — by which he meant the state — to prevent our mechanical impulses from tipping society into interminable civil war.[17] Spinoza, later followed by Leibniz, would attempt to square the circle by identifying freedom not with the capacity to override these chains, but with the positive affirmation of our status as 'spiritual automata'.[18]

Although mentioned infrequently, at best, the spectre of Vaucanson's androids also haunts the work of Immanuel Kant, providing a rare glimpse into the technical milieu from which the project of critical philosophy emerges. Famously, Kant's move is to separate out the mechanical determinism of the phenomenal world from that of an unknowable noumenal realm in itself, preserving autonomy in the 'necessary' metaphysical 'postulate' — one that exists beyond the bounds of pure rational comprehension — of an unconditioned causality able to act on phenomena from without the empirical determinations encountered in time and space. The third *Critique* writes of 'two entirely different kinds of causality, that of nature in its universal lawfulness and that of an idea that limits the latter' — 'the tool of an intentionally acting cause to whose ends nature is subordinated, even in its mechanical laws'.[19] In the second *Critique*, this separation of causal powers is presented as a noumenal gap, or opening, that differentiates us from otherwise lifelike automata:

> If a human being's actions [...] were not merely determinations of him as appearance but as a thing in itself, freedom could not be saved. A human being would be a marionette or an automaton, like Vaucanson's, built and wound up by the supreme artist; self-consciousness would indeed make him a thinking automaton, but the consciousness of his own spontaneity, if taken for freedom, would be mere delusion.[20]

Faced with the threat that freedom is a 'mere delusion', the function of the noumenon is to salvage humanity from automation, or what Kant more routinely calls 'heteronomy', meaning the antecedent causes of our behaviour that originate outside the mooted noumenal core of the transcendental subject. Kantian philosophy thus inverts the alignment of automation and autonomy: the automaton is one who declines to draw on the spontaneous causal power of reason to wrest themselves free from the automatic, habitual behaviours of the heteronomously conditioned body that lives in hock to the pursuit of pleasure. There is thus a decisive slippage between mechanical automation and the automation of the nervous system. As Kant puts it in his lectures on anthropology, the 'neural stimulus' of alcohol 'does not *reveal* the *natural* temperature', or underlying disposition, of the human condition, but 'rather *introduces* another one' that overcodes free will with causal determinism.[21] Nonetheless, despite the existence of transcendental freedom by default, automation is still the general tendency, rather than the exception. The ease with which heteronomous forces strengthen the mechanical grip of our corporeal being means that the intervention of reason is comparatively rare — and made more so by the prevalence of technological *pharmaka*, including a growing number of industrially produced and intensified intoxicants, able to impinge on our functioning. Notes taken during his lectures on ethics record Kant as having described drunkenness in terms of the short-circuiting of the transcendental by the empirical, leaving the drunkard incapable of acting freely.[22] In a rare discussion of habitual intoxication in the late *Metaphysics of Morals* (1797), the abjuration of autonomy is further equated not just with immorality, but with animality and, worse still, 'debasements, even below the nature of an animal', who, after all, has no choice but to live heteronomously. To allow one's actions to be determined by 'fermented drinks' and other narcotics, Kant continues, amounts to such a violation of 'duty to oneself' that the drunk is 'not to be treated as a human being', though he stops short of specifying the (presumably inhumane) ways with which they should accordingly be dealt.[23] Humanity, in this respect, consists in the willingness to accept the responsibility of 'freedom and dominion over oneself' made possible by reason, which is precisely what is surrendered by the subject who 'finds its pleasure and satisfaction in a slavish mind'. The refusal is 'evil', but moreover 'incurable', for the simple reason that 'the sick person does not want to be cured and flees from the dominion of principles, by which alone a cure could occur'. The proto-addict resorts to drink to escape life's miseries, but remains, for all that, reduced to misery by the haunting 'summons to inner freedom' of reason, which leaves him 'groan[ing] in his chains'.[24] With this emphasis on the curative powers of reason, let it be noted how it is rational philosophy — the 'dominion of principles' — and not yet medicine that is charged with treating what Kant classifies as the 'passions'. Equally, it is not quite clear how far (proto-)addictions would really fall into this category. His classification distinguishes between innate inclinations and culturally acquired 'manias', including for dominance and possession, but states of drinking and gambling that 'one does not exactly call these various inclinations or disinclinations so many passions', as much as abuses of '*mere passivity* in the faculty of desire'.[25]

In sliding between two kinds of automation, technological and behavioural, Kant affords us another rare glimpse at the general socio-historical and technological context so routinely elided by the abstraction and transcendence sought in philosophical writing. This is a context where mechanization goes hand in hand with the growth of incapacitating habits of consumption; one that also pre-dates the more recent separation of pharmaceuticals from a broader array of techno-pharmacological intoxicants; where besides alcohol and drugs stand books, deemed similarly capable of short-circuiting the exercise of reason. The splitting of categorical hairs points to an uncertain ontological status and, perhaps in turn, to a world where addictions are emerging into view but not yet squarely in the sights of a philosophical-medical gaze.

Technologies of Addiction

Only a couple of years before La Mettrie mused on the ability of intoxicants to reprogramme the man-machine, and but months after Vaucanson had first exhibited his automata to the upper echelons of London society, Britain's capital reached the nadir of a 'Gin Craze' whose social and economic impact had become increasingly troublesome over the course of the eighteenth century. In 1743, the average Londoner drank 2.2 gallons of fermented spirits per annum, up from 1.3 gallons in 1729, and only a third of a gallon at the turn of the century.[26] The causes of this rising consumption were multiple, ranging from a ban on imported French brandy and the corresponding deregulation of domestic production, to the development of cost-reducing distillation technologies, the rise of gambling, and the social devastation occasioned by the South Sea Bubble. Perhaps the most visible factor, however, was a massive influx of itinerant workers from the countryside, exacerbated by the absence of a social system able to absorb their precarious, rootless existence.[27] Agrarian capitalism grew from the increasing enclosure and privatization of once-common land, combined with new agricultural technologies including crop rotation and phosphate fertilizers. Its effect was to create a surplus of rural labour, which gravitated in desperation towards towns, above all London. The newly urbanized, pre-industrial precariat tended to find there neither stable work, nor the kind of welfare support available back home from families and local parishes. But there was enough cheap, effective solace in the city's many gin houses for excessive drinking to generate a crisis of serious ill-health and declining productivity. The historian of narcotics, Wolfgang Schivelbusch, recounts how liquor first entered everyday life via military daily rationing, where its power of 'anaesthetization' set out 'the rudiments of later industrial discipline', by serving 'as a sort of psychological and physiological lubricant to guarantee' the 'smooth functioning' of the early-modern soldier as 'a cog in the wheel of a mathematically and rationalistically organized corps of troops'.[28] The same logic of artificial integration is taken to extremes in the case of the dislocated urban poor, for whom the delegation of life's decisions to an autopilot powered by gin worked all too well — in a formulation of Bruce Alexander that significantly complicates the Kantian separation of reason from intoxication — as a 'rational', 'adaptive' substitute for meaningful psychosocial belonging.[29]

The first formulation of alcohol dependence as a 'disease' in need of specifically medical treatment came from the American physician and signatory of the Declaration of Independence, Benjamin Rush, in 1784, the same year as Kant's famous essay, 'An Answer to the Question: What Is Enlightenment?', to which we shall return in due course.[30] The consolidation of capitalism would usher in subsequent spikes in the consumption of intoxicants, including caffeine, which was sourced through the catastrophic off-loading of Indian opium on China, and also cocaine and opioids. In an age still beset by the brutality and boredom of much labour, the later rise of the pharmaceutical industry both commercialized and legitimated the consumption of new forms of pain medication, including laudanum, morphine, and subsequently heroin. The last of these, like the hypodermic syringes that underpinned the rise of morphinism, were initially thought to prevent increasingly documented phenomena of addiction.[31] Much like another intoxicant enjoying a boom period at the time, albeit one less conventionally recognized as such, they were also deemed especially corruptive of the supposedly weaker and certainly less stimulated sex.[32]

We have known at least since Avital Ronell's *Crack Wars: Literature Addiction Mania* (1992) that *Madame Bovary*, by Gustave Flaubert, can be read as a novel about addiction.[33] Entrapped by the uninspired rural drudgery of nineteenth-century France, the fate of Emma Bovary tracks that of the stereotypical terminal addict, beginning with the search for escape, excitement, and pain relief, before obsessional pursuit escalates into child neglect, debt, prostitution — a means of repaying her dealer, the pharmacist Homais — and ultimately suicide by overdose. Emma's gateway and drug of choice, and the high she thereafter labours in vain to recapture, is romance fiction, her novels functioning exactly in the terms of what Natasha Dow Schüll, writing on contemporary addiction to gambling machines, describes as the 'zone' opened up by the fetishized prosthesis: the therapeutic space of retreat into which the anxious and dopamine-starved addict withdraws from the chaos of a society that offers little prospect for world-building.[34] In much the same way that, like early proponents of heroin and the syringe, some still write off the non-pharmaceutical, 'soft' addictions of screens and the digital as mere metaphors for the real deal, there is a temptation to downplay Flaubert's fictitious case study as the product of misogynistic parody.[35] Even allowing for hyperbole, however, Emma's drama is in keeping with the broader experience of the printing revolution, diagnosed by Kant as a product of the automation of thought through the reckless consumption of reading material.

In another instance of disadjustment caused by the inability of social norms to keep up with, and regulate, the effects of accelerating technological change, the second half of the eighteenth century witnessed the intersection of a relatively anomic population and a rapid expansion in the supply of books. The combination led to fears that reading had become a 'fever', a 'mania', and even an 'addiction' in continental Europe.[36] In pre-unification Germany, the scale of *Lesesucht* and the thirst for written stimulation were deemed sufficiently dangerous to constitute a subversive menace to the social order, including an existential threat to the viability of the university. The progressive spread of literacy into the middle classes and the decreasing cost of mass-printing technologies generated a 'journal addiction', borne out, in the period 1700–1800, by a twenty-fold increase in the number of periodicals on the market, the majority of which were pitched to a new and 'unlearned "public"'.[37] What Wellmon describes as an 'Enlightenment form of technological disruption' caused a transformation in the hierarchy of social relations comparable to that of alphabetization in ancient Athens. The ready availability of books undermined the epistemic authority of the German university, causing enrollment to drop to the point that over half of them would eventually collapse.[38] The number of new publications dedicated to fiction moreover unleashed governing-class anxieties over inexperienced and unregulated amateur book fiends, able to consume disruptive material in inconspicuous silence. The unpoliceable private space between the page and the eye worked as a conduit for hacking into the brain, whereupon readers' heads could be filled with the kind of norm-violating fantasies that would encourage them to abandon their allotted stations in life.

Critique as (Limited) Therapy

The heteronomic potency of the book is identified at the outset of Kant's essay on enlightenment, which begins with something like wariness towards the unregulated consumption of information that Bruno Latour would later theorize as 'double click'.[39] Kant complains that, in spite of a capacity for reason that allows us emancipation from the 'alien guidance' of material corporeality, we still all too lazily seize the chance for 'a book to have understanding in place of me, a spiritual advisor to have a conscience for me, a doctor to judge my diet for me [...] I need not think, so long as I can pay'. So long as I can uncritically consume the answers thrown in my direction by the (unchecked) appearance of authority.[40]

This consumerist, abnegationist mentality is the very opposite of the value that Kant deemed fundamental to the age, namely 'maturity'. Maturity would consist in learning to think for oneself; and more pointedly, in distinguishing between the unregulated consumption of information and the critical engagement with ideas that underwrites the possibility of knowledge. It demands, furthermore, that one — albeit a certain, qualified, one — never surrender autonomy to the heteronomous forces that seize hold of and automate the body and mind. But that does not entail Kant rejecting automation under all circumstances. On the contrary, as he indicates later on in the same essay, the principle of freedom — the notional capacity to exercise one's noumenal-transcendental autonomy, without its causal power being heteronomously short-circuited, as it is in the case of the perennial drunkard — seems to count for rather more than the practice. Criticism can be offered up in private, but in public one must 'act as part of a machine', disciplining the mind and body in accordance with the 'imperative' of 'civil obedience'. Beyond the confines of domesticity, the citizen is bound by respect for the institutions of state, much as the clergyman is required to respect the doctrines of the Church.[41] In saying this, Kant builds towards the argument of his last major work, *Der Streit der Fakultaten*

[The Conflict of the Faculties] (1798), on the composition of the university. There, he makes a distinction between the public-facing and 'higher' faculties of law, medicine, and theology, whose subject-matter — namely the 'eternal', 'civil', and 'physical' well-being of the people — necessitates their subordination to and determination by the established legal, medical, and doctrinal norms established 'on the command of an external legislator',[42] and the 'lower' faculty of philosophy, which alone is granted the 'power to judge autonomously — that is, freely'.[43] Although Kant does not employ the term himself, the higher faculties are effectively 'heteronomous', in the sense of being governed by external causality. Theology derives its power from, and is bound by fidelity to, scripture; members of the faculty of law take their interpretive cue only from the statutory laws of the land. The medical profession is 'freer' than the other higher faculties, insofar as it 'must derive its rules of procedure not from orders of the authorities, but from the nature of things themselves'. To resist the temptation to exploit immaturity through quackery, however, it still needs to be policed and regulated by a 'board of public health'.[44] In addition to being subject to heteronomy, the higher faculties are also deemed liable to inculcate heteronomy in others, by slipping into the kind of seductive metaphysical dogma that Kant elsewhere equates with fanaticism, and which serves to circumvent the thought of, and thereby automate, the masses.[45] The autonomy of philosophy is required to keep this tendency towards dogmatic excess in check, but is itself conditional on the philosopher's criticisms remaining beyond the reach of the public, privately enclosed within the scholarly sphere of the university.[46] Withdrawal from the *polis* and into what might look like hermetic self-containment is built into the very structure of the discipline.

Echoing his earlier complaints about the prevalence of intellectual minority, in the later text, a proto-existentialist Kant concedes that the freedom of philosophy is not for everyone, the 'public' being broadly disinclined to take the arduous route towards a life lived well. 'The people want to be *led*, . . . to be *duped*' and 'naturally adhere most to doctrines which demand the least self-exertion and the least use of their reason'.[47] This general preference not to think elevates the 'businesspeople' of the higher faculties into magicians and 'miracle-workers', who indulge in regressing the masses to automation by demagogically setting forth 'doctrines in keeping with the people's inclinations', and manipulating their 'habits' and 'feelings' by pandering to popular reckoning with snake oil and cheap maxims of self-help that absolve us from the 'work' of duty.[48] While philosophical learning is not a prerequisite for living 'moderately', philosophy's behind-the-scenes, disautomating, work of critique is fundamental for curbing the hubris of those disciplines which, on account of their potential for rabble-rousing, fanaticism, and exploitation, risk sowing the seeds of insurrection. For the same reason of preserving social stability, however, Kant is by no means against automation — at least, not against the right kinds of automation. His 'account of true enlightenment and its relationship with governmentality hinged on careful specification of the mechanization of the subject', in the words of Simon Schaffer.[49] Just as the addict has effectively abnegated humanity and regressed to (sub-)animality by declining to circumscribe heteronomy through transcendental reason, Kant accepted industrial automation, the disciplinary formatting of workers around the rhythms imposed by the machine, as the lot of those not cut out for freedom. This ambivalence lingers over his concept of freedom, too, insofar as Kant (paradoxically) insists on autonomy being strictly law-governed. All that really differs is the kind of law — empirical or 'moral' — by which one's actions are determined. That the two kinds are distinguished only by what Kant himself acknowledges to be a mere 'postulate' furthermore becomes increasingly problematic in light of ongoing work, most notably by Catherine Malabou, on whether the transcendental can survive in an age of neurobiology.[50]

Recalling Aristotle's suggestion that we are differentiated from mechanical automata only at the level of subjective experience, that is, by the transformations of affect that coincide with the forces acting on our decision-making, Kant states that determination by the moral law will be qualitatively distinct from the experience of heteronomous, mechanical automation. Although grounded in reason, and not empirical, sensory, or corporeal in origin, we might still hazard that autonomy effectively amounts to a superior kind of automation, one marked by 'respect' rather than by the cravings associated with addiction. The distinction is weakened by Kant's admission that autonomous behaviours must first be inculcated and rehearsed to the point of becoming automatic, with 'appraisal of actions by moral laws a natural occupation and, as it were, a *habit* accompanying all our own free actions'.[51]

If the distinction between 'heteronomous' and 'autonomous', deterministic and free, causality begins to break down, then what is to stop us from wondering whether the philosopher's fetishistic pursuit of the moral law couldn't also serve as the object of an addiction? Such a reading would be in keeping with the earliest uses of the term. Although connoting servitude and habituation, the word 'addiction' acquires its predominantly negative undertone only over the course of capitalist modernity, its consumerist-era diagnosis as an (inherited) disease serving to insulate the majority against fears that their consumption is pathological. In a Christian tradition stretching from Saint Paul to the King James Bible of the early seventeenth century, one would still speak favourably of being submissively 'addicted [...] to the ministry of the saints' (1 Corinthians 16:15).[52] Religious experience has been identified with the dopamine highs more typically associated with intoxication, and is also thought potentially addictogenic.[53] Current neuroscience attests to the positivity of some addictions, highlighting the 'striking similarity' between pathological dependence and forms of automatized habituation associated with neuroplastic learning.[54]

The same mentality of affirming superior modes of addiction permeates throughout the history of philosophy, which, like Christianity, has revolved since Plato around the elevation of baser compulsive drives into a higher form, most notably the sublimation of *eros* into *agape*. In line with the idea that addiction is pharmacological, which is to say, can have therapeutic value in itself, both Stiegler and Malabou also write of the replacement of toxic addictions with 'better', more therapeutic ones.[55] And Kant, too, is inevitably no exception to this philosophical mainstream. His move is to substitute enslavement to and automation by the mechanistic causality of the passions with non-passionate voluntary servitude before a moral law that nonetheless still claims to draw its authority from an external source of causality, namely God. As Kant writes in both the second and so-called 'fourth' (posthumously published, unfinished) *Critiques*, it is the speculatively necessary postulation of God that underwrites the distinct existence of an ('unconditioned') self-positing subject of transcendental freedom, that is, a subject able to wrest itself free from the automations of heteronomy; God who exists as the point of externality to which we can anchor ourselves and so break out of the vicious circle of the addict's craving.[56]

From here, we might go further still and suggest that Kant's invocation of God as an idea presages that of Alcoholics Anonymous, most famously immortalized in the 'suggestions' of the *Twelve Steps*. AA's legendary programme for disautomation repeatedly outlines how allowing oneself to 'depend upon a Higher Power' preconditions the gaining of 'true independence of the spirit'.[57] The third step recounts how the organization's early adopters 'made a decision to turn our will and our lives over to the care of God *as we understood Him*', in a formulation that has caused consternation since its first publication in 1939.[58] Its stated intention is to extend the method of self-treatment to non-believers, though the remainder of the text strongly indicates that atheistic adhesions to the maxim will performatively lead any atheist towards true belief. The examples chosen to illustrate the breadth of possible interpretations of 'Him' are nonetheless philosophically interesting. Comparing dependence on God to a householder's dependence on electricity, or to that of a polio sufferer on their iron lung, the overt message is that God can be treated as a kind of supplementary help, or prosthetic will, allowing the concupiscent to outsource their own defective agency to a force that, like the *pharmakon* of the addict, effectively desires on their behalf. What matters more, of course, is whether this kind of treatment — of 1) generating a point of exteriority that stands outside the addict's automated craving for their specific stimulus of choice; and 2) of supplanting worse with better addictions — works. Recent research suggests that 2) does not, or does so only rarely: sticking rigidly to what has been reified as the dogmatic prescriptions of the *Twelve Steps*, it is argued, offers a differential success rate of just over 5 per cent, up against the commonly cited 50–80 per cent success rate of 'spontaneous' (untreated) remission.[59] Tried and trusted AA methods of religiously attending meetings, accepting powerlessness, abdicating one's will to God, and counting days of abstinence merely reinscribe the very neuronal pathways that identify the addiction as the go-to behaviour of choice, accelerating 'ego fatigue' and the risk of relapse.[60] There is thus a question over whether the method of inculcating a new and supposedly better addiction really goes far enough in creating an exit point from automation by something worse. Returning to 1), a promising alternative might therefore consist in empowering addicts to explore a multiplicity of ways of living, exposing addled brains to greater varieties of stimulation, so as to reverse the effect of neuronal pruning and the narrowing of attention around a single and overriding object of focus.

Salve Christina

Philosophy takes shape in response to the changing nature of automation, not just differentiating us from mechanical simulacra, but creating a space and moreover an agency through which to combat the *pharmaka* that take hold of and reprogramme the body. Yet the artifactuality of the will, namely the ease with which it is shaped, and freedom attenuated, by *pharmaka* makes for an ambivalent fascination. Kant's reaction to Vaucanson and the printing revolution offers one example of philosophy's role in what Stiegler terms 'disautomation', the creation of new techniques of critical learning to wean us off the bad habits of outsourcing desire to technology that works in our place. It serves as a mechanism for the reorganization of technologically diasdjusted societies. But philosophy, too, is forever at risk of becoming just another bad habit, a means of retreat from the chaos it is otherwise charged with stilling.

Plutarch's *Parallel Lives* records the tale of a Greek philosopher in Rome who exerted such powerful charms that 'he instilled in the young men of the city a fierce passion which caused them to banish all their other pleasures and pastimes, and succumb to love of knowledge'.[61] But what would it even mean to be debilitated in this way? Referencing Plato, Jean-Pierre Vernant wrote of the discipline that it was born in, and will forever continue to occupy, the ambivalent space between the *polis* and the debauchery of the symposium; between political engagement and its very opposite, namely withdrawal into the private intoxication of abstract intellectualism.[62] On a similar note, Bernard Stiegler has told me on more than one occasion that 'il arrive un moment où il faut arrêter de faire la philosophie pour être un citoyen' [there comes a time when one needs to stop being a philosopher and start being a citizen]; when, in other words, one needs to stop looking to the sublatory potential of philosophical solutionism to do away with the weight of the world, and just get stuck in with collective projects to alleviate it. Like everything else, in other words, philosophy is pharmacological, both therapeutic and toxically intoxicating. We see the curative side of what he has begun to call *penser/panser*, or *pænser*, on show in his recent writings on madness. Stiegler analyzes at length the role that reading and especially writing have played in carving himself an escape route, by turns from prison, addiction, and institutionalizing bouts of depression, and above all from entrapment in the constitutive nothingness of our interiority. As he puts it in *Dans la disruption* (2016) and again in *Qu'appelle-t-on panser?*: 'Écrire, c'est-à-dire de travailler — c'est-à-dire de *me* soigner [...] j'avais tenté de me soigner en prison par cette "technique de soi" que l'on appelle écrire, mais aussi lire — deux pratiques d'un autre *pharmakon*' [Writing, which is to say, working, which is to say, taking care of *myself* [...] I had tried to take care of myself in prison by means of this 'technique of the self' that we call writing, but also through reading — two practices of another *pharmakon*];[63] 'Penser, c'est panser le *pharmakon* qui *transduit* de manière toujours quasi-causale (et *jamais* de façon *simplement* causale) les pulsions de vie et de mort en tant qu'elles forment dans l'exosomatisation' [Thinking is salving the *pharmakon* that quasi-causally (and *never simply* causally) cuts across the drives of both life and death insofar as they are formed in exosomatization].[64] To think —

through writing — is to heal, by creating through technology a point of exteriority that takes us back outside of ourselves, a (retroactively, or 'quasi'-, causal) future that acts on the present by transporting us beyond the entropic, tightening noose of short-term impulses. And yet herein, in the second quotation, one also tastes the poison of this philosophical *pharmakon*: a language that writes more for itself than for the *polis*; whose function is *self*-medicatory, over and above communicational; one so obscure and hermetically intricated as to risk collapse back into the heady zone of its composition, at the cost of undercutting its ambitions towards super-philosophical citizenship.

It is perhaps to keep such intoxications at bay that French philosophy, in the wake of Derrida, has come to speak of philosophy's need to break out of itself, to become *anti-* or *non-*philosophical, by disautomating its inheritance of past habits. Badiou and Laruelle are the most explicit proponents of this approach, though they — and particularly Laruelle — can hardly be absolved from the accusation of getting high on their own writing.[65]

An alternative kind of ambassador to the *polis* might look something like Christina Howells, as a deconstructive existentialist but moreover as a person. Her published work is often only implicitly political, at best, and her thoughts on passion and freedom only occasionally cross over into ideas of addiction.[66] But she is remarkably free of those traits that characterize the philosophy addict, the one who preaches against the *esprit de sérieux* while simultaneously clinging to an inviolable core of their own thought; who teaches the lightness of being while wearing their work so heavily as to prevent them from living. The mentality is captured in the Sartrean motto of *qui perd gagne*, which she habitually recites to the overwrought and underworked in her function as teacher and therapist to all and sundry, be they her students, colleagues, random acquaintances, or the retinue of eccentric protégés she has redeemed and cultivated over the years. I count myself lucky to have numbered among at least two of those categories, and to have been coaxed out of hermetic intellectualism by her habit of never doing philosophy in abstraction, always treating it as a technique of anthropology, for the interminable analysis of everyday life.

Notes to Chapter 14

1. Peter Sloterdijk, 'Rules for the Human Zoo: A Response to the Letter on Humanism', *Environment and Planning D: Society and Space*, 27 (2009), 12–28 (p. 16).
2. Bernard Stiegler, *La Société automatique, 1: L'Avenir du travail* (Paris: Fayard, 2015), pp. 45–48 (§12).
3. A much more extensive reading of the overlaps between Stiegler and current addiction science is given in Gerald Moore, 'The Pharmacology of Addiction', *Parrhesia*, 29 (2018), 190–212; and Gerald Moore 'Addiction Epidemics from Athens to Fake News', *New Formations*, special issue on *Automation Anxiety*, ed. by Ben Roberts and Patrick Crogan (forthcoming). Both articles also defend these newer approaches against the accusation of emptying out the meaning of addiction.
4. On the 'automatization of behaviour' as a learned response to dopamine cues, see Barry J. Everitt and Trevor Robbins, 'From the Ventral to the Dorsal Striatum: Devolving Views of their Roles in Drug Addiction', *Neuroscience and Biobehavioural Reviews*, 37 (2013), 1946–54 (p. 1950).

5. Made in the closing comments to a paper given at the European Graduate School in Saas-Fee, 2015, which Malabou is in the process of working into a fuller treatment of addiction: <https://www.youtube.com/watch?v=eDdTqr-5APg> [accessed 20 February 2019]. The published version of the paper is 'The Brain of History, or, The Mentality of the Anthropocene', *South Atlantic Quarterly*, 116.1 (2016), 39–53.

6. Sylvia Berryman, 'Ancient Automata and Mechanical Explanation', *Phronesis*, 48, 4 (2003), 344–69 (p. 356).

7. Aristotle, 'Movement of Animals', in *The Complete Works of Aristotle*, ed. by Jonathan Barnes, 2 vols (Princeton, NJ: Princeton University Press, 1984), I, 1092 (701b1–15).

8. Berryman, 'Ancient Automata and Mechanical Explanation'.

9. Georges Canguilhem, *La Connaissance de la vie* (Paris: Vrin, 2009), p. 135 [106]; *Knowledge of Life*, ed. by Paola Marrati and Todd Meyers, trans. by Stefanos Geroulanos and Daniela Ginsburg (New York: Fordham University Press, 2008), pp. 79–80.

10. Aristotle, 'Problems, Book XXX', in *The Complete Works of Aristotle*, II, 1499–1500 [9–23].

11. Canguilhem, *La Connaissance de la vie*, p. 136 [106]; Canguilhem, *Knowledge of Life*, p. 80.

12. Ian Hacking, 'Canguilhem amid the Cyborgs', *Economy and Society*, 27, 2–3 (1998), 202–16 (p. 207).

13. See Bruce K. Alexander, *The Globalization of Addiction: A Study in the Poverty of Spirit* (Cambridge: Cambridge University Press, 2008), p. 321; Gerald Moore, 'Automations, Technological and Nervous' (forthcoming).

14. Elizabeth King, 'Perpetual Devotion: A Sixteenth-Century Machine That Prays', in *Genesis Redux: Essays in the History and Philosophy of Artificial Life*, ed. by Jennifer Riskin (Chicago, IL: Chicago University Press, 2007), pp. 268–73.

15. Simon Schaffer, 'Enlightened Automata', in *The Sciences in Enlightened Europe*, ed. by William Clark, Jan Golinski, and Simon Schaffer (Cambridge: Cambridge University Press, 1999), pp. 126–65 (p. 144).

16. Julien Offray de La Mettrie, *L'Homme-machine* (Paris: Mille-et-une nuits, 2000), pp. 24–25; *Man a Machine and Man a Plant*, trans. by Richard Watson and Maya Rybalka (Indianapolis, IN: Hackett, 1994), pp. 32 [70].

17. Thomas Hobbes, *Leviathan*, ed. by Richard Tuck (Cambridge: Cambridge University Press, 1991), p. 10 [2].

18. Baruch Spinoza, 'Treatise on the Emendation of the Intellect', in *Ethics, with Treatise on the Emendation of the Intellect and Selected Letters*, ed. by Seymour Friedman, trans. by Samuel Shirley (Indianapolis, IN: Hackett, 1992), p. 256 [85].

19. Immanuel Kant, *Critique of the Power of Judgment*, ed. by Paul Guyer, trans. by Paul Guyer and Eric Matthews (Cambridge: Cambridge University Press, 2000), p. 290 [5:422].

20. Immanuel Kant, *Critique of Practical Reason*, trans. by Mary Gregor (Cambridge: Cambridge University Press, 1997), p. 85 [5:101].

21. Immanuel Kant, *Anthropology from a Pragmatic Point of View*, ed. and trans. by Robert B. Louden (Cambridge: Cambridge University Press, 2012), p. 65 [172].

22. Immanuel Kant, *Lectures on Ethics*, ed. by Peter Heath and J. B. Schneewind, trans. by Peter Heath (Cambridge: Cambridge University Press, 1997), p. 81 [27: 288].

23. Immanuel Kant, *The Metaphysics of Morals, revised edition*, ed. by Lara Denis, trans. by Mary Gregor (Cambridge: Cambridge University Press, 1997), p. 194 [6:427–28].

24. Kant, *Anthropology from a Pragmatic Point of View*, p. 166 [266–67].

25. Ibid., p. 169 [269–70].

26. Jessica Warner, *Craze: Gin and Debauchery in an Age of Reason* (London: Profile, 2003), p. 3.

27. Patrick Dillon, *Gin: The Much-Lamented Death of Madam Geneva* (Boston, MA: Justin, Charles & Co., 2004), pp. 29–37.

28. Wolfgang Schivelbusch, *Tastes of Paradise: A Social History of Spices, Stimulants, and Intoxicants*, trans. by David Jacobson (New York: Vintage, 1993), pp. 152–53.

29. Alexander, *The Globalization of Addiction*, pp. 62–64.

30. Lucy Inglis, *Milk of Paradise: A History of Opium* (London: Macmillan, 2018), p. 152.

31. Ibid., pp. 212–13.

32. Ibid., p. 229.
33. Avital Ronell, *Crack Wars: Literature Addiction Mania* (Champagne: University of Illinois Press, 1992), esp. pp.74–75.
34. Natasha Dow Schüll, *Addiction by Design: Machine Gambling in Las Vegas* (Princeton, NJ: Princeton University Press, 2012), pp. 2–3.
35. See, for example, Sherry Turkle, *Alone Together: Why We Expect More from Technology and Less from Each Other* (New York: Basic Books, 2011), pp.293–94.
36. Roger Chartier, 'Reading and Reading Practices', in *Encyclopedia of the Enlightenment*, ed. by Alain Charles Kors (Oxford: Oxford University Press, 2003), p. 399; see also Chad Wellmon, *Organizing Enlightenment: Information Overload and the Invention of the Modern Research University* (Baltimore, MD: Johns Hopkins University Press, 2015), p. 67.
37. Wellmon, *Organizing Enlightenment*, pp. 68, 66.
38. Ibid., pp.164, 161–62.
39. Bruno Latour, *Enquête sur les modes d'existence: une anthropologie des modernes* (Paris: La Découverte, 2012), pp. 136–40.
40. Immanuel Kant, 'An Answer to the Question: What is Enlightenment?', in *Political Writings*, ed. by Hans Reiss (Cambridge: Cambridge University Press, 1991), p. 54.
41. Ibid., p. 56.
42. Immanuel Kant, 'The Conflict of the Faculties', in *Religion and Rational Theology*, ed. and trans. by Allen W. Wood and George Di Giovanni (Cambridge: Cambridge University Press, 1996), pp. 248–51 [7:18–23].
43. Ibid., p. 255 [7.28].
44. Ibid., p. 254 [7: 26–27].
45. Immanuel Kant, *Observations on the Feeling of the Beautiful and Sublime and Other Writings*, ed. by Patrick Frierson and Paul Guyer (Cambridge: Cambridge University Press, 2011), p. 57 [2:251].
46. Wellmon, *Organizing Enlightenment*, p. 146.
47. Kant, 'The Conflict of the Faculties', p. 258 [7:31–32].
48. Ibid., pp. 257–58, 261, n.1 [7: 30–31, 34].
49. Schaffer, 'Enlightened Automata', p. 153.
50. Catherine Malabou, *Avant demain: épigenèse et rationnalité* (Paris: Presses universitaires de France, 2014).
51. Kant, *The Critique of Practical Reason*, p. 127 [5:159].
52. As discussed by Alexander, *The Globalization of Addiction*, pp. 29–30.
53. Michael A. Ferguson, Jeffrey S. Anderson, and others, 'Reward, Salience, and Attentional Networks are Activated by Religious Experience in Devout Mormons', *Social Neuroscience*, 13, 1 (2018), 104–16; see also Cheryl Zerbe Taylor, 'Religious Addiction: Obsession with Spirituality', *Pastoral Psychology*, 50, 4 (2002), 291–315.
54. See, for example, Ann M. Graybiel, 'Habits, Rituals, and the Evaluative Brain', *Annual Review of Neuroscience*, 31 (2008), 359–87 (p. 369).
55. Malabou, 'The Brain of History', p. 52; see also, for example, Bernard Stiegler, *Mécréance et discrédit, 3: L'Esprit perdu du capitalisme* (Paris: Galilée, 2006), p. 116 (§24).
56. Immanuel Kant, *Opus postumum*, ed. by Eckart Förster, trans. by Eckart Förster and Michael Rosen (Cambridge: Cambridge University Press, 1993), p. 230 [21:25–26].
57. *Twelve Steps and Twelve Traditions* (New York: Alcoholics Anonymous World Services, 1953), p. 36.
58. Ibid., p. 34.
59. Lance Dodes and Zachary Dodes, *The Sober Truth: Debunking the Bad Science Behind 12-Step Programs and the Rehab Industry* (Boston, MA: Beacon Press, 2014), pp. 53–56.
60. Marc Lewis, *The Biology of Desire: Why Addiction is not a Disease* (New York: PublicAffairs, 2015), pp. 15–16, 184–85.
61. Plutarch, *Roman Lives*, trans. by Robin Waterfield (Oxford: Oxford University Press, 1999), p. 30 [Cat22].
62. Jean-Pierre Vernant, *The Origins of Greek Thought* (London: Methuen, 1982), p. 60.
63. Bernard Stiegler, *Dans la disruption: comment ne pas devenir fou* (Paris: Les Liens Qui Libèrent, 2016), p. 300.

64. Bernard Stiegler, *Qu'appelle-t-on panser? L'immense régression* (Paris: Les Liens Qui Libèrent, 2018), p. 85.
65. See, for example, Alain Badiou, *Nietzsche, L'Antiphilosophie 1: Le Séminaire 1* (Paris: Fayard, 2015); François Laruelle, *Principes de la non-philosophie* (Paris: Presses universitaires de France, 1996).
66. See, for example, Christina Howells, '*Le Défaut d'origine*', in *Stiegler and Technics*, ed. by Christina Howells and Gerald Moore (Edinburgh: Edinburgh University Press, 2013), p. 150.

CHAPTER 15

Frantz Fanon: Freedom, Embodiment, and Cultural Expression

Jane Hiddleston

The work of Frantz Fanon is a striking example of voracious interdisciplinarity. A psychiatrist by profession, Fanon's most famous works are an eclectic mixture of philosophy, psychoanalysis, political theory, and cultural critique. He received a literary education, having met Aimé Césaire — a figure who was to become one of the major influences on his thought — at the Lycée Schoelcher in Fort-de-France, Martinique. Yet he went on to study psychiatry in Lyon in 1946 and was appointed at the Blida-Joinville Hospital in Algiers in November 1953 before moving to Tunis in 1957, where he practised at the Manouba and Charles-Nicolle hospitals. In his clinics he was deeply committed to the ethical treatment of his patients, who were often damaged by the colonial conflict, and he read and wrote prolifically about psychiatric methods in North Africa and about the need for practices that would take cultural specificity into account. Alongside his medical work, however, he was also a political activist, closely engaged in Algeria's struggle for independence and writing frequently for the Algerian newspaper *El Moudjahid*. He was passionately committed to the principle of freedom, at once in the political context and in the treatment of psychiatric disorders; he was instrumental, for example, in setting up a day centre at the Charles-Nicolle hospital to allow patients greater agency and independence. His most famous works, *Peau noire, masques blancs* [Black Skin, White Masks] published in 1952, and *Les Damnés de la terre* [The Wretched of the Earth] published in 1961, moreover, both draw on his medical knowledge and on his political commitment, and yet are also above all steeped in philosophy. His interlocutors here range from psychoanalysts Freud, Adler, and Octave Mannoni, to Hegel and Marx, with heavy influences from Husserl, Sartre, Beauvoir, and Merleau-Ponty, all of whom are again read and critiqued for their contributions to the conceptualization of freedom.

   Yet alongside Fanon's psychiatric, political, and philosophical work, his passion for literature remains evident in much of his writing. His library, the contents of which is detailed by Jean Khalfa and Robert Young in *Écrits sur l'aliénation et la liberté*, contains a diverse range of literary works alongside medical, philosophical, and political studies, including in particular theatre and poetry. Khalfa's presentation of the library includes comments by Raymond Péju, the bookseller in Lyon whom Fanon frequented as a student, who emphasizes in particular his love of poetry and the long conversations they had together about figures such as Césaire, Char, Aragon, Breton, Eluard, Damas, and Senghor.[1] As David Macey notes, Fanon was also keenly interested in drama from an early age, writing two plays of his own recently published in Khalfa and Young's volume, and I would suggest that his theoretical works are on some level themselves theatrical in their language and structure.[2] Dictated and transcribed first to his wife Josie and later to an assistant at the day clinic in Tunis, Marie-Jeanne Manuellan, the works were originally spontaneous spoken performances, and can also be understood as a form of literary creation in themselves. *Peau noire, masques blancs*, in particular, is a formally experimental piece of writing and has been characterized both as a rewriting of Césaire's *Cahier* and as an echoing of Dante's descent into Hell.[3] Yet the place of literature, or more broadly of cultural production, in Fanon's thought has tended not to be the main focus of many of his critics and commentators, even if his relationship with Césaire has been well documented.[4] Jean Khalfa has discussed the connection between the various dimensions of the neurological, the psychiatric, and the social in Fanon's concept of the 'pathologie de liberté' suffered by mental health patients in North Africa, but Fanon's cultural interests tend to be treated separately.[5] How, though, does Fanon's interest in literary and cultural creativity relate to his psychiatric, political, and philosophical work? How can cultural activity contribute to his over-riding commitment to the principle of freedom?

This chapter will analyze how Fanon's eclectic interests can be seen to coalesce in a conception of embodiment, a conception that informs his understanding of psychiatry, politics, and culture, and that is also central to the creation of freedom towards which his thinking always tends. Indebted to phenomenologists such as Merleau-Ponty, Fanon situates the body at the centre of human perception and experience, and corporeality is referred to frequently through his writings as he discourses on medical, philosophical, and political questions. His critique of racism and colonialism is to a large extent based on the destructiveness of their 'schéma corporel', their oppression and forced alienation of black and colonized bodies. It is also the colonial system that is responsible for many of the health problems of the North African patients that Fanon discusses in 'Le "Syndrome nord-africain"', published in 1952, and in the case studies printed in *Les Damnés de la terre*, as colonial oppression produces harmful effects on both mind and body, conceived as inseparable from one another. Resistance to colonialism and freedom from oppression are for this reason in turn conceptualized by Fanon as bodily acts, requiring the girding of muscles as well as the brain.

Furthermore, the body is not just a physical presence for Fanon but also a form of expression, a language, and is shaped and channelled by language in turn. Racism overdetermines the body from the outside, so that freedom from racist oppression requires a new, liberated language of the body, a form of expression that allows bodily agency. It is culture, and sometimes more specifically literature, that for Fanon is able to give expression to this bodily agency, to overturn the violence of the colonial inscription of the colonized body and to allow it to produce its own significations. When he cites literary works for their assertions of revolt, for example, this is because he sees in them an immediacy, an immersion in lived experience, formulated in a creative language able to capture and touch the senses in ways that abstract discourse cannot. The rest of this chapter will trace the centrality of the body in Fanon's interweaving of medicine, philosophy, and politics, before demonstrating how cultural activity, including literature, might give expression to the liberated body.

Fanon's body is palpably present in his written work and is responsible for much of the rawness and the force of his rhetoric. If Lewis Gordon's recent study *What Fanon Said* reads Fanon, according to Sonia Dagan-Herzburn, 'through the eyes of Dante', this literary reading at the same time situates the body at the centre of his work: 'Fanon's body, a troubled, frenetic body that was simultaneously elegant, rhythmic (he did, in spite of his protestations, dance the beguine), and beautiful, is a subtext of all his writings. It gropes at reality, it shivers, it quakes'.[6] Although it is problematic to identify a clear autobiographical perspective in Fanon's works, given the slipperiness of the textual persona, the prose of *Peau noire, masques blancs* in particular nevertheless betrays a material body in its representation of physical violence and sensory experience through the voice of the narrating 'je'. The Introduction clearly positions the work in the present moment and in the lived experience of its narrator. It aspires to construct a future free from the shackles of the past, but, 'cet avenir n'est pas celui du cosmos, mais bien celui de mon siècle, de mon pays, de mon existence' ('this future is not the future of the cosmos but rather the future of my century, my country, my existence').[7] In a covert rebuttal of Césaire and the vision of the integration of poetry into the cosmos elucidated in 'Poésie et connaissance', Fanon here announces the subjectivity of his discourse and its anchoring in the material concerns of the immediate present.[8] This focus on materiality is felt most intensely, moreover, in 'L'Expérience vécue du noir', which traces the narrating persona's visceral reaction to the white boy's interpellation, '"Sale nègre!" ou simplement: "Tiens, un nègre!"' ('"Dirty nigger!" or simply, "Look, a negro!"') (*PN*, p. 88; 82). One of Fanon's most famous and most powerful passages evokes the alienation produced by the racist cry in physical terms; it is 'un décollement, un arrachement, une hémorragie qui caillait du sang noir sur tout mon corps' ('an amputation, an excision, a haemorrhage that spattered my whole body with black blood') (*PN*, p. 91; 95). The subjective voice experiences here a physical violation, a wound to the body which at the same time resists healing in its stubborn display of scabs of black blood encrusted on the persona's skin. Far from an abstract, philosophical denunciation of racism, the chapter tracks the attack on the body of the narrating 'je', who is at once sufficiently 'anonyme' not to be equated unproblematically with Fanon himself and at the same time tangibly embodied. Moreover, whilst the narrator traces this bodily violation using the vocabulary of wound, amputation, haemorrhage, and also nausea, he seeks an expression of resistance by reaffirming the power of his body, as if 'ma poitrine a une puissance d'expansion infinie' ('my chest has the power to expand without limit') (*PN*, p. 114;

108). If, as Fanon writes in the conclusion, revolt is necessary at the moment when it becomes 'impossible à respirer', liberation will start with this expansion of the breath. The persona's defeat, however, again associates bodily and linguistic disablement, as 'le silence éviscéré reflua vers moi' ('the disembowelled silence fell back on me'), and he is reduced at the end of the chapter to tears (PN, p. 114; 108).

The body in *Peau noire, masques blancs* is also conceptualized as intrinsically bound up with language; it is actively violated by the discourses of racism and colonialism and must provide the starting-point for a liberated expression of agency. Early in the chapter on 'Le Noir et le langage', Fanon cites Valéry's assertion that language is 'dieu dans la chair égaré' [god gone astray in the flesh], as if language, and indeed Valéry's poetry, is the result of a fusion between spirit and flesh (PN, p. 14; 9). The image at the same time attributes to this complicity between language and flesh an 'extraordinaire puissance' [remarkable power], as if the ownership and embodiment of one's language symbolizes a form of mastery, one that is denied to the black Martinican who, in speaking French, finds his body alienated by the discourse of the other. This non-belonging in language is conjured in the chapter, moreover, as a sort of bodily disability, as Fanon describes the Martinican's attempt to master the French 'r', 'se méfiant de sa langue, organe malheureusement paresseux' ('suspicious of his own tongue — a wretchedly lazy organ'), and pronouncing 'Garrrçon! Un vè de biè' ('Waiterrr! Bing me a beeya') only to betray his tongue's inability to form consistently the necessary sound (PN, p. 16; 11). While Fanon's chapter offers no suggestion of any alternative language of resistance, lamenting rather both the alienating 'mask' of the French language and the reductive stereotyping facilitated by the 'parler petit-nègre' [pidgin], it is evident that the Martinican's creation of linguistic agency will only take place through a reintegration of speech and body. The famous concluding words of *Peau noire* are indeed a prayer to the body, 'O mon corps, fais de moi toujours un homme qui interroge!' ('o my body, make of me always a man who questions!'), as if the necessary questioning of oppression will be triggered by the will of the body (PN, p. 188; 181).

The very production of Fanon's major volumes was also ostensibly a physical act bearing the trace of the effort of their creator. Marie-Jeanne Manuellan's testimony to her experience of transcribing the essays of *L'An V de la révolution algérienne* stresses the physical activity involved in the dictation, as if Fanon's whole body was implicated in the production of the words: 'il marchait et "parlait" le livre comme si de ses pas, du rythme de son corps en marche, jaillissait sa pensée' [he would walk and 'speak' the book as if his thoughts sprang from his steps, from the rhythm of his body as it was walking].[9] The texts are the product, then, of a moving body, of physical gesture, as if it was indeed this corporeal movement that generated the speech to be transcribed. At the same time, Manuellan emphasizes that it was crucial to Fanon to address another person, another body, as he spoke. The printed volumes we now have are in this way a record of a lived encounter between physical bodies. Manuellan as well as Fanon's various biographers have also commented on the relationship between the urgency of *Les Damnés de la terre* and the rapid degeneration of the author's body as he dictated the essays during the months leading up to his death of leukaemia in December 1961, just two months after the volume's publication. Indeed, Lewis Gordon accompanies his discussion of the work's production with photographs of Fanon betraying his increasing weakness.[10] The impassioned call to the 'damnés de la terre' to resist violence by seizing their bodily agency is, perhaps, made more real and more palpable by the knowledge that the body from which those words were issued was itself failing.

Fanon's conception of the centrality of bodily experience and its place in the expression of resistance is evidently rooted in his reading of phenomenology, particularly of Merleau-Ponty. Fanon attended Merleau-Ponty's lectures when he was a student in Lyon, and the latter's conception of the association between the body and perception clearly resonates with Fanon's thinking, in particular in *Peau noire, masques blancs*. Jean Khalfa has analyzed Fanon's use of Merleau-Ponty's conception of the body as '*notre point de vue sur le monde*' [our point of view on the world], and there will not be space to detail the full resonance of this phenomenological perspective in Fanon's thinking here.[11] It is worth noting specifically, however, that the body is for Merleau-Ponty as for Fanon the origin of human expression, not only of perception. The production of language, from this point of view, begins in the movement of the body, with gesture or breath, and human expression needs to be understood as embodied, as reliant on corporeal action and sensation. According to Merleau-Ponty:

> The body converts a certain motor essence into vocal form, spreads out the articulatory style of a word into audible phenomena, and arrays the former attitude, which is resumed, into the panorama of the past, projecting an intention to move into actual movement, because the body is a power of natural expression.[12]

Merleau-Ponty is here discussing the place of the body in reconstructing memory and bringing it into the present, but the observation is relevant also because it offers a way into thinking through the fusion of impulse with thought, movement, and then speech. Expression is crucially from this point of view not a translation of a preconceived idea but the product of a gesture, crystallized in the form of words.

Carrie Noland's ground-breaking study of agency and embodiment offers a compelling reading of Fanon through Merleau-Ponty and a number of other theorists of embodiment, and traces how Merleau-Ponty's 'schéma corporel' is translated by Fanon into a 'historical-racial schema' and a 'racial epidermal schema' in the analysis of the racist gaze in *Peau noire, masques blancs*.[13] Showing how Fanon also draws on Jean Lhermitte's *L'Image de notre corps*, Noland glosses Fanon's conception of the way in which the racist label interrupts the subject's apprehension of his or her body. Again, however, this interruption to the 'schéma corporel' is significant to Fanon because it results in the colonized subject being deprived of agency and also expression. Noland argues first that the black subject is stripped of his or her dynamism, movement, and self-creation:

> As Fanon demonstrates in 'The Lived Experience of the Black Man', it is precisely an ability to feel the body poised or moving through space (a body *schema*) that the black subject lacks. To exist solely as a legible surface without

depth, as a black skin with cutaneous sensation, is the '*malédiction corporelle*' — the embodied curse — of the *racialized* body.[14]

Next, moreover, Noland traces how Fanon's chapter seeks to imagine how the body might be reclaimed, notably here in an individual and subjective manner, as the narrating subject attempts to find a body schema with which he can be reintegrated.

Yet if Noland stresses the importance of this re-established connection with the subject's corporeal being, I would suggest that this connection necessarily calls, in Fanon's view, for bodily expression of a sort that he still struggles to achieve in the chapter but that remains the horizon of his thought. Noland argues that the tears with which the chapter ends signify a return to the 'involuntary, autonomous body', one closer, in fact, to an integrated expression of bodily experience than cultural activity tends to allow. These tears, however, must also be the starting-point for a fuller form of expression that would create a sense of agency and ultimately, for Fanon, liberation. If what is wrong with the 'historical-racial schema' is the representation, the 'mask' it imposes on the body, then the liberated and active body requires for Fanon another language: he demands, in Penelope Ingram's words, 'a resignification of the visual grammar of the body'.[15] Fanon's own creative production, and, I want to suggest, his readings of literary works, can be conceived as efforts to imagine this integrated, embodied expression.

It is perhaps pertinent to Fanon too that Noland opens her study of agency and embodiment with a reflection on the way in which a graffiti artist makes gesture into a form of inscription. The example shows how artistic production is always in some form the product of a gesture, of a movement of the body through space, and bears the trace of bodily agency in a way that poststructuralist emphases on pure textuality tend to occlude. This attention to corporeal movement is significant for Noland because, she suggests, it is also the result of learning or conditioning: when a body is able to accomplish a gesture, a memory is then created that allows the gesture to be repeated. Gesture is from this point of view a product of acculturation, and always participates in a set of existing cultural systems. At the same time, however, she insists that it is also an activity that can challenge cultural givens; the movement is also not fully circumscribed by its cultural meaning. Fanon's active, dynamic scenes of dictation might be conceived to perform something of this double aspect. His production of text is clearly also the result of corporeal movement, since as we have seen, the utterance of words is for him a gesture involving the whole body. This production also enacts the entry of the body into a certain cultural space, a space of conceptual analysis, of political and cultural expression. Yet Fanon's dynamic mode of production is also an affirmation of individual agency, his embodied form of enunciation is at the same time aesthetically new, unique, and singular. The creative, oral form of his writings bears the trace of a body in movement, as the language is also eclectic, often idiomatic, capturing the aleatory modulations of its original spoken form and recording the rhythm of the speaker's movement by switching between perspectives, idioms, and argumentative threads. Manuellan's testimony allows us to think of Fanon's writings as the record of a series of gestures that perform his notion of the centrality of the body to the subject's expressivity, and demonstrate how embodied expression can forge agency through the creation of a new form.

In 'L'Expérience vécue du noir', Fanon's narrating persona searches for a form of expression that would resist the stultification that the 'masque blanc' places on the body of the black subject. Poets such as Senghor, Césaire, and Diop are cited as their lines potentially give voice to the black man's body, and although Fanon's critique of their methods suggests he is not quite content with the form of this expression, he cites them precisely because their poetry captures a sensuality and materiality that exceeds colonial reason. Of all the thinkers to whom he refers across his work, then, it is these sorts of literary figures who come closest to a language of resistance and liberation, even if at this stage Fanon laments the falling of their imagery into stereotype. Having charted the violence against the black subject's body, Fanon first quotes Senghor's celebration of the use of rhythm to imagine a reintegration with the body, with the breath, in both art and experience:

> C'est l'élément vital par excellence. Il est la condition première et le signe de l'Art, comme la respiration de la vie; la respiration qui se précipite ou ralentit, devient régulière ou spasmodique suivant la tension de l'être, le degré et la qualité de l'émotion.

> [It is the archetype of the vital element. It is the first condition and the hallmark of Art, as breath is of life: breath, which accelerates or slows, which becomes even or agitated according to the tension in the individual, the degree and the nature of his emotion.] (*PN*, p. 98; p. 93)

The quotations from Césaire's *Cahier d'un retour au pays natal* that follow the Senghor passage, moreover, are replete with imagery of the body in contact with the physical world, and Fanon notes both the vocal vibration produced by the cry and the inscription of the violence carried out against black bodies: '"Sang ! Sang! Tout notre sang ému par le cœur mâle du soleil"' ('Blood! Blood! All our blood stirred by the male heart of the sun') (*PN*, p. 101; 95). The difficulty with the imagery used by Senghor and Césaire, Fanon complains, is that it risks reproducing the stereotype of the black man's simplicity, of his 'irrationality' as it is constructed and excluded by colonial reason. Nevertheless, it is famously Sartre's conception of negritude as merely a passing phase in a dialectic that is denounced most viscerally in the chapter, and that triggers Fanon's renewed determination to recreate black identity, again, in a way that implicates the body in the process of reconstruction. If Sartre's dismissal also destroys the body's stability and grounding, as 'mes épaules ont glissé de la structure du monde, mes pieds n'ont plus senti la caresse du sol' ('my shoulders slipped out of the framework of the world, my feet could no longer feel the touch of the ground'), Fanon's narrating persona affirms in response, 'je prends cette négritude et, les larmes aux yeux, j'en reconstitue le mécanisme. Ce qui avait été mis en pièces est par mes mains, lianes intuitives, rebâti, édifié' ('so I took up my negritude, and with tears in my eyes I put its machinery together again. What had been broken to pieces was rebuilt, reconstructed by the intuitive lianas of my hands') (*PN*, p. 112; 106). The chapter ends, as I have mentioned, with the narrator breaking down in tears, but as Noland's analysis suggested, this passage indicates that the tears might also be the starting-point for a reconstruction of the black subject, conceived here as a reshaping crafted by his hands.

Fanon's relationship with negritude is highly complex and seems to shift through the text, and there will not be space to explore its ambiguities here.[16] Senghor's and Césaire's endeavours to give expression and agency to the black body may, in 'L'Expérience vécue du noir', be conceived as flawed. Yet it is perhaps his immersion in their poetry that triggers Fanon's own creative vision in the conclusion, and later, as we shall see, more fully in *Les Damnés de la terre*. Poetry, then, is the catalyst for Fanon's call for a new, more liberated and embodied form of expression, but if he remains ambivalent towards Senghor and Césaire, his conclusion attempts a form of poetics of his own in its highly evocative, sensual, and at times corporeal language. Its staccato form from the outset mimics on some level the rhythms of the original spoken dictation, as the short, punchy paragraphs seem to be marked by pauses for breath. Once again, moreover, the powerfully moving affirmation of self-invention and agency explicitly draws on the energy and movement of the body. If the white man's view of the black man is based on a kind of mirage, for example, Fanon's narrating persona is determined that, 'je lui montrerai, en faisant peser sur sa vie tout mon poids d'homme, que je ne suis pas ce "Y a bon banania" qu'il persiste à imaginer' ('I will impose my whole weight as a man on his life and show him that I am not that "sho' good eatin'" that he persists in imagining') (*PN*, pp. 85–86; 178).[17] The insistence on the body's weight here figures its materiality as a crucial part of the speaker's humanity and of the rejection of colonial dehumanization by means of false chimera.

In the famous sequence of contestatory aphorisms celebrating self-invention and creation, moreover, Fanon uses imagery evocative of bodily movement: 'je dois me rappeler à tout instant que le véritable *saut* consiste à introduire l'invention dans l'existence. Dans le monde où je m'achemine, je me crée interminablement' ('I should constantly remind myself that the real *leap* consists in introducing invention into existence. In the world through which I travel, I am endlessly creating myself') (*PN*, p. 186; 179). The black man does not only reclaim his physical presence, his bodily mass, but also his ability to jump, to move, to make his way forward: the movement of the muscles here and, as we shall see more extensively in *Les Damnés de la terre*, is an integral part of the process of self-creation. Finally, Fanon's embodied aesthetics of liberation in the conclusion ends with an address not only to the speaker's own body but also to the body of the other: 'pouquoi tout simplement ne pas essayer de toucher l'autre, de sentir l'autre, de me révéler l'autre?' ('why not the quite simple attempt to touch the other, to feel the other, to explain the other to myself?') (*PN*, p. 188; 181). While he addresses Josie here in his dictation, Fanon also conjures a sensual contact with the body of the other, as if colonial and racist discourse never caresses but only violates the other's body, and resistance must consequently harbour a different ethics, a corporeal embrace.

It is perhaps in his work in Algeria, however, that Fanon's vision of freedom and resistance through embodied self-expression reaches its fullest significance. First, it is worth recalling again in this context that colonial oppression harms the neurological, the psychological, and the physical health of the colonized. Fanon's psychiatric writing suggests that colonial discourse damages the mind and body of its victims. The early essay 'Le "Syndrome nord-africain"', published in 1952 and describing North African immigrants in France, studies complaints of unspecified pain in various parts of the body, as well as muscular tension and sexual dysfunction as responses to the experience of alienation in France.[18] In the case studies that occupy the last chapter of *Les Damnés de la terre*, Fanon goes on to outline a number of disorders that he explicitly links with 'l'atmosphère sanglante, impitoyable, la généralisation de pratiques inhumaines, l'impression tenace qu'ont les gens d'assister à une véritable apocalypse' ('the bloody, pitiless atmosphere, the generalization of inhuman practices, of people's lasting impression that they are witnessing a veritable apocalypse').[19] Some of the cases refer to reactions to specific traumatic events, including an Algerian man's impotence after witnessing the rape of his wife, another man's murderous impulses after a massacre in his village, as well as a European patient traumatized by his experience as a perpetrator of torture (it was the difficulties surrounding the treatment of this patient that contributed to Fanon's decision to stop treating perpetrators and confront the political dimension of his own position as a doctor). Others stem more broadly from the violent atmosphere, though there is a section devoted specifically to the after-effects of the experience of torture on its victims. A section on psychosomatic disorders reinforces the association between mind and body in Fanon's thinking, moreover, as the experience or witnessing of violence can trigger stomach complaints, sleep disorders, disruption to menstruation, irregular heart rhythms, the whitening of hair, and, perhaps revealingly for Fanon's vision of resistance, muscular tension.

At the same time, Fanon's political writings on the Algerian War of Independence often draw on the medical terminology found in the psychiatric work. If one of the pathologies described in the case studies of *Les Damnés de la terre* is a constant, rigid contraction of the muscles, 'd'emblée contracturé, incapable du moindre relâchement volontaire le malade semble fait d'une pièce' ('immediately rigid and incapable of relaxing of his own free will, the patient seems to be made in one piece') (*DT*, pp. 348–49; 219), the political essay 'L'Indépendance nationale, seule issue possible', published earlier in 1957, betrays a related medical framework as it describes the whole of Algerian society as caught in 'un état de tension permanent' [a permanent state of tension].[20] And in 'La Conscience révolutionnaire algérienne', also published in 1957, the seizing of independence is associated with corporeal movement, as if in a rejection of the muscular spasms evoked above: the people need to be implicated in the movement, 'catalysant leurs énergies' [catalyzing their energies] and 'mises en branle' [set in motion].[21] Liberation will start, it seems, in this summoning of energy and setting in motion of the body. By 1958, and as a result of the coup d'état in Algiers, this movement becomes more frenzied, and again Fanon uses a medical vocabulary to describe the urgency of the situation, though the symptoms are conceived here as a prelude to healing:

> Cette fièvre qui règne sur les forums et les places publiques d'Algérie, ce
> délire collectif qui s'est emparé de la populace vociférante des grandes villes,

ces spasmes qui secouent ces généraux qui se découvrent soudainement une vocation de prophètes, tout cela ne saurait tromper. Ce sont les signes annonciateurs de la fin.[22]

[This fever which governs over public spaces and forums in Algeria, this collective delirium which has seized the shouting rabble of the big cities, these spasms that affect the generals who suddenly find themselves with the vocation of a prophet, all of this does not deceive. They are signs anticipating the end.]

Resistance, then, is a fever, a delirium, a spasm, an extreme physical state, evidently, but one that nevertheless embraces combat rather than remaining paralyzed in the state of fixity evoked above.

In the light of the pathologizing effects of colonial oppression, 'De la violence' repeatedly equates freedom with the release of muscular energy. Again, the colonized is constantly tense, his muscles contracted, and his dream of liberation is figured by the movement of the body:

Je rêve que je saute, que je nage, que je cours, que je grimpe. Je rêve que j'éclate de rire, que je franchis le fleuve d'une enjambée, que je suis poursuivi par des meutes de voitures qui ne me rattrapent jamais.

[I dream I am jumping, swimming, running, and climbing. I dream I burst out laughing, I am leaping across a river and chased by a pack of cars that never catches up with me.] (*DT*, p. 82; 15)

This assertion of muscular strength and movement goes some way to explaining the essay's defence of violence, since freedom requires for Fanon this physical release and the destruction of the system used to contain the colonized's agency and mobility, a destruction accomplished through freely chosen corporeal acts and gestures. Yet as in *Peau noire, masques blancs*, this embodied resistance is also a mode of expression and is enacted and crystallized through cultural activity. Various forms of cultural creation are seen to emerge from and give voice to this assumption of bodily agency, with literature, perhaps, achieving this most fully both in 'De la violence' and in 'Sur la culture nationale'. First, however, in 'De la violence' Fanon discusses dance as a release of energy, as a cultural form allowing for a liberated expression of the colonized body, where the tension created by the colonial system and harboured in the muscles is channelled into expressive movement. The practice of dance provides a controlled setting for this embodied expression, as Fanon describes how on these ritualized occasions, 'par des voies multiples, dénégations de la tête, courbure de la colonne, rejet en arrière de tout le corps, se déchiffre à livre ouvert l'effort grandiose d'une collectivité pour s'exorciser, s'affranchir, se dire' ('the exorcism, liberation, and expression of a community are grandiosely and spontaneously played out through the shaking of the head, and back and forward thrusts of the body') (*DT*, p. 88; 20). It is significant, however, that dance is evoked here as an example of cultural expression early in the conflict, and yet as the violence develops, Fanon insists on a form of action more directly contributing to the cause of the resistance. This struggle will remain nevertheless both a strategy for combat and a cultural act, and it is important to remember in the light of the criticisms of Fanon's no doubt disturbing call for violence that he is recommending here not only armed struggle but also a re-imagination of colonized humanity, the reassertion of a body able to construct and express itself in its own terms.[23]

Fanon's citation of Césaire's *Et les chiens se taisaient* in 'De la violence' serves to crystallize his vision of embodied expression, this time with particular intensity, through poetic drama. Whilst there can be no denying that struggle on the ground is Fanon's main priority in the chapter, the use of Césaire here again shows how his political thinking evolves through his literary reading, and the passage is particularly relevant because of the way in which it verbalizes the moment of revolt. A part of the same passage is also quoted in the chapter on 'Le Nègre et la psychopathologie' in *Peau noire, masques blancs*, moreover, and yet while in the former text Fanon comments on the self-destructiveness of the Rebelle (who jumps into the 'trou noir' of negritude) (*PN*, p. 161; 154), in 'De la violence' the character is taken as an inspirational figure because he physically acts out a revolt that is then able to resonate with, and offer significance to, the oppressed for whom he stands.[24] The section quoted dramatizes the Rebelle's confession to his mother of his murder of the slave master, and Fanon notes both its prophetic quality and its insistence that the violence was inevitable. What is also striking, however, is the Rebelle's claim to embody a revolt that stands for liberated humanity more broadly: '*mon nom: offensé; mon prénom: humilié; mon état: révolté; mon âge: l'âge de la prière*' ('my family name: offended; my given name: humiliated; my profession: rebel; my age: the stone age') (*DT*, p. 118; 44). Césaire conceives the tragedy here as bearing universal significance, and Fanon's choice of this powerful moment in his discussion of the Algerian conflict suggests that despite the Rebelle's own demise, his poetic text has a wider ability to inspire. Although by this time Fanon is committed to addressing events in their historical specificity, the literary text is perhaps one that he conceives can forge a bridge between individual lived experience and a broader commitment to human freedom.

At the same time, the passage picks up on Fanon's broader concern with expression and embodiment. The Rebelle's self-naming and self-definition in the quotation above enact an assertive statement of refusal to the slave master and to the colonizer's discourse. At the same time, his self-identification with the act of revolt clearly also implicates the physical body: '*c'est moi avec ma révolte et mes pauvres poings serrés et ma tête hirsute*' ('I with my revolt and my poor clenched fists and my bushy head') (*DT*, p. 119; 44). And while he claims to represent the suffering bodies of every lynched, every tortured man in the world, it is by killing the slave master with his own hands that the Rebelle performs his gesture of liberation. His language, moreover, has a sensuality and immediacy even as it resonates beyond the present moment in ways more palpable, and perhaps more forceful to Fanon, than theory. It is, finally, perhaps revealing that Fanon is most convinced and inspired by Césaire's theatrical work, as the oral performance and physical presence of the actor announce a literary form wholly embedded in bodily expression. Fanon's own *Les Mains parallèles*, which there will not be space to discuss here, is also significantly most inspired by Césaire's *Et les chiens* in its performance of a moment of murderous revolt in both language and gesture.

It is in 'Sur la culture nationale' that Fanon repeatedly and explicitly links cultural expression with the muscles, with bodily movement, and lived experience. One of the main polemical arguments of the essay is its vilification of bourgeois intellectuals whose cultural vision of the new nation is too abstract and not sufficiently embedded in the concrete and material experience of the masses. Rather than situating his critique purely on the level of ideas, the intellectual needs to implicate his own body in the struggle and immerse himself in the lived suffering of the people: he is 'condamné à cette plongée dans les entrailles de son peuple' ('to journey deep into the very bowels of his people') (*DT*, p. 256; 148). Some of the forms of writing that Fanon conceives to be insufficiently productive for the cause of independence, moreover, suffer from pathologies comparable to those described in the psychiatric essays, as he detects a 'style heurté' ('jagged style') or a 'style nerveux' ('energetic style'), often excessively fixated on the past rather than the future (*DT*, p. 266; 157). Rather than offering readings of any Algerian literary sources, however, Fanon quotes the poem 'Face à la nuit' by the Haitian writer René Depestre, first noting its character's excessive reverence towards Western culture, and next its more virulent condemnation of the ignorance of a culture that cuts itself off from flesh and blood:

> La dame n'était pas seule
> *Elle avait un mari*
> *Un mari qui savait tout*
> *Mais à parler franc qui ne savait rien*
> *Parce que la culture ne va pas sans concessions*
> *Une concession de sa chair et de son sang*
> *Une concession de soi-même aux autres*
> *Une concession qui vaut le*
> *Classicisme et le romantisme*
> *Et tout ce dont on abreuve notre esprit.*

> [The lady was not alone
> She had a husband
> A husband who knew everything
> But to tell the truth knew nothing
> Because culture does not come without making concessions
> Without conceding your flesh and blood
> Without conceding yourself to others
> A concession worth just as much as
> Classicism or Romanticism
> And all that nurture our soul.] (*DT*, p. 272; 162)

Depestre's poem echoes Fanon's preoccupations in its affirmation of bodily experience, its embrace of physical suffering, and its belief in the immersion of culture in lived experience rather than in the great literary movements of the past. Fanon too, it seems, believes in the power of poetry because of its capacity to evoke flesh and blood.

There is of course a certain irony in Fanon's celebration of the poet's immersion in lived experience when his literary references in this essay and indeed throughout the volume are themselves not Algerian, and clearly not at all embedded in the conflict for which he writes. Fanon's most extensive quotation in the essay is that taken from the poem 'Aube africaine' by the Guinean writer Keita Fodeba, again chosen for its aesthetics rather than for its relationship with Algeria. Christopher Miller discusses in *Theories of Africans* Fanon's inappropriate use of Fodeba, pointing out that Fanon's concept of national culture fits uneasily with Fodeba's Guinean context, and that he pays insufficient attention both to ethnicity and to the use of particular cultural and musical forms.[25] Miller's arguments are certainly justified, and it is clear that when Fanon draws on literature it is not so much in order to read it carefully as to find imagery in it that gives a vivid and palpable form to his own preoccupations. It is nevertheless revealing for my current purposes that Fanon chooses Fodeba's poem because he reads it as fully embedded in the colonized's struggle. It notably focuses on the physical experience of its hero, Naman, an impressively muscular and strong labourer, chosen to fight for the French, but killed by white men when he returns to Dakar. The poem helps Fanon to illustrate his argument, then, because it directly calls its readers to fight through its conjuring of the violation of its protagonist. The language of the poem closely captures the effort and sensation of Naman's body: as he works, '*il suait, infatigable, toujours courbé, maniant adroitement son outil*' ('sweating, untiring, constantly bent, he skilfully worked with his hoe') (*DT*, p. 274; 164). Just as with *Et les chiens se taisaient*, however, Fanon admires the poem because it captures embodied experience but also serves to inspire readers in other contexts: Naman's murder is, Fanon claims, mirrored in Sétif in 1945, Fort-de-France, Saïgon, Dakar, and Lagos. Literature, perhaps, can create this unique connection between the lived experience of an individual subject and the wider suffering of humanity, not in order to proclaim a falsely universal culture but in order to issue a call for the liberation of human subjects from all forms of oppression.

The final section of 'Sur la culture nationale' evokes a rousing fusion between bodily agency and cultural production. The moment of liberation, promises Fanon, 'suscite un nouveau rythme respiratoire, des tensions musculaires oubliées et développe l'imagination' ('brings an urgent breath of excitement, arouses forgotten muscular tensions and develops the imagination') (*DT*, p. 289; 174). Just as in 'L'Expérience vécue du noir' the persona imagined his assumption of power through the expansion of his chest, so here is the breath liberated at the same time as the nation; equally, the muscles are relaxed as if to heal the psychosomatic disorder described in the case studies and quoted above. Crucially, however, it is here that the imagination is alluded to directly in tandem with these bodily functions, as if the healing of mental and physical sickness is indissociable from cultural and literary creation. The description of the emergence of new artisanal forms also combines the vocabulary of bodily regeneration with that of cultural production, as 'le masque inexpressif ou accablé s'anime et les bras ont tendance à quitter le corps, à esquisser l'action' ('the expressionless or tormented mask comes to life, and the arms are raised upwards in a gesture of action') (*DT*, p. 290; 175). If the combat heralds an attempt to 'moderniser les formes de luttes évoquées' ('modernise the types of struggle') (p. 288; 174), moreover, it will also require a modernizing of cultural and artistic forms, and these forms, Fanon explains, will be born not from tradition but from recent lived experience. The colonial administration was right, he suggests, to demand the arrest of story-tellers, since they too respond to changes in the lived reality of the people by using their imagination to create new kinds of narrative impacting in turn directly on people's lives. In short, for Fanon national liberation will bring a reinvention of the human in all its dimensions. The concluding pages of this essay aptly blend Fanon's complementary commitments to politics, medicine, and culture in this vision of human renewal.

Finally, although *Les Damnés de la terre* is less formally eclectic, less resonant with its original orality, and less aesthetically experimental than *Peau noire, masques blancs*, its dynamic form and language still enact something of the visceral poetic expression with which it is preoccupied. It should be remembered, perhaps, that the title quotes at once the poem 'L'Internationale' by the French revolutionary Eugène Pottier, and the Haitian Jacques Roumain's 'Nouveau sermon nègre' and 'Sales nègres'. In citing these literary predecessors, Fanon directly associates his own text with poetry, as well as championing Pottier's and Roumain's aesthetics embracing the physical and mental suffering of the oppressed. Fanon's own writing in *Les Damnés de la terre* too, in its rhetorical vibrancy and vivid imagery, has a poetic dimension, woven closely into the political and psychological analyses, and again, steeped in the language of materiality. The conclusion in particular recalls the fragmented, rhythmical structure of *Peau noire, masques blancs*, as rousing lines conjuring insurrection and change are seemingly punctuated with pauses for breath while juxtaposing striking images of destruction and renewal. The closing lines deploy two triadic sets of repetition, for example, at the same time as they call for innovation at the level of mind and body for every human: 'pour l'Europe, pour nous-mêmes et pour l'humanité, camarades, il faut faire peau neuve, développer une pensée neuve, tenter de mettre sur pied un homme neuf' ('for Europe, for ourselves and for humanity, comrades, we must make a new start, develop a new way of thinking, and endeavour to create a new man') (*DT*, p. 376; 239). As Nicholas Harrison has also argued in the context of Fanon's shifting between relativist and universalist perspectives, this is an intensely rhetorical exercise, and indebted to the literary in its deployment of images and sounds to produce its mobilizing effect.[26] Even when cultural activity is not so explicitly the focus of his arguments, then, Fanon's writing bears the traces of the aesthetics of embodiment that has been the focus of this chapter. The literary imagination too, alongside political revolution and psychiatric treatment, can accomplish the liberation and self-expression of the oppressed body.

Notes to Chapter 15

1. Jean Khalfa, 'La Bibliothèque de Frantz Fanon, liste établie, présentée et commentée par Jean Khalfa', in *Frantz Fanon: écrits sur l'aliénation et la liberté*, ed. by Jean Khalfa and Robert Young (Paris: La Découverte, 2015), pp. 585–655.

2. David Macey, *Frantz Fanon: A Biography* (London: Verso, 2012).

3. Gary Wilder compares *Peau noire, masques blancs* to Césaire's *Cahier* in his 'Race, Reason, Impasse: Césaire, Fanon, and the Legacy of Emancipation', *Radical History Review*, 90 (2004), 31–61. Lewis C. Gordon associates the work with Dante's *Inferno* in *What Fanon Said: A Philosophical Introduction to his Life and Thought* (New York: Fordham University Press, 2015).

4. See for example Pierre Bouvier, *Aimé Césaire, Frantz Fanon: portraits de décolonisés* (Paris: Les Belles Lettres, 2010).

5. Jean Khalfa, 'Alienation and Freedom: Fanon on Psychiatry and Revolution', in *Poetics of the Antilles: Poetry, History, and Philosophy in the Writings of Perse, Césaire, Fanon and Glissant* (Oxford: Peter Lang, 2017), pp. 209–53.

6. Sonia Dagan-Herzbrun, 'Foreword', in Gordon, *What Fanon Said*, p. 8.

7. Frantz Fanon, *Peau noire, masques blancs* (Paris: Seuil, 1995) p. 10; *Black Skin, White Masks*, trans. by Charles Lam Markmann (London: Pluto Press, 2008), p. 6; this work subsequently referred to as *PN* in the main text.

8. See Aimé Césaire, 'Poésie et connaissance', *Tropiques*, 12 (1945), 157–70.

9. Marie-Jeanne Manuellan, *Sous la dictée de Fanon* (Paris: L'Armourier, 2017), p. 114.

10. See Gordon, *What Fanon Said*, pp. 107–10.

11. Jean Khalfa, 'Corps perdu: A Note on Fanon's Cogito', in *Poetics of the Antilles*, pp. 183–208 (p. 188). The whole chapter is relevant to the present discussion.

12. Maurice Merleau-Ponty, *Phenomenology of Perception*, trans. by Colin Smith (London: Routledge, 2002), p. 211.

13. Carrie Noland, *Agency and Embodiment: Performing Gestures/Producing Culture* (Cambridge, MA: Harvard University Press, 2009), p. 199.

14. Ibid., p. 201.

15. Penelope Ingram, *The Signifying Body: Toward an Ethics of Sexual and Racial Difference* (Albany, NY: SUNY Press, 2008), p. 108.

16. I discuss in particular the relationship with Césaire's vision of negritude in my 'Fanon and the Uses of Literature', *Nottingham French Studies*, 54, 1 (2015), 38–51.

17. 'Y a bon banania' is a phrase referring to the image of a black colonial infantryman eating something from a billy can and pronouncing 'c'est bon, Banania' in a Creole dialect.

18. Frantz Fanon, 'Le "Syndrome nord-africain"', in *Pour la révolution africaine* (Paris: La Découverte, 2006), pp. 11–25.

19. Frantz Fanon, *Les Damnés de la terre* (Paris: Gallimard, 1991) p. 302; *The Wretched of the Earth*, trans. by Richard Philcox (New York: Grove Press, 2004) p. 183; this work subsequently referred to as *DT* in the main text.

20. Frantz Fanon, 'L'Indépendance nationale, seule issue possible', in *Frantz Fanon*, ed. by Khalfa & Young, pp. 461–66 (p. 463).

21. Frantz Fanon, 'La Conscience révolutionnaire algérienne', in *Frantz Fanon*, ed. by Khalfa & Young, pp. 485–86 (p. 486).

22. Frantz Fanon, 'Logique de l'ultracolonialisme', in *Frantz Fanon*, ed. by Khalfa & Young, pp. 497–501 (p. 497).

23. On the problems of Fanon's defence of violence, see for example Hannah Arendt, *On Violence* (New York: Harcourt Brace, 1970).

24. In 'Antillais et Africains', Fanon again cites Césaire's image of the 'trou noir' to describe the trap of claiming an African culture for Caribbean people; 'Antillais et Africains', in *Pour la révolution africaine*, pp. 26–36 (p. 36).

25. Christopher Miller, *Theories of Africans: Francophone Literature and Anthropology in Africa* (Chicago, IL: University of Chicago Press, 1990), pp. 51–62.

26. See Nicholas Harrison, 'Afterword: Theory and Relativism (Fanon's Position)', in *Postcolonial Criticism: History, Theory, and the Work of Fiction* (Cambridge: Polity Press, 2003), pp. 151–63.

CHAPTER 16

Fanon and the
Pathology of Freedom

Robert J. C. Young

Frantz Fanon's ideas of freedom, best known from his 1961 classic *Les Damnés de la terre* [The Wretched of the Earth],[1] with its famous and still controversial preface by Jean-Paul Sartre, are generally understood to comprise a postcolonial freedom for a people who have achieved the sovereign independence of a decolonized state. While much of the book is concerned with how to achieve that freedom, mentally, culturally, and politically, it is also deeply concerned with how that freedom can be maintained, how the postcolonial state itself can avoid succumbing to the control of a bourgeois comprador class of the colonized. Decolonization, and its long, violent process in the case of Algeria, involves, according to Fanon, a process of re-subjectification that enables a people to challenge and transform the alienated state of being to which they, as colonized people, have been subjected. Fanon's ideas of political freedom, through a form of disalienation that leads towards an existentialist state of authentic personal freedom, were developed much earlier in the context of his psychiatric work which was the field in which he was professionally involved for all of his adult life. For Fanon, colonialism, like madness, could be analyzed as a pathology of freedom.

Recently published material by Fanon, written for the most part in the late 1940s and 50s, enables us to reframe his politics within the context of his psychiatric work which has been until now often neglected outside specialized discussions of the history of colonial psychiatry.[2] While Fanon is generally described as a psychiatrist, or even, improbably, as a psychoanalyst, which he was not, his field of specialization was neurology — the study of the disorders of the nervous system, a specialization perfectly suited to someone who by all accounts seems always to have lived on the edge of his nerves. After qualifying as a psychiatrist in Lyon in 1952, Fanon moved to St Alban for his internship, then to Ivry, then to Blida-Joinville in Algeria and finally to Tunis, where he continued to practice on a daily basis even while working for the Front de libération nationale. Soon after moving to St Alban, he became part of a community of radical psychiatrists and began to publish research essays with them in academic and professional medical journals. His work from that period gives a very vivid sense of the very particular intellectual milieu of psychiatry in

France of the early 1950s, a largely unfamiliar environment for non-specialists very different from the more recognizable landscape that emerged in the 1960s. Yet the seeds of what developed in the 1960s are already there in the radical writings of the previous decade — the beginnings of the anti-psychiatry movement that would appear in the work of Félix Guattari, and of which Michel Foucault would also be a product. Foucault's general approach shares many of the presuppositions developed in France in the 1950s about the role of the asylum in the history of French society, for example, in the work of Georges Daumézon.[3] The formative intellectual milieu of Fanon and Foucault was in fact very similar, though they made different intellectual choices from the ideas and positions available to them.

The dominant figure in French psychiatry in Fanon's time and indeed for decades after his death was Henri Ey (1900–77), an almost exact contemporary of Jacques Lacan and Jean-Paul Sartre. His *Manuel de psychiatrie* (1960) would become the standard textbook of its time in France.[4] Fanon's own ideas and subsequent practice were fundamentally indebted to the positions and ideas developed in Ey's work. The mode of the latter's extensive writings helps to explain the curious mixture — to Anglophone readers — of experimental psychiatry, psychoanalysis, philosophy, phenomenology, and surrealism to be found in Fanon's work. All these domains formed part of the exploration of consciousness and mental illness, from a philosophical as well as a medical perspective, that constituted Ey's and Fanon's writings alike. Ey's work began from a critique of the effects of Cartesian dualism, a position which Fanon also adopted as the basis of his thought and which explains the apparent correlations between his anti-dualism and that of later post-structuralist philosophers such as Deleuze.[5] Ey's philosophical commitment to anti-dualism was to some degree mediated by professional interests: he argued that the consequence of the conceptual differentiation which separated mind from body, psychology from biology, was to prevent psychiatry operating as a regular medical discourse and practice. His professional mission was to make psychiatry a part of medicine proper rather than a para or pseudo-medical adjunct to it. His strategy to achieve that was to separate psychiatry, which views mental illness as an organic illness like any other bodily malfunction, from the psychology which presents mental illness as purely psychogenetic in origin. Ey found in the work of the British neurologist John Hughlings Jackson (1835–1911) an approach to neurology which he adapted to psychiatry, that allowed him to resolve the mind-body dichotomy through an integrative approach which continued to differentiate psychiatry from any kind of psychology or psychotherapy based on psycho-genetic assumptions. Hughlings Jackson's work enabled Ey to develop a form of psychiatry that could incorporate both body and mind in a dynamic, dialectical relation to each other.

For his part, Hughlings Jackson himself drew on the work of Herbert Spencer (1820–1903) in order to develop a model of evolutionary psychiatry in which the higher structures and capacities of the brain evolved from the lower and were integrated with them. Instead of a mind/soul-body split, Hughlings Jackson argued that there were different layers of complexity in the brain: while bodily movements were controlled by the lower, complex forms of conceptualization and abstract thought were controlled by the higher. Hughlings Jackson was the first neurologist to argue explicitly that far from involving any metaphysical element, 'the nervous system is an exclusively sensorimotor machine', with each organ or function organized through cerebral localizations, a view that remains essentially the same today.[6] According to Hughlings Jackson, the mind is altogether an evolutionary product which has developed higher out of lower forms of organization: while the lower organize the functions and movements of the body, they overlap with the higher which involve cognitive abilities, language and consciousness. The lack of specific knowledge about the localization of functions within the brain in that period (which would really only be established with the development of neuropsychology using brain scanning technologies from the 1960s onwards) meant that Hughlings Jackson was able to leave the exact locations of these different layers, and the modes of transitions between them, somewhat vague. The advantage of Hughlings Jackson's work for Ey was that it allowed him to relate all mental phenomena directly to the body, and thus allow psychiatry a claim to belong fully to medical science. Ey's 'organo-dynamic psychology' emphasized the continuity of organic or neurological and psychodynamic factors within an evolutionary, hierarchical framework with consciousness as its apex. Here Fanon describes it, in a somewhat schematized way, in terms of a simple two-fold division:

> Pour Ey, le système nerveux se répartit en deux 'plans' : 1) le plan des fonctions sensorimotrices et psychiques élémentaires ou instrumentales (appareils réflexes de coordination des mouvements, de régulation du tonus, de la marche...) ; 2) le plan des fonctions psychiques supérieures ou énergétiques (par exemple se souvenir, juger, croire, aimer). Les fonctions instrumentales sont spécifiquement et morphologiquement inscrites dans le cerveau.

> [According to Ey, the nervous system is divided into two 'planes': 1) the plane of elementary or instrumental sensorimotor and psychic functions (reflex apparatuses for the coordination of movements, the regulation of tonus, of walking ...); and 2) the plane of higher or energetic psychic functions (e.g. remembering, judging, believing, loving). The instrumental functions are specifically and morphologically inscribed in the brain.] (*AL*, p. 207; 248)

Fanon's utilization of this framework, which emphasizes a fundamental distinction between the neurological and the psychiatric while accepting both, does not really change from his thesis to his last article of 1959 and provides an essential component for understanding his work.

With respect to Fanon, the key element that follows from this relates to questions of pathology. Ey's evolutionary psychiatry, extended from Hughlings Jackson's neurology, took over a fundamental model from the Englishman, namely that of evolution, dissolution, and reconstruction. This conceptualization of mental illness proposes that psychological problems are the result of the disintegration of the organization of the mind, where the upper levels of organization have been destroyed or dissolved, and the mind has reverted to its more basic functions. Mental illness is based on a positive and negative structure: the negative involves the dissolution of the mind's usual higher functions, the positive consists of the ways in which the mind then puts distorting substitutes in place.[7] These substitutes construct the abnormalities of mental illness. In explaining this process, Ey begins with the everyday example of sleep, where the mind loses its normative rational control, and substitutes the fantasies of dreams.

It was on the basis of this perspective that Ey argued that 'Psychiatry is [...] the pathology of freedom', a phrase which Fanon also invokes twice in his 1959 essay written with Charles Geronimi on 'L'Hospitalisation de jour en psychiatrie' (*AL*, pp. 419, 422; 497, 501).[8] Freedom itself forms the basis of the sovereign capacities of the individual; a pathology of that freedom results from its falling under the control of lower forms of neurological organization, which is then characterized as a mental illness in which the subject has lost his or her autonomy. Ey took the concept of the pathology of freedom from Gunther Anders's essay of that name of 1936–37, an essay which is often claimed to have also influenced Sartre's statement in *L'Être et le néant* [Being and Nothingness] (1943) that 'la liberté est condamnée à être libre' [Freedom is condemned to be free].[9] Fanon owned a copy of the issue of *Recherches philosophiques* in which Anders's essay first appeared (in French translation), and cites the essay in *Peau noire, masques blancs*: 'Certains hommes veulent enfler le monde de leur être. Un philosophe allemand avait décrit ce processus sous le nom de pathologie de la liberté' ('Some men want to inflate the world with their being. A German philosopher has described this process as the pathology of freedom').[10] As this comment suggests, Fanon himself was not altogether sympathetic to Anders's Nietzschean argument that in a world deprived of God and divorced from nature, man is condemned to be both alone and free. The problem for Fanon was not with the freedom, but with the account of freedom itself as a pathological state. Anders, moreover, with his claim that '*l'artificialité est la nature de l'homme et son essence est l'instabilité*' ('*artificiality is the nature of man and his essence is instability*'), reinstitutes the very split between human consciousness and the body that Ey was concerned to resolve.[11] As a psychiatrist, Ey strategically reversed Anders's argument to propose that psychiatry deals with the pathology of freedom, namely situations when mental illness has the effect of preventing freedom for the individual. As Fanon describes it:

> La maladie mentale, dans une phénoménologie qui laisserait de côté les grosses altérations de la conscience, se présente comme une véritable pathologie de la liberté. La maladie situe le malade dans un monde où sa liberté, sa volonté, ses désirs sont constamment brisés par des obsessions, des inhibitions, des contre-ordres, des angoisses.

> [In any phenomenology in which the major alterations of consciousness are left aside, mental illness is presented as a veritable pathology of freedom. Illness situates the patient in a world in which his or her freedom, will and desires are constantly broken by obsessions, inhibitions, countermands, anxieties.] (*AL*, p. 419; 497)

The dissolution of higher functions allows a freedom to the lower that in fact imprisons the mental patient in uncontrolled activities, obsessions, and desires. The role of the psychiatrist is to remove these formations and help the patient to reconstruct his or her normative forms of consciousness in which the self is autonomous and in full control.

Fanon's differences with Jacques Lacan (1901–81) revolve around comparable issues. Fanon's medical thesis demonstrates the extent to which he knew Lacan's work, a knowledge which may have later been reinforced when he began working in the hospital in St Alban with François Tosquelles, the radical Catalan psychiatrist and great admirer of Lacan. Fanon was sympathetic to Lacan's stress on social and group relations, and wrote in positive terms with respect to his focus on language, commenting 'Pourtant, à la réflexion, nous devons reconnaître que tout phénomène délirant est en définitive un phénomène exprimé, c'est-à-dire parlé' ('Nevertheless, upon reflection, we ought to recognize that every delusional phenomenon is ultimately expressed, that is to say, spoken') (*AL*, p. 225; 268). Tantalizingly, in the thesis Fanon remarks that he would have liked to have written at length on the Lacanian theory of language but has stopped himself because it would go off the main topic. However, Fanon was no Lacanianist and in certain respects differed from him fundamentally. Though clearly interested in, and sympathetic to, Lacan, Fanon did not sign up to what he described as Lacan's Jungian understanding of the psychogenesis of mental disease, that is the argument that mental illness is entirely determined psychically (*AL*, p. 225; 269). This was the core issue that Ey was contesting and the one in which Fanon loyally followed him. After reviewing different positions among contemporary psychiatrists towards the conclusion of his thesis, Fanon stated his preferred authority explicitly: 'Nous pensons comme Ey' ('I subscribe to Ey's viewpoint') (*AL*, p. 219; 261).

Fanon's discussion of Lacan draws on two sources: he briefly characterizes Lacan's position by summarizing parts of the argument of Lacan's thesis, *De la psychose paranoïaque dans ses rapports avec la personnalité* [On Paranoiac Psychosis and its Relation to the Personality] which had been published in 1932.[12] He gives no source or page numbers, and does not include the thesis in his bibliography, and so seems here to be simply recalling Lacan's arguments from memory.[13] His primary source is a volume published in 1950 that contained the proceedings of a congress held in Bonneval in 1946 which had been set up by Henri Ey. The congress involved a debate between Ey himself, Lacan, and other psychiatrists over the key theoretical question of the relative claims of psycho- or organogenesis. Following a short opening position statement by Ey, Lacan offered a serious critique of Ey's work in three parts, and it is from these three *rapports* that much of Fanon's knowledge of Lacan is derived.[14]

Although, as has been suggested, Fanon is in some ways sympathetic to Lacan, he characterizes Lacan's position overall with the slightly sarcastic remark, 'Personnellement, si nous avions à définir la position de Lacan, nous dirions qu'elle est une défense acharnée des droits nobiliaires de la folie' ('Personally, were I to define Lacan's position, I would call it an unremitting defence of the nobility rights of madness') (*AL*, p. 220; 263). In support of this view he cites Lacan's statement from the first *rapport* that:

> Loin donc que la folie soit le fait contingent des fragilités de l'organisme de l'homme, elle est la virtualité permanente d'une faille ouverte dans son essence. Loin qu'elle soit pour la liberté une 'insulte', elle est sa plus fidèle compagne, elle

suit son mouvement comme une ombre. Et l'être de l'homme non seulement
ne peut être compris sans la folie, mais il ne serait pas l'être de l'homme s'il ne
portait en lui la folie comme la limite de sa liberté.

[So rather than resulting from a contingent fact — the frailties of man's organism — madness is the permanent virtuality of a gap opened up in his essence.
And far from being an 'insult' to freedom, madness is freedom's most faithful
companion, following its every move like a shadow. Not only can man's being
not be understood without madness, but it would not be man's being if it did
not bear madness within itself as the limit of his freedom.] (*AL*, p. 220; 262)

Despite his interest in surrealism, Fanon was to be no espouser of the psychoanalysis
or philosophy of *délire*, and thus positions himself very differently not only from
Lacan but from contemporaries influenced by Lacan's fundamental arguments,
such as Deleuze and Foucault. This division comes down to the fundamental one
highlighted by Ey, namely the choice between the psycho- and organogenesis of
mental illness and the role of liberty in this dichotomy. As Fanon puts it: 'il y a
une organogenèse de la maladie mentale et la psychiatrie, refusant toute valeur
au concept de psychogenèse pathologique, se réserve un domaine d'étude n'ayant
aucun rapport avec celui de la liberté' ('mental illness involves organogenesis,
and psychiatry, refusing any value to the concept of pathological psychogenesis,
reserves itself a domain of study with no relation to that of freedom') (*AL*, p. 213;
254). Madness, in other words, is not freedom's most faithful companion. The
only relation that psychiatry has to freedom is that its therapeutic aim is to help
the patient return to it. Madness for Fanon is a deprivation of freedom. Fanon
saw his role as a psychiatrist as one that enabled his patients to move from a state
of alienation (psychiatrists in France were themselves of course called 'aliénistes')
towards that of freedom. Despite his differences with Foucault with respect to
psycho- and organogenesis, in later life Fanon also became increasingly convinced
that the psychiatric hospital was itself an institution that successively diminished
human freedom, putting doctor or nurse and patient into a master-slave relationship.
Instead of restoring and deepening the inhibited freedom of the patient, treatment
in a psychiatric hospital only lessened it. The institution too was a vehicle for a
pathology of freedom.

Notes to Chapter 16

1. Frantz Fanon, *Les Damnés de la terre* (Paris: Maspero, 1961).
2. Frantz Fanon, *Écrits sur l'aliénation et la liberté, Œuvres II*, ed. by Jean Khalfa and Robert J. C. Young (Paris: La Découverte, 2016); *Alienation and Freedom*, rev. ed., trans. by Steve Corcoran (London: Bloomsbury, 2018); this work subsequently referred to as *AL* in the main text. On Fanon's psychiatry, see Hussein Abdilahi Bulhan, *Frantz Fanon and the Psychology of Oppression* (New York: Plenum Press, 1985); Alice Cherki, *Frantz Fanon, portrait* (Paris: Seuil, 2000); Richard Keller, *Colonial Madness: Psychiatry in French North Africa* (Chicago, IL: University of Chicago Press, 2007); Jock McCulloch, *Black Soul White Artifact: Fanon's Clinical Psychology and Social Theory* (Cambridge: Cambridge University Press, 1983), and *Colonial Psychiatry and the 'African Mind'* (Cambridge: Cambridge University Press, 1995).
3. Georges Daumézon, 'Le Poids des structures', *Esprit*, n.s. 197, 12 (December 1952), 935–44.
4. Henri Ey, Paul Bernard, and Charles Brisset, *Manuel de psychiatrie* (Paris: Masson, 1960).

5. Henri Ey, *Études psychiatriques*, 3 vols (Paris: Desclée de Brouwer, 1948–54), I, 33–35.
6. George K. York, III, and David A. Steinberg, 'Hughlings Jackson's Neurological Ideas', *Brain: A Journal of Neurology*, 134, 10 (2011), 3106–13 (p. 3108).
7. John Hughlings Jackson, 'Croonian Lectures on the Evolution and Dissolution of the Nervous System', *The Lancet*, 3161 (29 March 1884), 555–58 (p. 555).
8. Ey: 'La psychiatrie est [...] la Pathologie de la Liberté' (*Études psychiatriques*, I, 57).
9. Jean-Paul Sartre, *L'Être et le néant, essai d'ontologie phénoménologique*, rev. ed. with index, ed. by Arlette Elkaïm-Sartre (Paris: Gallimard, 1976), p. 554. The veracity of the oft-claimed connection between Anders and Sartre is probed by Christopher David in 'Deux faux jumeaux: Jean Paul Sartre et Günther Anders', in *Sartre, le philosophe, l'intellectuel et la politique: les actes du colloque d'Amiens, mai 2005*, ed. by Arno Münster and Jean-William Wallet (Paris: L'Harmattan, 2006), pp. 207–29.
10. Frantz Fanon, *Peau noire, masques blancs* (Paris: Seuil, 1952), p. 217; *Black Skins, White Masks*, trans. by Richard Philcox (New York: Grove Press, 2008), p. 200, translation modified.
11. Günther Stern [Gustave Anders], 'Pathologie de la liberté: essai sur la non-identification', *Recherches philosophiques*, 6 (1936–37), 22; 'The Pathology of Freedom: An Essay on Non-Identification', trans. by Katharine Wolfe, *Deleuze Studies*, 3, 2 (2009), 278–310 (p. 279). Fanon's own copy of Anders's essay is marked in several places (Fanon, *Écrits sur l'aliénation et la liberté*, p. 612).
12. Jacques Lacan, *De la psychose paranoïaque dans ses rapports avec la personnalité* (Paris: Le François, 1932); reprinted as *De la psychose paranoïaque dans ses rapports avec la personnalité, suivi de Premiers écrits sur la paranoïa* (Paris: Seuil, 1975).
13. For the correlations, see *AL*, pp. 221–24; 263–67.
14. Lucien Bonnafé, Henri Ey, and others, *Le Problème de la psychogénèse des névroses et des psychoses* (Paris: Desclée De Brouwer, 1950).

INDEX

Lightning Source UK Ltd.
Milton Keynes UK
UKHW030707050619

343806UK00004B/29/P

9 781781 887332